ROCK STAR

ADVENTURES OF A METEORITE MAN

Geoffrey Notkin

Introduction by Neil Gaiman

Edited by Suzanne and Norma Morrison

D1206900

STANEGATE PRESS

Photography

Suzanne Morrison
Steve Arnold
Sonya Gay Bourn
Sonny Clary
Leigh Anne Delray-Crowell
Lindsay Eklund
Margaret Haddad
Nick Harman
Jacqueline Ho
Anne Husick
Stu Jenks
Maureen Maloney
Judith Mizrahi
Lisa Marie Morrison
Andrew Notkin
Geoffrey Notkin
Sam Notkin
Caroline Palmer
Pablo del Rio Larrain
Andy Shuford

Portions of chapters 7, 9, 11, and 14 originally appeared,
in a different form, in the May 1998, August 1998, November 1998,
and February 2006 issues of *Meteorite* magazine, and are presented
here by kind permission of founding editor and publisher, Dr. Joel Schiff.

Design and art direction by Stanegate Studios, Tucson, AZ
Published by Stanegate Press, LLC
www.stanegate.com

FIRST EDITION
ISBN 978-0-9847548-2-3

Printed in the United States of America
© 2012 by Stanegate Press, LLC, except where noted

For my mother,
Gay Nelle Flint Notkin, 1926–1998,
without whom there would have been no
life of adventure. Send a shooting star my way,
once in while, so I know you're okay.

Notes on the Lyrics

In addition to being a meteorite man, I am a rock 'n' roller. I have played music professionally for most of my life and I felt it important that a musical thread should run through this book. Each chapter, therefore, commences with a few lines of lyrics that particularly appeal to me and demonstrate, at least in my mind, some relevance to, or commentary upon, the tale that follows.

I am extremely grateful to my friends—past and present bandmates—for the generous permission to use excerpts from their original compositions in this work. Many of the lyrics quoted in *Rock Star* are from songs that my bands have performed and recorded over the years, and they all have a special place in my heart.

"Edge of Yesterday" © Anne Husick

"She Loves the Moon" © Geoffrey Notkin

"Stuck" © Norman England

"Army, School, or Work" © Lach and Norman England

"Mr. Bitterman" © Lach

"Lighthouse" © Geoffrey Notkin and Chris Gibson

"Last Truckstop" © Geoffrey Notkin and Anne Husick

"Alien Street" © Lach

"Undecided Dream" © Chris Gibson

"Questions" © Lach

"Tight Genes" © Krista Khrome

"Every Party" © Anne Husick

"Strange Days" © Anne Husick

"Five Highways Home" © Geoffrey Notkin

"Gasoline Blue" © Lach

"My Shoes" © Krista Khrome

"Let's Make a Movie" © Lach

"Civilized Fun" © Paul Martino and 4 Way Ping

"Haircut Like Captain Kirk" © Dave Hall, Graham K. Smith and Geoffrey Notkin

"Radiate, Baby" © Geoffrey Notkin

"Coffee Black" © Lach

"Shutting Out the Red Light" © Martin Brett

"Reset to Zero" © Geoffrey Notkin

ACKNOWLEDGEMENTS

A LARGE PART OF WHO I AM, and where I am today, has its roots in the brilliantly unorthodox influence of my remarkable friend Neil Gaiman. When we were eleven or twelve years old, who could have imagined that the fascinating boy sitting next to me, inventing comic books in Mr. Harlow's French class, would go on to become one of the greatest writers of our generation? Neil was not only my pal, but my comrade. We were misfits in the oppressive wasteland of British school in the 1970s, and we first connected through a shared love of American comics. From there to here; it's a hell of a long road. Neil told me I should play music, and started a band with me in 1976. He introduced me to creators as diverse as Robert Heinlein and Lou Reed, and wrote the introduction to this, my memoir. I thank you, Neil, partly for delighting so many millions of people around the world with your writing, but mostly, and somewhat selfishly, I suppose, for being such a good friend to me for forty years.

Steve Arnold, my friend and hunting partner since 1997, goofball, King of Brenham, and think-outside-the-box idea generator, is a cornerstone of this book. Without his courage and foresight as a meteorite hunter *Rock Star* would not exist, and neither would *Meteorite Men*. Thank you for the laughs, the brain waves, the bottle of vodka that time in Moscow, and everything else. You rock. And ditto for you, Qynne.

The Cereus Writers' Group—Deborah Mayaan, Betsy Krause, Lisa Harris, Susan Dawson-Cook, Lynn Rae Lowe, and especially Dennis Hull—read and commented upon significant portions of this book, sometimes repeatedly. They encouraged me, berated me (in the nicest possible way) for the overuse of words such as "tremendous," and served as editors, friends, and supporters. Part of you lives in this work.

Dr. Joel Schiff, founding editor and publisher of *Meteorite* magazine, was one of the first people to put my non-fiction work in print. He helped make my career as a writer. His contributions to the world of meteorites are immeasurable, and he kindly gave me permission to reproduce some of my early work in this book.

Ruben Garcia and Sonny Clary are valued and trusted friends and highly experienced meteorite experts. We have shared many an adventure together. I learned from them, and hopefully they learned a little from me. They both guested on the TV series, and Sonny is the only hunter—apart from Steve and me—who appeared in all three seasons of *Meteorite Men*. I owe you both.

Mike Miller is an extraordinary meteorite hunter and a fine friend. I respectfully call him "The Human Tank." We once embarked upon an expedition so strange, so entertaining, and so memorable, that it would certainly have made for one of the best chapters in this book. That tale must, however and alas, remain locked within the X-Files for now, as the location is still a secret. Maybe one day.

Geoff Cintron used to run one of the best companies in our strange business—Island Meteorite. He is also an aircraft engineer, amateur historian, and one of the smartest people I know. Thank you for sharing your wisdom and whisky with me.

My former bandmates and music colleagues are legion. Working with them not only filled a void in my heart during the rock 'n' roll years, but also helped prepare me for television. If you can entertain an intoxicated crowd in a punk rock club without getting beaten up, then you can probably do so on the box as well. Anne Husick and Lach, in particular, have been the closest and most trusted of friends for decades. Also, Norman England, Chris Gibson, Martin Brett, Al Binney, Richard Barone, Chuck Metaxas, Billy Ficca, The Washington Squares, Dave Rave, Joe Bendik, both Jon Bergers, Graham Smith, Dave Hall, Krista Khrome, Paul Martino, and soul singer extraordinaire, J. Miguel Carter. Thank you for tearing it up with me!

Team Aerolite are Suzanne Morrison, Beth Carrillo, Lisa Marie Morrison, Timothy Arbon, and Norma Morrison. I couldn't have done it without you. Suzanne took many of the photos in *Rock Star*, and she and Norma assisted greatly with editing. Paul Martino is my proofreader, and Guy Rovella of Aardvark is my print manager.

José Guggiari and Eduardo Jawerbaum are two of the true gentlemen in the meteorite business. Their trust and generosity helped me build Aerolite Meteorites.

I made many friends working on *Meteorite Men* and special mention goes to Sonya Gay Bourn, Bob Melisso, Ruth Rivin, Kathy Williamson, Debbie Myers, Per Larsson, Dave Marlin, Joe "Boots" Parker, James Rowley, Andy Shuford, and Jeff Fisher.

Others who shared kindness, insight, or inspiration during the journey were Dan Sullivan, who taught me how to camp in the desert, Jim Kriegh, Twink Monrad, Paul Harris and Jim Tobin of *Meteorite Times*, Blaine and Blake Reed, Bob Holmes, Mike and Bill Jensen, Dr. Art Ehlmann, Matt Morgan, Robert Matson, Allan and Iris Lang, Al Mitterling, Anne Black, Bob Falls, John Sinclair, Dr. Alain Carion and Louis Carion, Nancy and Dr. Larry Lebofsky, Chris Cokinos, Leigh Anne Delray-Crowell, Dr. Carleton Moore, Dr. Andy Tomkins, Dr. Chris Herd, Dave Eicher, Art Jones, Richard and Dorothy Norton, Stu Jenks, Mike Martinez, Marlin Cilz, Alan Traino, Marcin Stolarz, Iwo Szklarski, Bill Mason, George Winters, Tom Caggiano, Dima Sadilenko, Serge Afanasyev, Martin Altmann, Mike Scott, Andrzej Pilski, Professor Andrzej Muszynski, Warren Lazar, Jeff Kuyken, Ivy Bernhard Brown, Pam Huggins, Maureen Maloney, Jackie Ho, Cindy Johnson, Judith Mizrahi, Leslie Ballard da Silva, Grant Sanders, Rob Seulowitz, Maria Haas, Rob Wesel, Mike Bandli, Charles Elias, Professor Roy Gallant, Katya Rossovskaya, Jason Philips, McCartney Taylor, Katherine Rambo, Greg Thompson, Wendy Townsend, Darryl Pitt, Derek Yoost, Kelly Kennedy, Joe Strummer, Joey Ramone, and the Australian guy with the detergent in Iceland.

An extra special tip of the hat to Xpo Press, Dr. Laurence Garvie of ASU (the "Third Meteorite Man"), Mark Evans and TucsonCitizen.com, the Australian National Park Service, Dan's Toy Shop, Dr. Hobart King and Geology.com, the Flandrau Science Center, Tucson's Science Café, and the Space Tweep Society.

Fisher Labs and Teknetics, 5.11 Tactical, PulseStar, Lorenz, Hydratrek, David Ho and HoTech—thank you for the *great* gear! You helped keep me in one piece.

My teachers—Henry Maslin, Derek Melotte, Suzanne Guest, and Ginny MacKenzie—were beacons of creativity in a world gone mad. Art Spiegelman and Françoise Mouly-Spiegelman gave me my first job out of art school, and I learned so much from them, as I did from the great Will Eisner and the great Harvey Kurtzman.

My brother, Andrew, had enough of digging in the dirt when we were kids and is now an airline pilot. The memory and influence of my late parents, Sam and Gay Notkin, live on in my work, always. I would, literally, be nothing without you.

My love, Libby Egleson, waited patiently for me while I traveled over one hundred thousand miles. She gave me something to come home to. It's all about you, Sweets.

And cheers to everyone else who held my camera, shared a glass of wine, helped fix a flat, or otherwise carried a little of the weight for me.

TABLE OF CONTENTS

INTRODUCTION

SOME PEOPLE CHANGE. Kids you knew at school become investment bankers or bankruptcy specialists (failed). They fatten and they bald and somewhere you get the sense that they must have devoured the child they once were, eaten them bit by bit, mouthful by mouthful, until nothing is left of the smart, optimistic dreamer you knew when you were both young.

On a bad day, I worry that it's happening to me.

And then I see Geoff Notkin, and everything's all right.

True, sometimes, when he looks in the right direction, I see his father, Sam Notkin, a man so cool we used to talk obscure 1940s American science fiction authors together. But mostly I see Geoff, and he hasn't changed.

Geoffrey Notkin in 1976 was impetuous, brilliant, obsessed, really funny, easily angered but someone who would just as quickly forget that he'd ever been angry. We were both outsiders at school, Geoff because he was semi-American, me because I lived in books, and we bonded over music and comics. I took Geoff to a Lou Reed concert at the New Victoria, and we started a punk garage band, literally in his garage. Geoff was a terrific and passionate drummer.

We drew comics together, in the back of classes that bored us. Most classes bored us. We were smart kids who ignored most of school (we liked the art rooms, I liked the school library) and taught ourselves, because that seemed like more fun. We liked being disliked by the teachers, and neither of us actually got around to graduating.

We were friends. We dated the same girls (although never at the same time). We read the same comics and listened to the same music (often at the same time) and even dyed our hair blond, or tried to. Geoff's parents did not mind that he had dyed his hair blond. My father minded that I had dyed my hair a straw orange, and made me dye it black, which was even stranger. We signed to a record label as young punks, and none of our music is around anywhere except possibly tapes somewhere in Geoff's storage lockers, and I like to think that as long as I get him this introduction on deadline any tapes will stay there. Geoff put me into the ambulance when I needed to get my faced stitched up after a grumpy punter expressed his dislike of our band by throwing an (unopened) beer can at me...

I think it was after the beer can incident that I stopped dreaming of being a rock star.

I would see Geoff every few years, our lives strobing: the last time I saw his parents, introducing them to my infant daughter Holly, and found that I had been forgiven for the unfortunate events of the night of Geoff's party; the all-consuming envy of Geoff for inking Will Eisner at the School of Visual Arts, of knowing Will Eisner and Art Spiegelman and Harvey Kurtzman, people who were the gods and demigods of a 24-year-old journalist in London who dreamed of one day doing comics; Geoff Notkin rocking-man-about-town as I started stumbling into New York as someone who made his living writing comics; and then the emails from Geoff, in which he was going off to Siberia to look for meteorites . . .

Truthfully, it had never occurred to me that anyone actually ever looked for meteorites. I assumed that you noticed them when they hit your house or your car, or landed, green and pulsing, in your meadow before they transformed you into something monstrous. I did not think that people went out and looked for them with rare-earth magnets and madness.

I watched *Meteorite Men* because Geoff was on it, and I was delighted to observe that Geoff is still, so obviously that it comes through the television screen, impetuous, brilliant, obsessed, really funny, and capable of losing his temper really entertainingly whenever he's frustrated and in forgetting and forgiving almost instantly. But I kept watching it because I was hooked: Geoff has an autodidact's love of knowledge. He does not stop marvelling at the universe, and, for Geoffrey Notkin, the quickest way to touch the rest of the universe is to find something that came from another part of it and landed here, like a meteorite.

He gave me a meteorite of my own for my 50th birthday. It has a hole in it. He is in love with a ballerina.

And in my head, it's still 1977 somewhere, and Geoff Notkin and I have taken the afternoon off school to hit the second-hand book stores, and some record stores that have the real American Punk Imports that Geoff loved and the Velvet Underground bootlegs I dreamed about, and Geoff is standing on the side of the road shouting "We mean it mannnnnnn" at the cars going by, and we are kids in school uniforms and it's also now, thirty-five years later, and nothing's changed.

He still means it, every word.

Neil Gaiman
May 2012

ONE

EXCITING LIFE OF A METEORITE HUNTER

Look up in the sky, turn the other way
Walk the lonely road, there's nothing left today
Living history, waiting to be found
A rock from space, hiding underground
Standing here on the edge of yesterday
Standing here, you take my breath away
Standing here, on the edge of something grand
Standing here, I need to understand

From "Edge of Yesterday"
By Anne Husick

DURING MY CHILDHOOD YEARS IN LONDON, *Monty Python's Flying Circus* was easily the most controversial and talked-about show on television. My father wryly encouraged me to stay up until 9:25 p.m. and watch each new weekly episode on the BBC. It aired on a school night, which worried Mom and, anyway, she found the racy and provocative content almost entirely inappropriate for a young lad such as myself. My mother was a brilliant woman and that was one of the few instances in which I remember her being clearly in error. I remain a *Python* fan to this day and recently purchased the entire collected episodes in a DVD boxed set.

Decades after their initial broadcast some *Python* sketches feel dated, while others remain wonderfully timeless, and are as funny and original as when they first aired. In the "Vocational Guidance Counselor Sketch," Michael Palin—my favorite Python— plays a delightfully timid chartered accountant who visits a career advisor, acted out in a typically snide and officious manner by the uniquely weird John Cleese. Mr. Palin's sweet and mousy character complains, delicately, about how bored he is after spending twenty years as an accountant, and how he yearns to switch to a truly exciting new vocation, such as lion taming.

Palin's lament reminded me of how often I hear the remark: "What an exciting life you lead!" from people I meet while pursuing my unusual profession. Yes, it is exciting, at times; and, yes, I am lucky to be able to make a living from my passion, but the realities of international adventuring can be quite taxing. So, before recounting some of my favorite adventures, I feel I should first present an overview of some less glamorous moments in the exciting life of a meteorite hunter.

Whilst in the pursuit of space rocks I have suffered from sunburn, windburn, sun stroke, altitude sickness, exposure, exhaustion, food poisoning, concussions, dehydration, broken toes, benign paroxysmal positional vertigo, plus scores of other everyday, run-of-the-mill maladies.

1

I have been accused of being "overenthusiastic" in the field, and even though I do my best to stay focused and act in a semi-sensible manner, the sheer number of days spent in remote areas has resulted in my exterior surface being scratched, cut, burned, or otherwise injured by barbed wire, regular wire, rusty vintage farm machinery, a portable gasoline stove, ATVs and 4WD trucks, poison ivy, scorpion weed, other unidentified allergens, rocks, rock hammers, bamboo, corn stalks, every type of thorn, bramble and cactus, and shocked by electric fences. I also got knocked senseless by a heavy truck door blown shut by a micro burst, had a finger crushed between two shockingly powerful rare earth magnets, and was very nearly struck by lightning on an Arizona mountaintop.

I have been bitten by mosquitoes, gnats, chiggers, black flies, robber flies, fire ants, various types of spiders and a cattle dog. I have experienced close encounters with rattlesnakes, many kinds of other snakes, dog-sized lizards with blue tongues, alligators, wild boar, tarantulas, black widow spiders, two swarms of killer bees and one forest full of hornets' nests, scorpions, the venomous giant desert centipede (*Scolopendra heros*), two angry bald eagles with very large talons, the Sonoran lynx (*Lynx rufus*) and more than one pack of hungry coyotes.

During the execution of my duties, I was very nearly arrested and incarcerated by three armed and jackbooted Chilean police officers (it got as far as their hands on the guns), after getting into an altercation with a crooked bar owner in San Pedro de Atacama. I have been accosted by uniformed Russian soldiers and police, and the Mexican Army, and twice had my passport confiscated. While meteorite hunting or transporting meteorites, I have been stopped and searched by police, customs officers and security officers in numerous different countries, detained by immigration officials, interrogated by the U.S. Department of Homeland Security, British security services, and U.S. Border Patrol. I have been accused of being a terrorist by an Illinois sheriff, and barked at by a park ranger who thought I was using a metal detector on the site of a national monument (I wasn't; it's illegal).

Items stolen from me during regular operations include: the Aerolite Meteorites LLC company checkbook, pens and field notebooks, maps, sunglasses, a Nikon

[left] Riding Orange County Chopper's *Meteorite Men* bike around the Henbury Craters, Australia, 2010.

camera, a suitcase, an Acculab digital scale, important business records, the charger for my cell phone, and a recently worn and likely smelly "I Dig Space Rocks" t-shirt. Why anybody would steal such a thing is beyond my comprehension.

While traveling in strange parts of the world, and when there was literally no alternative, I have been required to subsist on Cliff Bars, reindeer burgers, porridge with flies in it, steamed abalone which had the consistency of truck tires, and some type of large, slimy and hideous freshwater eel plucked from a frigid lake far north of the Arctic Circle. While this dietary supplement list may not sound too appalling to some, please consider that under normal circumstances I am a strict vegetarian!

I survived a drinking competition involving vodka, wine, "And now the Georgian brandy!" on a pebble island in the middle of a river, inside a 100-kilometer wide meteorite crater with the field support staff of the Siberian Geological Survey—and a tougher bunch of guys I never met—and then foolishly accepted a dare which resulted in me leaping into a frigid river at 2 a.m. and swimming a few hundred yards. I received a standing ovation and round of applause from our comrades, so I did it a second time, just to show them.

I have lived through several earthquakes, two hurricanes, a stranded truck in the heart of the Atacama Desert, a dead ATV in the middle of a winter blizzard in the snow belt of upstate New York, encounters with desert pirates in Nevada and Arizona, a gurgling uncapped oil well at the bottom of an excavation hole in Kansas, an impromptu margarita party at the edge of Area 51, an unexploded air-to-air guided missile which somehow came to rest atop a large rock outcrop in the Arizona desert, and a 1000-pound bomb which we almost drove into while hunting near a secret testing range in Utah. I crossed the Arctic Circle three times, and nearly fell into an active volcano in Iceland.

While hunting, or on the way to suspected hunting zones, I have traveled by foot, horse, mountain bike, scooter, dirt bike, a custom-built Orange County Chopper weighing 900 pounds, ATVs, regular cars, vans and buses, 4WD vehicles including Steve Arnold's canary-yellow Hummer and my heavily customized Tacoma known as *The Mule*, a wooden raft handmade from pine trees, air force life rafts, a hydrofoil, two amphibious tracked Hydratreks, an ex-Russian military Mi-8 cargo helicopter, and every type of airplane from a Cessna to a Jumbo Jet.

While searching for meteorites with metal detectors, I have accidentally found or helped excavate Frontier-Era wagon wheels, coyote traps, Civil War bullets and belt buckles, a 30-gallon steel drum inside of a 55-gallon drum, artillery shrapnel, bullets, shotgun shells, .50-caliber shells, a clip of live 9-millimeter ammo, ball bearings, hundreds of hot rocks, unidentifiable pieces of machinery, 19th-Century forged iron tools, a chain big enough to hold down a battleship, beer cans, cans of beans, rusted buckets, and parts of several old cars.

By this point the reader may well be thinking: "Then why do you do it?" Simply put, there really is nothing that could possibly engage me more than digging for space rocks except, maybe, working with Michael Palin as a lion tamer.

When asked how I became a meteorite hunter, I tend to fall back on that most comfortable and reliable of answers—as we all do—and blame my parents. In order, however, to provide a more sensible explanation of how I came to venture down this strangest of all paths, we must journey back to the wistful, and long-vanished London of the 1960s.

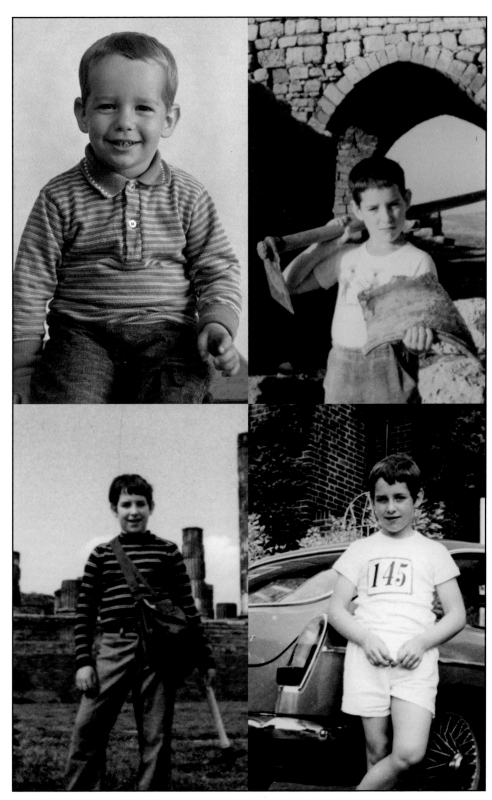

TWO

FROM ETERNITY TO HERE

She lies alone in bed at night
And knows the stars are dancing
Movements of the asteroids
Are measured by her heartbeat
Telescopes live in constant darkness
Confined by a world of stone
That whisper, from the canyon
Is us calling you home

From "She Loves the Moon"
By Geoffrey Notkin

IN 1968, I WAS A SHY AND SOMEWHAT ECCENTRIC LITTLE BOY living in a sleepy, upper middle-class town at the edge of Greater London—not quite in the city and not quite in the country—and a relentless battle of wits between my parents and me consumed much of my time.

It was the year Stanley Kubrick released his masterpiece, *2001*, a film that forever changed the way we looked at science fiction. My father took me to see it during the opening run at London's grand Dominion Theatre and I still have the original program. James Watson published *The Double Helix* in 1968, and four meteorites are known to have fallen to Earth that year: Schenectady (New York), Awere (Uganda), Piancaldoli (Italy), Juromenha (Portugal).

Let me say at the outset that my parents were unlike any other adults that I knew, and probably unlike many or most parents of their generation. They were kind and unconventional, enlightened, tirelessly patient with my seemingly limitless number of hobbies, and well versed in unusual subjects that were of no interest to the parents of the children with whom I had the misfortune of going to school. And that was the root of the problem: my parents were far more interesting than school, so it was my intention not to go anymore. I had the most success with this plan when Father was away on business, which was much of the time when I was little.

Conundrum is the word that comes to mind when I think of my father, Sam Notkin, in the 1960s. We lived in a fairly posh neighborhood about fifteen miles south of the River Thames, in a desirable part of the County of Surrey known as "the stockbroker belt." A successful international businessman, Dad declined to purchase a respectable car suitable for someone of his station and, instead, delighted in driving a massive, cantankerous, one and three quarter-ton retired London taxicab that belched

[left] My father (at left) and his army buddy, Norm Zuckerman, with the United States 99th Infantry Division in 1943.

[below] I took this photo of my parents at their favorite restaurant, Chez Paul, on the Ile de la Cité in Paris, in the 1990s.

[following page] My mother, Gay Nelle Flint in Paris in the 1950s, before she married my father. Music runs in the family.

blue diesel fumes from its ancient engine. The car might as well have been a gunboat laying down a smokescreen, and it came across as unspeakably common to our class-conscious neighbors who, with their Bentleys and Jaguars, hated it.

Sometimes Dad wore a space helmet when he drove the taxi.

My father was also a twice-decorated World War II hero of such modesty that I was in my mid-thirties before he finally told me the details about what had happened between him and an SS Panzer Division during the winter of 1944, in a savage conflict known as the Battle of the Bulge. I think he always felt lucky to have survived. His best friend, after whom my younger brother Andrew is named, did not come home from the war. Dad could have been anything he wanted: a scientist, painter, historian, university professor, economist, or a world-class fencing coach, but he chose to enjoy himself in a mostly calm and contemplative manner. He devoted time to family, friends and international relations; and to gentlemanly pursuits like chess, tennis, good books and amateur astronomy.

During his career, my father was an admired professional with a responsible job which he executed diligently and respectfully, representing the Port Authority of New York and New Jersey from their London office, and later the American Chamber of Commerce in London. He helped found the World Trade Center in Tel-Aviv, and became a respected authority on world travel, commerce, and shipping. The downside was, he spent close to half my childhood traveling through Europe and the Middle East on business.

On those rare occasions when my father was both at home, and the night sky over southern England was clear enough so that you could actually see something other than sheets of grey clouds, he loved to take his small refracting telescope outside. He would set up its wooden tripod near the antique brass sundial which stood at the center of my mother's rose garden. I remember many instances, when I was very young, of being awakened by my father around 2 a.m., getting bundled up in a thick wool blanket and knitted blue and white ski cap with a bobbin on top, and carried outside like a papoose to the telescope. My mother would get quite upset and say: "But, Sam, it's the middle of the night and he has school tomorrow."

Dad would gently insist that seeing four of Jupiter's moons at the same time was more important than sleep or school and I, of course, heartily agreed with him, and still do. I was genuinely stunned by the concept that we could see actual planets in outer space from our genteel, Surrey garden lawn. As a bonus, any illness caused by sudden night time exposure would likely mean several days home sick from school, and any possible antidote to school became a source of immediate and intense interest for me. As a result, from an early age, I developed a very strong alliance with the science of astronomy.

I fondly remember my first school as a dictatorial, family-run institution, operated sullenly out of a retrofitted cream-colored Tudor house on the snooty side of town. We cowered daily, with genuine terror, under the rule of a large and angry headmaster who looked uncomfortably like Stalin.

In order to avoid the creaking terror of a British education, I routinely feigned all kinds of illnesses: stomach aches, headaches, dizziness, sore throats, ringing in the ears, and sometimes considered fainting in front of my mother but was never certain I could convincingly pull off so dramatic a stunt.

My mother, Gay Flint Notkin, was an exceptionally bright and intuitive woman: sunny, positive, empathic and trusting, but never naive. She had grown up in an orphanage in Mississippi, and later won a scholarship to the Women's College in Jackson. She passed the Foreign Service entrance examination and, as a young lady during the mid-1950s, made it all the way to France where she met my father, entirely under her own volition with no family to help or support her. She spoke fluent French and Spanish, which helped her win a desirable position with the American Embassy in Paris. In later years she also worked for the Rockefeller Foundation in New York and the State Department. As a worldly person, she could hardly have been fooled by my fake maladies, but she always was concerned about my health, as well as my accomplishments at school which—due to chronic boredom—were meager at best. So I often got away with staying home.

By late morning on any given sick day, with no possible chance that I might be sent in to school for a half day of brutality, I often miraculously felt much better and wanted to go to the chalk quarry. Somehow, Mom and I never really had the "If you're well enough for the chalk quarry, you're well enough for school" conversation. Looking back more than forty years, I believe those stolen afternoons hunting for fossils were as important for her as they were for me. Some sort of compromise along the lines of "Alright, we'll go to the quarry if you promise to go back to school tomorrow," would quickly be arrived at. With great speed and efficiency we would then pack sandwiches, orange juice, and my rock hammer into our red station wagon and drive a couple miles to the disused quarry high up on Marlpit Lane, "marl" being an old English word for clay or mud. We would sidle under a slowly-decomposing wire fence, and hunt for micrasters—beautiful heart-shaped fossil sea urchins—among the abandoned diggings. A cavernous open-face pit of stupefying size, bracketed by white dam-like vertical cliffs and dotted with hawthorne trees, that old chalk quarry was the birthplace of my lifetime of natural history collecting.

Occasionally, one of our missions would be starkly interrupted by the caretaker, a gruff and whiskered old man, wearing a grey flat cap, who would chase us away shouting: "Thems cliffs is dangerous, them is! Bloody dangerous. Ye can't come dahn 'ere!"

My mother did not much care for the term "bloody," and gently explained that it was only used by "coarse and vulgar" people.

Fascinated as I was by astronomy, my first true love was the study of fossils. Space was something I could only read about and look at from a distance. But fossils, the last remaining whispers of ancient life, were buried in the tranquil, rolling chalk hills all around our house. Nightly, I insisted on having *A Field Guide to Fossils in Colour* for my bedtime reading. I must have been a strange kid, but to me science was so much more engaging than toys, or the annoying children who happened to live in my neighborhood. In later life my mother liked to remark that she accidentally learned Latin because, as a child, I was forever asking her how to pronounce the scientific names of dinosaurs and fossils from my reference books.

My other love was the forest. Our garden backed onto an expanse of ancient woodland that is one of the oldest surviving habitats in Southern England. It has remained undeveloped and relatively untouched since at least the year 1600, and some naturalists believe it is much older and stretches back—virtually unchanged—to a time before the Iron Age. Birds, badgers, and foxes could be seen if you were quiet, and

9

ventured far enough. I adored the sassy magpies with their black and white plumage and long tails that made them look like imperious waiters in a fancy restaurant, and hardly a week would go by without me spying a fox on its dusk mission. They were bold and elegant with white faces and ginger fur, and not particularly frightened of humans. Badgers, on the other hand, are nocturnal and very wary of people. Seeing one was extremely unusual, but I did delight in my secret visits to "Badger City," as I called it—a small and completely hidden valley, filled with moss-covered trees, where those social and industrious animals had excavated scores of large burrows into the slopes. Close together, their dig holes tunneled deep into the chalk, creating a fantastic communal home that could have been the setting for a fantasy novel. In search of fossils, I always picked through the talus of white stones the badgers had thrown out while excavating their burrows.

I spent hours and days, almost always alone, exploring ancient paths that wound, seemingly forever, under ominous trees completely obscuring the sky. I observed robins, thrushes, sparrows, and, if I was lucky, a red-headed woodpecker. I collected rocks, hunted for fossils, and felt there could be nothing more mysterious and calming than the melancholy silence of the lonely forest.

In spring, a breathtaking tapestry of bluebells bloomed, deep in the woods, but only for a few days. Each year, my mother and I would walk out to see them in all their intoxicating violet beauty. Literally thousands of flowers opened at the same time, painting a dizzying carpet of petals below the giant oaks and chestnut trees. In all my travels I have never seen anything remotely like it—a place both glorious and tragic. Within a few short days the bluebells withered to grey, and some years we missed the spectacle entirely. That brief flurry of botanical wonder instilled in me, even as a little boy, a lingering sadness at the transitory nature of life, and a determination to make the most of the time I had.

Occasional fossil hunting expeditions with Mom continued but, over time, it became more and more difficult to evade capture at the chalk quarry. Eventually, and to my great distress, a modern steel fence was put up, barring me forever from my dream of finding a perfect fist-sized micraster at the site. Today, the quarry is home to an industrial compound and its grand white cliffs are all but hidden by nondescript, monolithic structures.

To pull me out of my despair, my mother suggested a visit to Central London where she claimed we could see "other fossils." We rode an old, green double-decker bus to the local 19th-Century red-brick train station, where we caught a train to Victoria and finally the underground to South Kensington. Another bus ride, followed by a short walk under giant and leafy horse chestnut trees delivered us before the mighty carved stone facade of the British Museum of Natural History and its little brother, the Geological Museum. Today they are both under one roof and known as the NHM, or Natural History Museum, London—one of the world's great repositories of natural history wonders.

I was both overwhelmed with delight at the exhibits and furiously envious of the displays. Looking at things in the museum was not good enough. I wanted to find, and to hold, such marvels for myself. I scrutinized the display cabinets—rows and rows of raised-up desks with glass tops—each one full of minerals and fossils, with every specimen perfect and carefully labeled. I developed a fascination with the minutiae of cataloging: all those meticulously handwritten collection numbers and identification cards. There is something about a tiny, painted calligraphic museum number that makes a specimen seem more real than one you might find in a quarry.

The Hall of Minerals was long and wide, with a high ceiling and brightly illuminated, even on a grey day, by its elegant Georgian-style windows. At the far end of the hall, stood the most mysterious and melancholy corner of the museum—the Hall of Meteorites. The centerpiece of the display was a 198-kilogram Imilac, one of the largest pallasite meteorites ever found. It had been donated to the museum in 1879 by a gentleman adventurer who brought it all the way to London from the high Atacama Desert in Chile. I always imagined that a good part of such a journey had to have been made on the back of a donkey or alpaca, and that's a heavy load for a thirsty animal in a desert with an 11,000-foot elevation. I could not have dreamed it at the time, but Imilac was to play a most important part in my adventures in the years to come.

Walking into the Hall of Meteorites was like entering a science fiction cave. I tiptoed through an archway into a silent, low-lit, domed room, tucked away in a corner like the mutant black sheep of exhibits. I went there time and again, and was almost always the only person in the exhibit. Giant, dark, iron meteorites of unknown origin sat there, magnificently and with immense gravitas. They were scarred and pitted, melted into impossible shapes by a fiery journey through Earth's atmosphere. What a revelation it was for a child so very enthralled, as I was, with geology and astronomy.

That was the moment when it all came together for me: rocks and space. Meteorites were, I realized, the unlikely progeny of my love for both astronomy and geology. They are, quite literally, rocks from space.

I could not fully absorb the puzzling enigma of the meteorite collection. It seemed unbelievably alien, at the very edge of understanding, and perhaps even somewhat frightening. The big irons, some of which weighed hundreds of pounds were moody, eerily sculptural, and they were from "out there," the depths of space. A little boy like me could actually reach out and touch them, run his hands over their otherworldly ridges and furrows, feel their points and thumbprints, and the cold, unforgiving density of a long-dead asteroid's core.

"How did they get to Earth?," I wondered, and were there more of them waiting somewhere out there, to be found by someone, maybe someone like me? I became entranced. I was also certain that finding a real meteorite would be the finest achievement of one's life. Or, at least my life. I would daydream about imaginary expeditions all the time, when I should have been paying attention in class. I had immersed myself in the films *Journey to the Center of the Earth* and *King Solomon's Mines* numerous times, and they instilled in me an idealized image of the gentleman adventurer. In my daring dreamworld travels, I sported a pith helmet and carried a worn leather satchel, full of compasses, maps, and scientific instruments.

At age seven, the idea of finding a meteorite seemed an impossibly difficult task, but I had little doubt that one day I would, somehow, manage to discover one for myself. The following year my family spent our summer vacation in the United States, on Cape Cod. Alone in the sand dunes late one afternoon, aged eight, and with the wind sighing through cream-colored dune grass, I dug a deep round hole in the sand, scattered rocks around the perimeter, and placed ashes and pieces of burned wood in the bottom. I pretended I had found a meteorite crater.

[top right] The author (far right) playing drums with my very first band circa 1966 at British school.

[above] One of my earliest expeditions: fossil hunting with my mother (in cap), and younger brother, Andrew, circa 1968.

[right] The volcanic island of Heimaey, off the southern coast of Iceland.

THREE

ARIZONA, ICELAND, AND THE ABYSS BETWEEN

Why'd you never tell me
Just what was really going on?
So now I'm in the middle
The middle of a time gone wrong
Some of you won't make it
But I've heard them say
I couldn't hear that bad advice
I've seen it just slip away
Leaving me stuck

From "Stuck"
By Norman England

AT THE OUTSET, 1971 HAD THE POTENTIAL, IT SEEMED, to be the best year of my life. I was ten. I had passed the entrance examination to a highly-regarded British school in the London suburb of South Croydon, and would start there in the fall. Before that great journey could begin, however, an even greater one, at least in geographical terms, awaited: the American West.

One morning in July a uniformed driver showed up wearing a smart black cap and took us to the port city of Southampton, where we boarded the magnificent Cunard liner *Queen Elizabeth 2*. Following a five-day crossing to New York, we flew to Denver, Colorado, and then to Albuquerque, New Mexico. How fantastic it all felt! There I was, in the Wild West, where real Indians walked around wearing black cowboy hats and silver belts with turquoise buckles. I am not sure which enthralled me more: the handsome, larger-than-life Navajo and Hopi people we met, or the grandiose robin's-egg blue turquoise stones set in their bolo ties, hatbands and bracelets.

The first night, we had dinner in an old adobe Mexican restaurant with a dirt floor and a tree growing right up through the ceiling. I had never seen anything like it. The town of South Croydon where I went to school boasted only the marginal culinary distinction of being home to one of England's first four McDonald's assembly-line hamburger joints. I had no idea what jalapeño peppers were but they looked extremely interesting from a botanical point of view, which prompted me to eat one. It was so hot I went temporarily blind, and poured glass after glass of ice water into my mouth in a vain attempt to drown the incandescent pepper. I remained wary of Mexican food for years, an aberration from which I fortunately fully recovered.

My parents, my brother Andrew, and I were to spend two weeks driving from New Mexico to California, where we would meet up with one of my father's friends. Our list of possible destinations sounded like a who's-who of the Geological Wonders of the World: the Grand Canyon, the Petrified Forest, the Painted Desert, Sunset Crater and, of course, the legendary Meteor Crater—universally recognized as the best preserved meteorite crater on earth. But there was a serious problem. I could not comprehend it, but apparently the rest of my family did not plan on spending the entire two-week vacation looking at geological and paleontological features. For some reason my mother intended to waste valuable rock-hunting time visiting her long-lost brother Jim in Las Vegas, Nevada, and my father had a strong desire to go boating on Lake Powell. It felt absurd and unfair, but a cruel edict came down from the driver's seat: we could see the Petrified Forest or Meteor Crater, but not both.

I was, therefore, forced into making a monumental decision.

In retrospect, it seems obvious that with my obsession with meteorites, a trip to the crater should have been an easy choice. But even at that early age I was very aware that fossils were much easier to find than meteorites. "What if we go to the crater and find nothing?" I asked myself. I could conceivably go back to England and my new school empty-handed, with no stories of discovery, no meteorites, and no petrified wood to add to my collection. I could not see taking such a risk. There was no chance of me not finding petrified wood at the Petrified Forest and so the forest it was.

In 1971 it was still possible to search for space rocks at Meteor Crater. Today, the removal of specimens is, for some reason, not allowed and I often wonder, had we gone, if I would have found anything. I now know that without a metal detector and some serious experience, finding a meteorite, even at a well-known site is difficult at best. If we had made the trip to Meteor Crater and if I had, against all odds, found something, would that have jump-started my career as a meteorite hunter? I shall never know, and my own discoveries of cosmic matter would have to wait a couple of decades. We found plenty of petrified wood outside the protected federal land, and had many other adventures before returning to England in late August, suntanned, happy, and full of wonder from a summer in the American West. As proof of our exploits on the frontier, all three of the Notkin males sported new cowboy hats and jeans, purchased from an authentic western outfitter in Truckee, California.

Up until this time I had never considered pursuing any career other than that of a scientist, preferably specializing in geology, except for flirting with the idea—as most boys have done, I'm sure—of becoming an astronaut.

At age ten I already had my own chemistry lab, a microscope, and an extensive rock and fossil collection, much of which I had found myself. I had amassed a considerable library of books on biology, paleontology, geology, prospecting, and astronomy. I considered myself a skilled amateur rocketeer and since solid-fuel model rockets were illegal in England, we smuggled them in from other countries, making it all that much more exciting. I had also experimented with designing and building remote-controlled vehicles, simple robots, and was hoping to somehow procure a Geiger counter.

The Wild West adventure was behind us, and a brave new world of science awaited me at the new school, with its state-of-the-art chemistry and physics labs and—joy of joys—a geology department. I was bursting with enthusiasm, eager to start my first term and ready to embark with great diligence and determination upon my soon-to-be brilliant career as a famous scientist.

I quickly learned that the school in which I was destined to serve a seven-year sentence had been founded in the 1500s by the then current Archbishop of Canterbury. It had slumped and shuffled into the Twentieth Century as a dark, damp, and intimidating Dickensian nightmare of endless corridors and identical classrooms, all of it gloomily constructed from antiquated, stained and dirty wooden boards. I had inadvertently become imprisoned in a totalitarian, excessively religious, all-boys school where teachers were called "masters" and the operative word was "compulsory": compulsory uniforms, compulsory prayers presided over every morning by the doddering gin-soaked headmaster, compulsory out-of-tune mumbling of hymns and recitations of "The Lord's Prayer," compulsory rugby, compulsory cricket, compulsory bible study, and compulsory memorial services for "Old Boys" (the British term for alumni) killed during two world wars.

We were required to call the teachers "sir," and they would call us "boy," or "that boy there, Notkin," or "crabs," "urchins" or "ungrateful wretches," and at one point inexplicably, my Latin master referred to me as "a black seal."

Savage physical beatings with a cane, gym shoe, ruler, or whatever was handy, for the smallest of infractions—forgetting to bring your towel to the swimming pool, for instance—were delivered regularly and with great vigor by several of the more sadistic masters.

My French master was a former rugby player for the New Zealand All-Blacks, a team noted for their intensity of play. It was evident to me that he had, in fact, been hired to train the school rugby team and the Board of Directors felt they needed to give him a real job as well, so he instantly became a French teacher. "How difficult can it be to instruct the boys in French?" I imagine them asking. He once hurled a piece of chalk at me, which caught me just above the left eye, with such tremendous force that I nearly blacked out. That was his response to me idly tapping a pencil on my desk.

The school motto was in Latin and roughly translated to "He who suffers shall return victorious," and how they loved to make us suffer.

The first blow to my scientific career came early on, but there were to be many more. I discovered to my horror that, as of 1971, the year as my inglorious arrival, geology would no longer be taught at the school and the Geology Department had been closed permanently. I once peered, wistfully and with great longing, through that locked door, just able to see drawers upon drawers of abandoned rock samples through the wire-reinforced glass window, before being soundly slapped on the head by my geography master for "dawdling." I can still remember the ringing in my ears.

The crushing tedium of physics class is painful to recall, even after all these years. Following a disastrous parents-teachers evening where my instructors once again made it clear how "disappointed" they were with my "lack of attention and progress in class," even my usually diplomatic mother shook her head and stated that the decrepit physics teacher was clearly a drunk and could barely stand.

In retrospect, I can perhaps feel a minute amount of pity for those glum men who were, I suppose, failed scientists themselves, relegated to teaching a white-bread cadre of frail Anglo-Saxon nerds who would go on to become the next generation of British politicians, CEOs, and sexual deviants. In a school of 860 boys, there was not one child of ethnic descent, and less than ten who were of any religious persuasion other than Church of England.

Our chemistry teachers were at least memorable: one, a severe, hollow, bony man had worked for the Ministry of Defence during World War II developing flame throwers. The other, a Scotsman, spoke with an accent so thick I wanted to ask for subtitles. He once earnestly warned me that I must never allow myself to be hypnotized. "Hypnotism is awful dangerous, lad, aye. If ye are hypnotized, yer mental guard is doon an' it allows evil spirits ta enter yer bodee." He was gravely serious, and this was one of my science teachers!

One master was quietly let go after molesting a number of ten-year-old boys in the swimming pool, and another—a hobbit-like woodworking teacher—referred to each and every student as a "Cane Hill candidate"; Cane Hill being a nearby asylum for the insane.

I did have a few, a very few, allies in that dreadful place.

One, a refined, soft-spoken art teacher who looked as if he belonged in a Manet portrait, took me quietly under his wing. He taught me to use a single lens reflex camera and print my own photographs in the darkroom—skills which would serve me extremely well in the years ahead.

The planners and architects had thoughtfully placed the Art Department in an isolated prefabricated building as far away as possible from the rest of the school. Situated on the other side of the military cadets' asphalt parade ground and next to the rugby fields, it seemed to imply that even having art at all must be some kind of embarrassment. That was fine by me. The further away from the rest of the school, the better. Inside that art building I was introduced to the work of M.C. Escher, and experimental electronic music by avant-garde composers like Stockhausen and Edgar Varèse. My art teacher somehow maneuvred the school into funding an animated short film which I directed, and he tutored me in drawing and painting with great patience over a period of several years. That one exemplary teacher helped me believe that I could be an artist.

Another ally was a curious and solitary boy in my class who seemed completely oblivious to the hardship and suffering around him. He happily wandered through our school days immersed in hefty and complex novels such as Robert Heinlein's *Stranger in a Strange Land*. We shared an intense interest in American comics and science fiction and sat together at the back of class writing and illustrating amateurish sword and sorcery tales, which usually featured our own teachers as the hideous villains. We were shouted at, routinely, by those same teachers and received much helpful encouragement along the lines of: "Comics are rubbish! You two will never amount to anything."

My friend's name was Neil Gaiman. He is now a successful novelist, comic book author, and screenplay writer of great international fame. We remain friends to this day, and he is the only person from that dismal period in my life with whom I maintain regular contact.

The only good thing I can recall about my second year at the new school is that it eventually ended. My memory of the 1972–3 term is a perpetually grainy mental snapshot in which I stare at a wall clock, willing the seconds to tick through to 3:30 p.m. and the end of daily classes.

Legend had it that our geography teacher, a violent alcoholic named O'Brien, carried a tiny piece of Nazi shrapnel lodged in his left eye—a memento of the minute role he personally played in the Battle of the Atlantic. O'Brien detested my tendency to repeatedly check the time and flew into a rage whenever he caught me doing it.

"Do you know what clock-watchers get, boy? Useless, wasted lives, that's what!"

He had a habit of getting uncomfortably close to you when he shouted, so you could not avoid getting peppered by his spittle. His eyes would open up extremely wide. I always tried to find the piece of shrapnel, but never could spot it.

"Clock-watchers will always be waiting for something that never happens. Are you a clock-watcher, you miserable boy? *Are you?*"

My father gave me a replica divers' watch for my eleventh birthday. I quickly learned to wear its luminous face on the inside of my wrist so I could check the time discretely without risking another tirade from O'Brien.

Halfway through the school year an event of literally Earth-shaking magnitude occurred. The isle of Heimaey, part of the Westmann Islands archipelago off the southern coast of Iceland, was split open by a massive volcanic eruption. Active volcanoes ranked second in my personal Science Top Ten list, after meteorite impacts, so all of my other activities were immediately suspended. I sat through the nightly BBC news broadcast in its entirety hoping to catch live footage of the fiery volcano filmed, as always, by the amazing Haroun Tazieff, a daring French volcanologist and geologist who was a personal hero. I implored my father to bring home a copy of every London newspaper, and I clipped and saved everything related to the Heimaey eruption.

My parents must have been relieved to see me excited and happy about something again, as my reaction to school had been to sink into despair. They were great supporters of the family adventure holiday concept, and to that end Dad made a surprise announcement one evening after dinner: our summer vacation plans would be amended to include a week in Iceland so we could visit the volcano!

We took an Icelandair jet to Keflavik and, from there, chartered a pair of four-seater Cessnas to the little island of Heimaey. I doubt there had ever been an airfield in the Westmanns; if they used to have one it now lay buried beneath twenty feet of volcanic cinder. The resourceful islanders had managed to get a bulldozer out there, somehow, and they flattened a patch of acrid fallout into something vaguely resembling a runway. We bounced down that landing strip like beans in a maraca and emerged from the airplanes into an alien landscape. The air smelled overwhelmingly of sulphur and noxious smoke rose up all around us. Everything was black, covered by millions of tons of granular black cinders. The steaming, smoldering surface was broken up here and there by orange triangles—roofs of the unfortunate islanders' buried homes poking through the fallout. I suppose it looked like hell to everyone else, but it was a dream come true for me. I filled my rucksack with everything I could pack into it: fine volcanic cinder, coarse volcanic cinder, volcanic bombs, intricate vine-like wreaths of dried lava.

We were warned not to enter any of the houses, as toxic gasses had accumulated in the basements and even a brief exposure could be deadly. I ran here and there, on my own, collecting specimens. I moved further and further away from my family and the lounging pilots, up the side of a long, steep slope, eager to see the view from the top. Looking back the way I'd come, from near the summit, the Cessnas looked like delicate toys sitting there: out-of-place, frail, and starkly white against an elevated plateau of coal-black igneous debris. As I turned around, I realized I had come right up to the crest of one of the craters. I also realized that there were no footprints anywhere around me. The fine, pea-sized rock grains started to slide down into the crater under my weight, taking me with them, and making a sighing sound, like a sack of rice being poured onto a concrete floor. The cascade grew in speed and volume, pulling more and more material along with it, down into the mouth of the smoking pit. I tried to jump to one side but my shoes filled with sharp cinders, I lost my balance, and fell hard on my back. I rolled over and, still sliding down, managed to bury my rock pick into a patch of denser ground which, slowly and grudgingly, brought me to a stop. Most of the gravel continued whooshing down and disappeared into the swirling smoke below. Very slowly and carefully, like an intoxicated guest tip-toeing through a house full of sleeping people, I moved back up the slope. Each step left a deep, plate-sized footprint and sent another minor cascade of black grit into the abyss.

For many years my father enjoyed telling the story about how the family visited an active volcano in Iceland when I was twelve. "We were walking around near the airplanes looking at the buried houses and the lava, when Gay realized that nobody had seen Geoffrey for a while. We called out for him for a long time, 'Geoffrey! Geoffrey!' and looked everywhere but couldn't find him. We were getting very worried when a tiny figure came up over the ridge from *inside* the volcano, waving, with a wall of smoke behind him and a bag of rocks on his shoulder."

I was quite shaken up by the near-fatal trip into the crater but, red-faced and breathless, I was not about to admit that to anyone. As I walked back to the group, pretending that nothing at all had happened, the pilot shook his head disdainfully. "Det's very denjer-us. Det's de vol-canho dare. Very hot, very denjer-us."

I tried to play it all off like nothing had happened, and said something like: "Oh, I was just collecting some samples over there on that hill," but I must have been unconvincing and was kept on a tight leash for the rest of the trip.

On the outbound flight, my father sat up front in the co-pilot's seat and had been invited by the captain to fly the plane for a while. On the return flight, I maneuvered for the front seat. I was too small to even see out of the cockpit, but the lunatic pilot asked me—in a totally nonchalant manner, like it happened every day—if I'd like to fly us back. And so, at age twelve, using instruments only, and to my considerable surprise, I put my hands on the controls and took our aircraft out over the cold, grey north Atlantic and headed north for Iceland.

In 1973 Iceland experienced next to no tourism. Back on the mainland, therefore, it was only after some searching and negotiating, that we managed to rent a very well-used but expertly customized Land Rover, stocked with spare tires, flares, ropes, and survival supplies. We spent a few days exploring the wild north—a landscape so remote and barren that NASA sent the Apollo astronauts there for Moon mission training.

We had seen the volcano and now I had to see the famous geyser—imaginatively named Geysir by the locals. We followed signs for "Geysir" for ages and when we got to the place, there was really nothing to see. The ground was grey, brown and rocky, with snow-covered mountains way off in the distance, and an empty, dirt parking lot with a beaten-up Volkswagen camper van sitting at the far end. There were no buildings or signs, or trees, or people, or anything at all except for a small amount of steam whispering up from a basketball-sized hole in the middle of a few square feet of cracked cement. I suppose kids always believe everything is happening all the time, and I imagined the geyser would be going full steam when we arrived, and that we would be able to see it from miles away.

"Is this it?" I asked. "This is rubbish."

I walked right up to the hole and looked down, expecting to see it full of hot water at least, but it was just a hole that went way down deep into the ground. You could not see the bottom.

We stood around and waited for what seemed like forever, but nothing happened. The sky looked like blue ice. Even in our Arctic-style parkas we were all cold. Our breath steamed out in front of us.

I went back to the hole and looked in again. It really was rubbish. I had seen photos of Geysir blasting away, and it was nothing like this.

Mom asked if we should think about going to see something else, and then we heard the VW's door creak open. A tall, wiry man with long hair, mirrored sunglasses and a wacky, brightly-colored hippie outfit appeared. He waved, and gave us the thumbs-up sign.

"G'day!" he boomed. "How're ya goin'?"

Clearly Australian—though somewhat inexplicably given the location—he walked right up to me as I stared sullenly into the steaming cement hole. He towered over me, and looked down with a raw, benevolent smile.

"D'ya wanna see the geyser go off, mate?"

"Oh yes, we were hoping to. Do you know when it's supposed to go off next?"

He let out a solid, hearty laugh. "Wait right here, mate." He strode back to the van and returned with a white plastic bottle, which he held up, for me to see. "Washing-up liquid."

He winked.

My new friend poured about half his bottle of detergent into the hole and then ran. "Okay everyone, let's move waaaaaaay back," he shouted.

We shuffled back about two feet.

"No seriously, lads, I mean let's move waaaaaaay back."

We started shuffling back a little further and far below us the earth grumbled. A monstrous, moaning, gurgling vibration roared up through the ground, and through us, and a jet of pressurized boiling water exploded into the atmosphere like Niagara Falls in reverse. It went on for entire minutes, spewing steaming water and an ocean of soap suds all over the landscape in every direction.

I have liked Australians immensely, ever since.

Coincidentally, upon returning to England we discovered that, during our absence, a family of Australians had moved in directly across the street from us. The good news was, they had three fun-loving and very cute daughters, roughly the same ages as my brother and myself. The bad news was, classes started again on Monday.

FOUR

ARMY, SCHOOL, OR WORK

They gave you thirst, then sold you relief
They gave you sin, then called for a priest
So, now they give you a choice
Because they know you're such a jerk
Yeah they know, you're such a jerk
Army, school, or work
Or exile

From "Army, School, or Work"
By Lach and Norman England

MY SCHOOL BOASTED A LONG AND PROUD MILITARY HISTORY ably documented in their private church named Big School by the gold leaf-embellished names of the many unfortunate boys who had been obliterated in combat between 1914–18 and 1939–45. Despite previous losses, a two-year stint in the school's army or air force cadet corps was for our generation, of course, compulsory.

Any kid who dreams of going into space knows that the fastest way to get there is to become a skilled military pilot like Gordo Cooper or Neil Armstrong and, once you have the experience, move on to NASA. In my position it made good sense for me to take the air force cadet route, just in case I decided to pursue a career as an astronaut at a later date. I had been thrilled by my first flying experience during the Iceland adventure; and, two years later, as a know-it-all fourteen year-old, I was quite certain that flight training would be infinitely preferable to crawling around in the mud with the infantry, poor misguided fool that I was.

That spring I was packed off to Crowborough Camp—a military training base in southern England—and placed under the absolute control of a savage maniac named Sergeant Ruddle. A member of England's elite Special Air Service, he had recently returned from a tour of duty in Northern Ireland. A rumor had it that his best friend was killed over there by the Irish Republican Army, and he certainly used every possible opportunity to take out his aggression on us. The camp's Survival Training Initiative focused on a daily program of smearing dirt on our faces and crawling around in the mud while Sergeant Ruddle kicked us with his perfectly-polished paratrooper boots.

A day-long orienteering exercise on the moors consisted of driving us cadets deep into the wastelands in Land Rovers, and throwing us out, one by one, with no food or

[facing page] The Jurassic Coast, near Lyme Regis in England, my favorite fossil hunting grounds as a child.

money, equipped only with an out-of-date map and a broken compass. We were informed that we could eat after we made it back to camp, whenever that might be. I imagine the damp bones of a few boys are still out there, somewhere, in the peat bogs.

We spent several rainy nights abandoned at a disused and overgrown WWII airfield, with a military surplus parachute for shelter, a couple of smelly sterno firelighters and a dehydrated meal package stamped: "Chicken Supreme Dinner. Ministry of Defence, 1948."

I am now a strict vegetarian.

Our sad little squad of four teenagers managed to construct a rudimentary tent from one sagging parachute, and coaxed a fire to life under dripping branches. We nodded off sometime during the night, propped up against trees, huddled together, and trying our best to keep dry. A surprise raid by a rival group of kids woke us around 2 a.m., when six thugs ripped through our melancholy camp, tearing the parachute and smashing all our supplies. We ambushed them in return, the following night. Leaping out from a roadside trench, we roughed them up, stole their flashlights and compasses and left them helpless in the darkness.

At that moment I realized a career in the military was not for me.

The unrelenting harshness of my incarceration at school eventually drove out all desire for learning and even civility. The quiet boy who loved to read and visit museums had been mutated by British public school into an anti-authoritarian malcontent. School life was propelled by the petty minutiae of absurd rules and regulations: certain stairwells were up only; others were down only. We all had to dress daily in matching uniforms and were not allowed to wear any buttons or badges unless they were sanctioned by the school. We were required to carry with us a very specific style and color of sports bag that was available from only one overpriced shop in town. We were forbidden to read comics, or bring toys, matches, or water pistols onto the grounds. The school even published its own pathetic little rule book, which we were required to study and memorize. I am not proud of this now, and I certainly do not recommend such behavior to school children today, but in 1976, when I was fifteen, I had been pushed, bullied, belittled, and shouted at for too long. I set myself on a new course of action and went on the offensive: I literally broke every school rule in the book, one by one, and in order.

At just about the same time, Neil Gaiman took me to my first rock concert—Lou Reed at the Rainbow Theater in North London. We were listening to Lou's records all the time, along with others by David Bowie and Iggy Pop. I found Lou Reed's monotone, sarcastic voice to be the perfect commentary on the political and social desolation of the 1970s. Neil favored his quiet, moody albums like *Berlin*, while I fixated upon the raucous live records such as *Rock 'n' Roll Animal*.

As we walked up to the Rainbow on that warm spring evening, I noticed two fascinating and very strange girls dressed in black vinyl jackets covered in safety pins and sporting purple hair, waiting to go in.

"What are they?" I whispered to Neil.

"Oh, they're just punk rockers," he replied.

It was the very dawn of punk, but Neil already knew what was going on.

We took our seats, about six rows back in the grand old auditorium. It was the start of the European leg of Lou Reed's famous Rock 'n' Roll Heart Tour. He walked out onto the big stage in front of us, with a full band, and blasted straight into "Sweet Jane." Within thirty seconds my life changed forever. From that day on I lived for rock music. I got a lousy part time job stocking shelves at Boots the Chemists for the sole purpose of spending all money on records.

I was a powder keg ready to blow, and Lou Reed and Neil Gaiman lit the fuse.

It is impossible to overstate the effect that the punk rock revolution had—and continues to have to this day—on every aspect of my life. It was a social movement existing at the very bottom of the hierarchy of British life, a stratum that was decidedly anti-establishment and in which every ounce of pretense and artifice had been stripped away. Punk bands were obsessed with the idea of "not selling out" and remaining true to their ideals. The searing guitars, spiky hair, leather jackets, and brilliantly colored homemade t-shirts were a rebellion not only against the square fashion and established music of the time, but also an in-your-face sneer at the British government of the 1970s—a corrupt and misguided political monolith that failed, in almost every way, to support the needs of ordinary people.

When the new punk bands were unable to generate interest from the major record companies, some of them started their own and put out records without any interference from the industry, and that pivotal moment in the history of music—the birth of indie labels—is lovingly described in the The Clash song "Hitsville UK." Such radical steps were born partly out of necessity—at the start most of the big record labels were too frightened or too close-minded to sign punk bands—and partly a deliberate decision by musicians not to participate in the corporate ownership of original music. It was a social and artistic revolution of the first order.

Fanzines also had their genesis in the punk years, so indie music and self publishing, as they exist today in all their splendor are, without a shadow of a doubt, the children of punk. I was part of all that and the music from those times lives in my bones. Above all else, the "do-it-yourself" ethic of the punk rock movement instilled in me the clear understanding that I could be unconventional, resist the tired programming of society, go my own way, and do things for myself without the approval of church or state. And I did.

Neil and I bought mirrored sunglasses and bleached our dark hair tangerine. In today's high schools such a thing would barely be noticed, but in 1976 such behavior—especially from "educated" boys at a "proper" school was unthinkable. We were ridiculed, once again, by the headmaster, in public. Shortly thereafter started our own band. Neil said it would be a great way to meet girls.

I learned to play the drums in six months. We recruited guitarist Baggy Wilson—a fellow student—called ourselves Impact, then quickly changed the name to Chaos, which was definitely more appropriate, and finally, after adding bassplayer Graham Smith to the lineup, settled on The Ex-Execs.

Neil understood guitar chords and was already good with words. Like me, he cared little for studies, but was easily the smartest kid in the entire school. To my amazement, he quickly wrote a slew of songs and we filled out our repertoire with covers of Lou Reed and David Bowie numbers. We would play absolutely anywhere at any time: parties, pubs, church halls. We once drove two hours, in the pouring rain, to play at a tiny bar late on a Tuesday night.

We constantly saw the best bands of that era—The Clash, The Ramones, Blondie,

The Jam, The Damned, The Stranglers, Generation X, The Buzzcocks, The Rich Kids, and many others—in small venues and, to this day, I have witnessed precious few concerts that can match the energy and passion of that era.

London was not all music and mischief in the 1970s. Unemployment was rampant. The police regularly harassed teenagers and ethnic groups. There were riots, car bombs, pub bombings, and youth gangs with their own uniform code of dress—rockers, skinheads, teddy boys, and others—routinely inflicted horrific violence on other groups in the street, in clubs and bars, and even on the trains and buses. One afternoon I was randomly attacked by seven or eight skinheads and arrived at school shaken and somewhat bloody.

In 1977 our band was approached by one of the first indie labels, Heat Records. They wanted to release Neil's song "Victims" as a 45, or a "single" as it was called in England. We felt ecstatic and believed we were already on the road to music stardom. But the label went broke and our record was never released. It was the first in a very long line of "almosts" in my life as a musician.

A year later, after a short but blazing career, The Damned—one of my most favorite bands—announced they were breaking up and would hold a farewell concert at The Rainbow in London. They have since reformed, several times, but it was a tragic night for me, and also the first time I was recognized in public. I returned to the same venue where I attended my very first concert, two years earlier, but now I was in my own my band, and my bassplayer, Graham, who disliked The Damned, reluctantly agreed to go along with me.

It was mayhem from the moment we arrived. The large seated venue was a shambles. Hundreds of punk rockers invaded the place, ignored the numbers on their tickets, and took whatever places appealed to them. When an usher pointed Graham and me in the direction of our assigned and very desirable eighth-row seats, we saw that a gang of evil-looking skinheads had already appropriated them and, not having a death wish, we declined to ask them to move. So did the usher, who said: "Oh, just come down here then," and took us to the front row, exactly in the middle—the best seats in the whole place.

It was only a few minutes to show time. Fans were hurling plastic beer mugs and pieces of their own clothing up on the stage, whooping, singing, leaping around, chanting, and generally acting like pirates on a bender. Graham and I were congratulating each other on our good fortune regarding the seating change when a breathtaking petite, svelte punkette ran up the narrow space between our front row seats and the stage. Heavily made up with black eyeliner, she was wearing black tights, a tiny colorful miniskirt, a sharp little leather jacket, and a sexy velvet choker around her white neck.

"Aren't you the drummer from The Ex-Execs!" she exclaimed, her dark eyes wide and glittering.

"Umm . . . yes, I am." I was nearly shocked into silence.

"Oh, you are just brilliant!" she beamed.

She moved closer, as if about to kiss me.

"Where did you see us?" I stammered.

She smiled at me—a hot, seductive, sweet and irresistible smile—opened her black-lipsticked lips and said: "At the … "

And at that very instant the lights went down and three thousand punk rockers and skinheads rose up and surged over us. The front eight rows of seats—including ours—were pulled out of the floor and many were hurled onto the stage before the first song was done. Unprepared for this catastrophe, Graham and I were slammed forward by the mob of Damned fans gone mad, and plastered hard against the stage. For a moment I caught a glimpse of the beautiful punk rock girl floating away, captured by the crowd, moving in the opposite direction, out of reach in the maelstrom, and waving sadly to me amid a sea of maniacs. I never saw her again.

Back in the daylight world, I was disgusted by the hypocrisy of day-to-day life at school. The headmaster preached to us first thing, every morning, about "the love of our Lord Jesus Christ" and then his henchmen would beat and humiliate us for the duration. I learned to distrust, and sometimes despise, authority figures and so-called moralists who felt the need to instruct me and my generation in what was regarded as proper and acceptable. At age seventeen, angry and battered by the psychic cost of "a good education" I left British school behind forever, determined to focus all of my energies on music.

The Ex-Execs disbanded, but Graham and I had a terrific rapport with similar tastes in music and humor. We stuck together with the intention of forming a power trio and spent some months auditioning prospects until we met Dave Hall, a strikingly handsome singer/guitarist who dressed in dashing mod fashions. I admired Dave's songwriting and style and the three of us formed a new band, Phazers on Stun, in 1978. After a performance one night at a South London club in Tooting, a dapper man came up to us with a boxy and bulky camera under his arm.

"Oi lads, take a look at this!" he said. He flipped up a small screen and played back part of the concert for us. 1978 was still the era of 8-millimeter film movie cameras and I was amazed by the ability to instantly view a scene on magnetic tape. It was the very first time I ever saw myself on video. Sadly the recording is lost in the mist of the punk years.

Despite my devotion to the new band, my parents implored me to go back to school, elsewhere, for my one remaining year, so I made a deal: I would be good, finish my final year of high school and—after that—I was on my own.

I am eternally grateful to Mom and Dad for guiding me at that difficult moment, because I completed my preliminary education at a school that was as different from the previous one as could be imagined. The American School in London (ASL) was a modern, progressive, international establishment in idyllic Saint John's Wood where we were not beaten or abused by our teachers. On the contrary, they called us by our first names, we could wear our own clothes, meet girls, and even go to the pub when we were not in class.

England did not enforce the drinking age in the 1970s, nobody knew what "I.D." stood for, driver's licenses did not even have photos on them, and the most severe interrogation you might receive in a bar would be a publican asking: "Are you sure you're eighteen?" as he poured your next pint of real ale.

At ASL I came under the influence of another exceptional art teacher—Suzanne Guest—a charmingly quirky former nun who shared my appetite for both pranks and pop art. She goaded me into painting a colossal Andy Warhol-style mural of Marilyn Monroe on the front of the school. To my considerable surprise that sort of thing went

[top] The Ex-Execs at Soho Market, London, in 1978 (left to right) Graham K. Smith, the author, Neil Gaiman, Al Kingsbury. [above] On stage with The Marines, Crawdaddy Club, South London, 1980. [facing page] The Marines in 1980 (left to right) the author, Al Binney, Martin Brett.

over quite well at ASL and, for the first time, I thought I might actually enjoy being at school, and possibly even learn something of value. I used to delight in walking down Loudon Road every morning before class and winking at Marilyn, gazing out over North London.

ASL offered a real geology course and I enrolled immediately. The entry-level curriculum contained little that was new to me, but the teacher had plenty of enthusiasm, and I spent actual school time playing with igneous rocks and invertebrate fossils. Early in the semester he organized a field trip for us to the South Downs—a gentle wave of rolling, treeless hills that were once the bed of an ancient sea, and quite close to the quarry I haunted as a kid.

We took a long lunch break during the day hike, and I clambered to the top of the nearest chalk cliff and got back to the serious business of looking for micrasters. Most of the class wandered off out of sight somewhere, including two vivacious and constantly-giggling brunettes whom I found most intriguing. They were Ivy Brown and Pam Huggins, became lifelong friends, and many years later owned up to being "a little freaked out" by the English kid who turned up for the field trip with a leather jacket and a bag of rock hammers. They also admitted that when I climbed up the slope to look for fossils at lunchtime, they laughed themselves silly about "the weird guy hanging off the edge of the cliff."

At roughly the same time, Neil Gaiman was commencing his soon-to-be-stellar writing career and is, today, one of the most celebrated and influential authors of our generation. He was one of the key figures in my life and if he had not suggested, back in 1976, that we start a band, I would have followed a very different and probably far less interesting path.

Neil's books *Stardust*, *Coraline*, and *Mirrormask* were made into motion pictures and *Neverwhere* was televised by the BBC. His fantasy novels have delighted millions around the world, and his comic book series *Sandman* is a milestone in the genre. I was honored when Neil gave an incidental character the name of Notkin in the very first issue of *Sandman*.

In 1979 Phazers on Stun disbanded and I joined an established London rock group, The Marines. My singer, Martin Brett, went on to great success in the late '80s and early '90s with the Anglo-American pop group Voice of the Beehive. He recently worked on the Martin Scorsese film *Hugo*, and still plays music in London.

Life with the band was packed with travel, night clubs, and excitement. The Marines played constantly during 1979 and 1980, and we built a modest but devoted following in southern England. In other words, the exact opposite of the dull and dusty laboratories where I had recently studied the Periodic Table of the Elements. I also found I had made another profound miscalculation: My true love in music was destined to be the bass guitar, not the drums. The Marines were the last band I would work with as a drummer. I bought a Fender bass guitar and, late at night, after I returned home from a concert, I would pick it up and practice for hours while foxes and badgers crept, unseen, through the woods behind the house where I played as a child.

I was still involved with geology, but I had become part of something very different and vital and undeniable. As a little boy I was an outcast at school. The punk rockers were displaced in their own way—a loud, vigorous, disenchanted generation of outcasts mired in Conservative Britain. They became my new family.

Following graduation from ASL, and due largely to my personal field experience collecting rocks and fossils, I landed a good job with an oil exploration company in South London. It was a time of conflict and indecision for me. The company director was an affable American geologist-turned-administrator who allowed us to wear blue jeans—provided they were clean and did not have studs on them—to the office. The American influence added a pleasant laid-back atmosphere at work, but it was still Thatcher's England and a gloomy, pessimistic attitude hung over most of the country like a wet sheepdog.

I should have been thrilled. Despite the grisly failure of my British education, I completed high school in a supportive and encouraging environment and almost immediately succeeded in finding a well-paying job in geology. I spent my days in a relaxed office looking for oil and my nights playing punk rock. But then again, I was not *really* looking for oil. This was not really geology. I prepared and analyzed data sent to us by the *real* geologists who worked in unpronounceable parts of the Middle East, laying big seismic charges deep underground and blowing them the hell up. If I was going to be in geology at all, I needed to be where the action was and that meant a desolate and hopefully slightly dangerous desert where I could find extraordinary things for myself. I realized I was not suited for the strictures of lab work.

At the age of nineteen I arrived at a significant crossroads. Pursuit of the sparkling scientific career I imagined for myself had lead me to a financially rewarding, but unfortunately dull, office situation. Many people told me I should devote my abilities to a career as a professional musician, or artist, and I became confused and despondent.

Science is hard work. You do not guesstimate, wing it, or go with the flow. It requires patience, dedication, and earnest, painstaking labor. Rock 'n' roll was fast, invigorating, and immediate, and both of my adored art teachers told me I could make a living as an artist. I simply did not have the temperament to go back to school again for years of numbers and graphs and charts, in order to earn the degrees that a research scientist would need.

I was torn. To me, science was and would always be Haroun Tazieff perching gracefully on the rim of an erupting volcano with his movie camera, not the analysis and measurement of charts in an office in South London. I did still want to be that adventurer, out in the screaming wilderness, discovering and documenting astonishing things, but I could not commit to the long course of study and lab work I thought I would need to get there.

At the time, I viewed my change of heart as both a personal failure of character and a betrayal of my true love of science, rather than seeing it for what it really was—evolution.

FIVE

INTO THE DEVIL'S CANYON

You look like a lizard
Jealous of the Empire State Building
You hate anyone who doesn't share your feeling
That everyone is stealing
From the floor down to the ceiling
Anything not nailed down by the logic of your fear
But logic is a rerun of a *Star Trek* long gone
And you're scared your time has never come
You're Mr. Bitterman

From "Mr. Bitterman"
By Lach

IN AUGUST OF 1981 I LEFT HOME, and England, for the United States at the age of nineteen. The Marines were doing well and I could easily have stayed on and played with them for years, but I yearned to see more of the America I visited as a child.

The Marines signed a record deal with a London label and even recorded our first 45, but the company went belly up just like the label Chaos signed with, and the disc was never released.

It was time for a major change in direction. I removed the neck from my Fender bass guitar, and crammed it into a suitcase along with my leather jacket, a photo album, my most frequently played cassette tapes, three favorite fossils I had found back in the old quarry as a kid, a couple of books, some good English tea bags and a few clothes. I was starting over.

The summers I spent on Cape Cod as a child drew me to Massachusetts, and I enrolled as a freshman in the School of Liberal Arts at Boston University. Although my parents and I had a "no more school deal," they still somehow convinced me that college was a good idea. I developed an instant affection for the city, but the university was too large and too impersonal for me with its 56,000 students and tedious regulations that reminded me altogether too much of British school. Once again, I found myself at a school that I did not much care for. All, however, was not lost.

Within two days I met Lach, a luminous, energetic and irreverent musician who would go on to great acclaim as the founder of New York's Antifolk movement. I saw him standing outside of my dormitory building on the first day of school, wearing a Clash t-shirt. I went up to say hello and we formed an instantaneous rapport. A day later we began putting a new band together—The Aliens—and by the end of the school year we decided to quit university, move to New York, reform Lach's old band, Proper Id, with me on bass guitar, and go for broke as rock 'n' rollers.

I stepped gleefully into an unfamiliar and intoxicating world full of New York bohemians and musicians. Lach and my other new bandmates had grown up there and seemed to know everyone. A rivalry existed between us and the other top outfit on our local circuit—4 Way Ping. I loved that band. Way ahead of their time, both sonically and musically, they carried an unusual lineup: two guitars, bass, drums, and a highly talented percussionist. The singer and rhythm guitarist, Paul Martino, intrigued me from the day we first met. A handsome, articulate, literary man, with impeccable manners, he was a startlingly original songwriter and also that rarest of things—a rock 'n' roll intellectual. We became fast friends, much to the confusion of the members of both Proper Id and 4 Way Ping. Evidently, it was not regarded as cool for the Id bassplayer to hang out with the rival Ping singer, but we did anyway and even formed a side project, The Dubcats, that reflected our mutual obsession with Jamaican reggae.

I played professionally in the New York rock scene for most of the next twenty years, with Proper Id and a number of other bands. I performed at most of the top clubs on the East Coast, some of them too many times to count: The Ritz, C.B.G.B., The Cat Club, The Mercury Lounge, The Stone Pony, The Knitting Factory, Beowulf's, Sidewalk, and many others.

One night at C.B.G.B., the so-called "Birthplace of Punk," on the Bowery in New York, I met Anne Husick. We went on to work in a band called The Big Picture, with producer and singer/songwriter Chris Gibson. Anne later performed with Band of Susans, The Ronnie Spector Band, Wilson Pickett, Joey Ramone and many other music legends. Anne had long, wavy dark brown hair, was an excellent musician with a keen ear, and presented a spiritual and somewhat New Agey, hippie demeanor. With my South London punk sensibility and spiky hair, we seemed as different as could be on the surface, but we remain the closest of friends to this day, and she has always been a moderating influence on me.

"Just learn to let things go," she would say, when I ranted on for too long about how evil British school had been, or how much various aspects of life in New York irritated me.

In 1983 a girlfriend invited me to attend a gallery opening at her school, a cutting-edge, privately-owned New York City art college named the School of Visual Arts. It was love at first sight. Slightly run down, with witty graffiti on the bathroom walls and undergrad art shows in every open space, SVA was populated by an odd mix of hippies, punk rockers, downtown art world dandies, and polite, well-dressed and well-spoken foreign students. I had never encountered such an eclectic microcosm of talent and individuality. A vaguely anarchic, highly progressive school, where every teacher was a professional working artist, and where the pragmatic student could write his own syllabus, SVA became my new home.

I commenced my freshman year that fall. A few years older than my classmates, and propelled by the excitement of being in the right place at the right time, I became—for the first time in my life—a good student. I regularly air mailed school reports back home to my parents, just to shock them, but nobody was more surprised than I was to see all those A grades. I had the good fortune to work with two admired professional photographers—Cora Kennedy and Walter Silver—and studied with some of the great artists of the times, including legendary cartoonist and publisher Will Eisner, who wrote and illustrated the influential comic book, *The Spirit*; Harvey

Kurtzman, creator of *Mad* magazine; and Pulitzer prize-winner Art Spiegelman. After I graduated I was offered a job as associate editor with Art and his wife, the brilliant designer and publisher Françoise Mouly-Spiegelman, with the avant-garde comics and graphics magazine, *Raw*.

In the late 1980s I worked for several major publishers in New York, learned the publishing and design business, then founded my own design firm, Stanegate Studios, in 1989. Design work paid my bills all through the rock 'n' roll years.

Proper Id, completed its first CD, *Contender*, in 1990. It came out under Lach's name as he had a solo deal at the time, and we threw ourselves a spectacular record release party at the Pyramid Club in New York's East Village. It was one of the best crowds we ever played to. People were jammed right up against the stage, their heads bobbing under the hazy red and green spotlights. Lach opened the show solo, then a couple of guests came on, and finally the whole band edged up the spiral staircase that threaded its way from the below-stage dressing room through the drum riser.

People I had never met, or even seen before, knew our music and were singing along with one of the crowd favorites, a Lach composition called "The John Glenn Song." As I watched a pair of saucy rock girls mouth the words: "I wanna be an astronaut, I wanna be an astronaut," I spun around, so the spotlights would illuminate my newly-painted jacket.

I wanted to wear something unique for the release party so I painted myself a Proper Id jean jacket. I cut the sleeves off and decorated it with a psychedelic multi-colored Id logo, an assortment of studs, a brass marshall's badge, the image of a gecko, and the words: "You look like a lizard, jealous of the Empire State Building. Proper Id Record Release Party, July 21 '90." Not your everyday line, and neither is the story of how it came to be.

A couple of years earlier, during my senior year at the School of Visual Arts, and on a misty spring night, Lach did a solo concert at 61 Fifth Avenue. The place is now an ordinary salad bar and deli but was once the famous Lone Star Café, best known to New Yorkers as "that building with the lizard on top," due to the enormous model reptile that squatted sullenly on its roof. Despite the lizard, or perhaps because of it, the Lone Star was a prestigious gig.

"You have to either be really happening, or be one of the good ol' boys to play there," Lach told me. I had recently seen British punk solo artist Billy Bragg at the Lone Star and could not help comparing Lach with Billy Bragg, even though Lach wrote better songs and resisted delivering a twenty-minute pro-Communist speech before each number. Lach confided to me that he was once thrown out of the Lone Star for hitting Bragg with a packet of Marlboros during just such a monologue, and yelling at him: "You're in America now, pal." Lach spent much of the evening of his own show worrying that he would be recognized and thrown out a second time.

Immediately after his set, Lach headed straight for me. He wanted to know the usual things: "How was the sound? Could you hear the words? Was it obvious that I messed up the second song?" all the while towing me upstairs.

"There's food and stuff in the dressing room. Let's grab some." Lach appropriated a mostly full bottle of Jack Daniels from the bar, and said over and over, in a loud animated voice that he needed to go up and see "that big lizard!"

"Come on! Let's all go up on the roof!" he bellowed, waving the bottle of Jack over

[page 30] The author at C.B.G.B. with Proper Id, New York, 1981. [top] As a young writer at New York's School of Visual Arts in 1984. [above] On stage at the Cat Club in New York City, with Anne Husick and the Big Picture, 1989. [following page] The author and Lach, performing with Proper Id, New York, Halloween, 1982.

his head. The backstage area was full of music business hangers-on, talent scouts, journalists, and so on, and as Lach continued to insist that we must all go to the roof, they started to look like they had somewhere to be and disappeared downstairs to see the next act.

"Come on, Geoff," Lach said, heading for the roof. "We don't need any of those record company posers to have a good time."

I had no idea how blustery it had become until we stepped outside. I cowered under the lizard's gigantic torso as it creaked and swayed over our heads. It was easily the size of a small airplane and did not look stable.

Lach walked right to the edge of the building and stood under the thing's throat, on a wet and narrow brick ledge, three stories above Fifth Avenue.

"Look!" he shouted. "This lizard is looking right at the Empire State Building." He pointed north, towards the famous skyscraper, lit up and glimmering through the rainy haze. Minute bursts of light twinkled down to us like microscopic neon diamonds—flashbulbs from tourist cameras on the 86th floor.

"You can tell it's jealous," Lach yelled through the wind. "This lizard wants to see the view from up there, instead of being stuck on top of this bullshit place."

"Lach, I think you ought to keep away from the edge."

I did not want to sound like a square, so I added: "These old buildings get very slippery in the rain, you know."

Lach staggered back over, and I was delighted that he was actually listening to my advice. He handed me the bottle of Jack Daniels.

"Here, hold onto this."

He bounded back towards the edge of the building leaping, at the very last moment, up into the air and grabbing onto the lower jaw of the lizard's gaping mouth. He hung there, swaying madly, leather jacket and plaid shirt flapping in the awful wind, with his feet dangling over the Fifth Avenue traffic eighty feet below, laughing and shouting out crazily into the night: "I am the lizard king. I can do anything!"

It was a spectacular stunt, but I was fairly certain that he was about to lose his grip and fall to his death, or tear the lizard's mouth off and then fall to his death. Or, possibly, bring the entire lizard crashing down on top of me, and then fall to his death clutching half a giant jaw.

"Hey Lach, come over and look at this!" I yelled, trying to feign astonishment.

"What?" He flung himself back onto the roof. "What is it?"

I ran over, grabbed him, and dragged him quickly back inside where he promised he would not climb onto the lizard again. Later that night he was accosted by a bitter old folk musician who complained relentlessly about his own lack of fame and success. That combined with the brooding lizard inspired one of Lach's best songs: "Mr. Bitterman."

Back at the Pyramid, on the night of the release party in 1990, the incident with the lizard was very much in my mind. We hammered through "Mr. Bitterman," and there was no doubt that we were better than ever.

I still had my eye on the two sing-along girls in the front. They were enjoying the new songs, too. They did not know the lyrics to "Mr. Bitterman" yet, but our first CD was finally out, and all seemed right with the world. In the stagelight euphoria of the moment, I thought it would be only a matter of time until everyone knew the words,

but it was not to be. Our drummer, Jon Berger, quit the band less than a year later and went on the road with a touring Broadway show for good money.

Lead guitarist Norman England was one of my closest friends, and also one of the most brilliant people I have ever met. I admired him tremendously. We shared a passion for science fiction, movies, literature, and irreverent humor and, to this day, I consider him the finest guitarist I have ever worked with. Always the most committed and hardworking among us, Norman became so disillusioned when the band splintered that he poured a can of lighter fluid over his red Flying V guitar, set fire to it, and moved to Japan, where he is now an accomplished film and television director, writer, and translator. I miss him.

I have attended hundreds, or more likely, thousands of rock concerts during the past thirty-five years. I have seen many, or most, of the world's greatest contemporary musical artists—some of them numerous times—including The Who, The Clash, The Ramones, David Bowie, Eric Clapton, Lou Reed, Iggy Pop, and I know objectively, and in my heart, that Proper Id was one of the best bands of that era. Today, when I re-watch the concert videos from our later shows during the 1990s, I am still amazed by the power, precision, and originality of our music. Most of those great songs Lach and Norman wrote never made it to the airwaves, or onto plastic. There remains within me, and the others too I imagine, a lingering dissatisfaction, as if we came back from the edge without fulfilling our mission. I have the tapes, and the photos, and the memories of incandescent live shows, but they are not enough.

After a time, Lach and I started again, recruited famed drummer Billy Ficca— formerly of Television and The Waitresses—and from then on, played under Lach's name. We put out several albums and had many adventures but, without Norman and Jon, it was never the same. As Joe Strummer said, after The Clash split up: "The circle had been broken."

In 1994, while browsing through bookstores in-between concerts, I happened upon O. Richard Norton's seminal meteorite work *Rocks from Space*. I devoured it in a few afternoons during that humid summer, sitting on a flimsy deck chair on the roof of a building in New York's Chelsea district. There is a mildly unsettling experience that many meteorite people have shared. It is the abrupt shattering of a vague pre-conceived idea that they are the only individual in the world interested in the obscure and outlandish field of meteorites except, perhaps, for a few super-educated academics. *Rocks from Space* was my own personal catalyst for that experience.

All through the rock 'n' roll years I had kept a rock hammer in the trunk of my car, and occasionally visited an abandoned mine or quarry to collect a few new geological specimens, but my heart wasn't really in it. The allure of geology and meteorites never left me, but it had been neatly sublimated by rock 'n' roll. During those sweaty rooftop afternoons, as I worked through *Rocks from Space*, page by page, all the wonder and anticipation I felt as a child poured back into me like heavy water into a bucket. I bought maps and a new compass, sanded the rust off of my rock hammer and oiled it for the first time in twenty years. Back in 1968 I had promised myself that I would find a meteorite and now, for the first time in my life, I was setting out in an attempt to fulfill that childhood dream.

[facing page] Promotional photograph for The Big Picture, taken in Hoboken, NJ in 1987 (left to right) Pat Ramsey, Anne Husick, the author, Chris Gibson.

[top] The author putting down bass tracks for the first Proper Id 45, "Electric Boy," at the Barge Studio in Wayne, New Jersey, 1981. [above] Listening to rough mixes while recording at Northcott Studios in New York City, 1982. In the background (left to right) are Lach, producer John Rutherford, and Norman England.

40

[top] On stage with Lach at the Pyramid Club, New York City, during the record release party for *Contender*.
[above] Proper Id at Beowulf's rock club in New York's East Village in 1991 (left to right) Lach, Jon Berger, Norman England, the author.

My girlfriend of several years, Jackie, an elegant and talented graphic artist of Asian descent whom I met while working for a big New York City magazine publisher, had never been out West, and barely done any camping. I invited her to join me on a tour of the Southwest that would include Monument Valley, the Grand Canyon, the Four Corners, the Hopi Nation's artist co-op on Second Mesa and, of course, the site that had been denied to me way back in 1971—Meteor Crater.

After overnighting in Phoenix, Arizona, we rented a four-wheel drive Pathfinder, loaded it with supplies, and headed north. I remember being impressed by a stern warning at the point where I-17 begins its 5,000-foot climb towards Flagstaff: "Avoid overheating. Turn off air conditioner." That sign made me feel as if we were heading somewhere vast, different, and possibly dangerous.

As you roll east down the long, fast stretch of I-40 between Flagstaff and Holbrook, the land flattens out and opens up, and a jagged, prominent ridge appears way off, near the horizon, and a little to the right. Jackie sat beside me in the Pathfinder, wearing dark sunglasses and quietly following our progress on the map.

As we drove closer, the ridge seemed to become more substantial, as if taking on more of a presence. After some time, squinting through the distance, and feeling a little silly, I said: "That can't be the crater up there, can it? It's huge!"

And it is huge. The awkwardly named Meteor Crater—craters are made by meteorites, not meteors—known to previous generations as Coon Butte, Crater Mound, Winslow Crater and Barringer Crater is a massive, mile-wide, beautifully preserved impact feature into which you could easily fit a not-very-small town, and is something of a mecca for meteorite enthusiasts. It is also, unfortunately, a privately-owned tourist attraction and commercial venture. Visitors must make their way through a crowded gift shop full of Meteor Crater patches and meteorite candy before arriving at the aerie—the observation point perched at the crater's rim. From there you can look out in dazed wonder at a stupendous hole punched in the earth's crust about 25,000 years ago by a chunk of iron-nickel asteroid core the size of a small building.

I had called ahead, and we took a brief meeting with one of the managerial staff. He was pleasant and courteous, but inflexible. I wanted to write an article about the crater, or do a photographic project, or maybe both, and I asked for permission to hike around in the off-limits areas. While we were out there we might, possibly, you know, pick up one or two small specimens. I was confident that my polite British manners and London accent would overcome any petty regulations that they might have concocted.

Not a chance.

The staff who run the Meteor Crater attraction maintain that collecting is prohibited in order to preserve any remaining meteorites for future study. It sounds good, but in reality is a thin argument when you consider that the great meteorite pioneer, H.H. Nininger, already spent half of his life carrying out exhaustive research at the site. The iron meteorite fragments with their attractive orange desert patina that still litter the area by the thousands are not being preserved in the ground; they are slowly rusting away.

[facing page] Apparently, rock 'n' roll never dies. The author (second from left) appearing with Krista Krome's Feed as the New York Dolls for a charity concert, Club Congress, Tucson, 2008. © Stu Jenks

[top] My first view of Meteor Crater in Arizona, 1994. [above] Harvey Harlow Nininger (1887–1986) was a biology teacher turned meteorite pioneer, and is regarded by many (including me) as the father of modern meteoritics. He is one of my heroes. This Canyon Diablo iron meteorite was collected by Dr. Nininger at Meteor Crater, probably during the 1950s, and bears one of his original hand-painted collection numbers.

"How much of the surrounding land do you own?" I asked. "I mean, at what point is it okay to get out and hike, and collect specimens?"

"Well, pretty much, if we can see ya, we're gonna arrest ya."

I was quite disappointed.

We walked back through the tacky gift shop and returned to our Pathfinder. We drove down to the main road, then headed off, away from the crater. Every so often we'd pass a severe red, black, and white metal sign informing us that "Removing meteoritic material from this area is against the law."

A meteorite is typically named after a known site closest to the spot where it was found, or seen to fall. In the United States that is usually the nearest town with a post office. If no town is available, a new discovery may be named after a recognizable geological feature, such as Elephant Wash or Coyote Flat. Confusingly, the space rocks found around Meteor Crater are not called Meteor Crater meteorites, but Canyon Diablo (Devil's Canyon) meteorites, after a rather treacherous ravine lying some miles to the west.

As we drove, we paralleled the steep-sided canyon for a while, and it did look like the sort of place where a devil might cower and scowl on a bad day.

Eventually, there were no more signs, and no more barbed wire fences and we were miles from the crater. I pulled the truck over on a flat patch of gravel and climbed out. It was spectacular view—a scene right out of George Herriman's *Krazy Kat* comic strip, with bright blue skies, petite sombrero-shaped clouds, and the crater ridge barely visible way off in the distance, like a dinosaur's backbone.

"Well, at least we got to see the crater," Jackie said, trying to cheer me up. She held out her hand. "Here, I bought you this Meteor Crater patch."

I wandered away from the truck, squinting at the brilliant sky, and absent mindedly taking some photographs. The ground was almost completely covered with tiny pieces of volcanic cinder. Eventually I came upon an old trench that appeared to have been dug by hand. I walked beside it, and after perhaps fifty feet noticed a big rusty ball protruding slightly from the trench wall. I marked the spot, went back to the truck, retrieved my handy digging tool, and poked at the ball for a while, until it just fell out of the dirt face and into my hands. I stood in the trench, puzzled, holding this odd and very heavy thing, and staring at it. I was completely calm because I did not think for a minute that the rusty rock could possibly amount to anything. The metal ball had a fractured surface and was extremely heavy. I asked Jackie to bring over my magnet. I placed the magnet on the rock and it stayed there.

I had found my first meteorite.

SIX

METEORHNTR

I am still naive enough to think
I could have some purpose
Still believe these words we sing
Should be much more profound
And sometimes when I'm lost at night
Alone without a friend
I wish I had a lighthouse
To guide me home again

From "Lighthouse"
By Geoffrey Notkin and Chris Gibson

I DISCOVERED AN OLD TOOTHBRUSH UNDER THE SINK and cleaned the Canyon Diablo with a lot more care than was necessary. It had fallen out of the sky and then sat in the desert for thousands of years. How much damage could I do with a toothbrush?

In the years that followed I would learn that I had, mostly by accident and as a result of dumb luck, become one of a very small group of enthusiasts who found their own first meteorite.

The majority of people who take that initial tentative, innocent step on the road towards total space rock obsession, purchase their first specimen from a dealer and then—later on when they have been savagely bitten by the bug—may try their luck at hunting. Most hunt and hunt, spend a lot of time and money, suffer sunburn or twisted ankles, and occasionally something much worse, never to find anything because successful meteorite hunting is hard work, time consuming, and requires a lot of specialized knowledge. In my case, it had been surprisingly easy to uncover that first visitor from outer space, after all those years of daydreaming about how great and challenging such a discovery would be.

My meteorite was weathered. It looked like a softball made out of rust-colored concrete toasted by a blowtorch. It was interesting in the same way that a hideous wild boar is interesting, but it did not have much in common with those fabulous sculptural specimens I gazed upon during my childhood visits to the Geological Museum in London.

I felt completely despondent. Jackie could not get me to snap out of it.

[facing page] The incomparable Steve Arnold at Gold Basin, Arizona.

"You should be over the moon," she said. "This is what you've always wanted!"

Despite my surprising and inexplicable disappointment, I gave my new find the highest possible honor in my New York apartment. I put in on a display shelf in the office, all by itself.

Just the one meteorite on the shelf.

I looked at it all the time. Some days I almost convinced myself that it was an excellent specimen worthy of a real meteorite hunter, and some days I wanted to cut it open to see if there was actually even any iron hidden away within its coarse exterior. I often stopped work, picked the rock up and examined it, sometimes with a magnifying glass.

I admitted to myself that I felt a miniscule but nagging doubt that it was not a real meteorite, and the whole thing had been too easy. I started to worry on a regular basis, and finally took my perplexing rock all the way up to the American Museum of Natural History on 79th Street in Manhattan, where I discretely compared it to their genuine iron meteorites which were safely displayed under glass. I was pleased to note that my find displayed an uncanny similarity to a specimen from Wolf Creek Crater in Australia.

Now that I understand meteorites, and have seen hundreds of Canyon Diablo specimens, I know that what I found was a "shale ball." Shale is a slang term for iron meteorites that have been heavily terrestrialized. In other words, oxygen, wind, and water, and thousands of years on our humid greenhouse Earth have caused much of the original iron to decay.

I delivered a final verdict: Yes, it was a meteorite. No, it was not good enough to count as the great meteorite find I imagined for myself while still a child. It just wasn't. I was extremely irritated with that seven-year-old boy I had once, apparently, been.

"You should have promised us that we were going to find a really *good* meteorite, you idiot!" I chided him retroactively. "Not one that looks like it came out of a junk yard."

I became vigorously involved with the Internet in the early days. My design firm counted a leading technology publisher among its clients, and one of their computer gurus hooked me up with a tiny modem and a fledgling Internet service provider. I included a list of hobbies in the simple user profile attached to my email account: fireworks, paleontology, scotch whisky, meteorites.

I only knew a couple of people who had email accounts back then, and I did not have a single friend with his or her own website. It is difficult to believe now that spam and invasive advertising have polluted almost every aspect of the Web, but there was a time when the arrival of a single new email from someone you did not know personally was an exciting event.

One morning in 1996 there arrived in my inbox an email with "Meteorites?" in the subject header. The sender's name was MeteorHntr. Two years had elapsed since the Canyon Diablo caper and I had fallen back into being continually busy with my design career. My Arizona meteorite was still in the office but it now had a lot of other bits and pieces piled around it: a Civil War mortar shell I had acquired in North Carolina; some fossils I found in Dorset, England; and a wind-up robot from Japan.

MeteorHntr had carried out a comprehensive search of existing online profiles, looking for any that contained the word "meteorite." After finding mine, he wrote to ask if I was a dealer or a collector. I wrote back and said I was not really sure what a meteorite dealer was, but I had found a Canyon Diablo ("A very nice one," I claimed), and planned on finding more when I got around to it.

"I have a meteorite hunting expedition to Chile planned for the spring of 1997 and I'm looking for a few more people to share expenses. Are you interested?"

MeteorHntr had already made the trip to Chile once, and found some meteorite fragments right at the end of his expedition. He wanted to return and was confident that he knew precisely how to get back to the site.

"Imilac, in Chile's Atacama Desert, is one of the few places on Earth where you're guaranteed to find meteorites," he promised. And we could also try our luck at Vaca Muerta and Pampa, two other sites along the way, where numerous other finds had been made.

MeteorHntr's real name was Steve Arnold; born in Kansas, but at the time residing in Tulsa, Oklahoma. Steve was 31—five years younger than me—had been hunting meteorites for several years, and was the president and founder of a company that was bizarrely named International Meteorite Brokerage. He held a business degree and was—to my amazement—making a living entirely out of hunting for, and trading and selling, meteorites.

After numerous emails and a few phone calls, I decided to spend three weeks in one of the most desolate and remote places on Earth, with a complete stranger. Jackie enjoyed traveling and was evidently somewhat reckless too, as she agreed to go along with us.

A few of my friends were quite concerned by our plans and another asked, puzzled, if we were going all the way to Chile because "meteorites fall there more often?"

[below] Steve Arnold and the author trying to figure out
where they are, and where they are going, in the Atacama Desert, Chile.

"Have you not seen *Treasure of the Sierra Madre!*" another friend exclaimed. "What if you get out there, find some meteorites that are worth more than gold, and he hits you over the head with a shovel and leaves you buried in a shallow grave in some godforsaken corner of the Chilean desert?"

Steve and I discussed everything in great detail: GPS units, camping equipment, 4WD trucks, maps and metal detectors, but I did not mention *Treasure of the Sierra Madre*, as I wanted to avoid making anyone unnecessarily nervous. We would be on our own, hundreds of miles out in the driest desert on Earth and there would be no room for error. With five team members we would be renting two 4WD Toyotas in case one got stuck or broke down. Then, sometime during March of 1997 the other two team members dropped out. It would be just the three of us traversing Chile, and in one vehicle.

I made a special trip to my favorite camping store, way up on Route 17 in northern New Jersey. We would be working at considerable altitude and were almost certain to experience harsh weather. While the American East Coast was enjoying a mild early spring, fall had already descended upon the Southern Hemisphere.

I bought cold weather sleeping bags, rated to 30 degrees; the latest high-tech miniature gasoline powered camp stove; collapsible army cots; and a dashing low profile three-man tent, which the expert staff promised me could handle almost anything. As an afterthought, I went back into the store once the gear was loaded into my car and bought two spare sets of extra long steel tent spikes. In a couple of weeks' time we would be very glad we had them, along with a pair of folding entrenching tools, purchased in the same store, that probably saved our lives.

The trip from New York to Santiago—the capital of Chile—via Buenos Aires, Argentina, took twenty-two hours. Crossing the Andes, our Aerolinas Argentinas jet was pounded by air currents spiralling up from the mountain summits a few thousand feet below. I stared down in wonder at vertical red-walled canyons, the size of small cities, where no person had ever walked.

We changed planes in Buenos Aires and flew low over the vast prairies and cattle ranches of Argentina which looked, I imagined, much as the American West had during the Nineteenth Century.

We had reserved a 4WD truck by phone, but options were very limited; once we reached Santiago we found that only regular two-wheel drive vehicles were available. I was not about to turn back just because the rental agency did not understand how to hold a reservation, so we took a 2WD extended cab Toyota instead, which looked pretty tough, but as a result of that decision we ended up putting ourselves in the riskiest of situations.

Navigating traffic in Santiago was as anarchic a driving experience as I have ever encountered. It made New York City seem tame in comparison. Once we fought our way to the hotel, tucked away in a cobbled cul-de-sac, and shoe-horned our truck into a tiny parking space, Jackie and I wandered, jet-lagged but too excited to sleep, through a new and strange city, far south of the Equator.

As sunset approached we climbed the brick citadel of Cerro Santo Lucia, where beautiful hilltop gardens made a vibrant contrast to the ugly modernist apartment buildings that surrounded it. A slender young Chilean man, dark and handsome and dressed in a white suit and Panama hat, stood alone under a palm tree singing a haunting aria in Spanish.

After dark, Jackie and I shared a meal of fresh vegetables and a carafe of local wine in an outdoor cafe off one of the main streets—the improbably named Avenida Bernardo O'Higgins. Our smartly-dressed waiter spoke a little English and with scores of birds singing in trees on both sides of the street and young starstruck couples, arm-in-arm and out for an evening stroll, we could easily have been in the most elegant neighborhood in Barcelona. The European Spanish influence on Chile was evident everywhere.

We had been awake for more than two days and were sorely in need of a long, quiet night's sleep. Of course, our hotel turned out to be cramped and noisy, and packed with an unsettling assortment of international misfits. Our room sat next to the elevator which squeaked and groaned relentlessly, and while I was showering the floor began to rumble and I nearly fell over in the tub.

"That's just great," I yelled out. "I *had* to pick a hotel right on top of the subway," but quickly realized that subways do not make buildings shake to that degree.

I ran out of the bathroom, clutching a towel, sensing that something was very wrong. We watched from our rattling fourth-floor window as locals poured into the darkened streets by the hundreds. They gathered in a square below us and all of them seemed to be pointing directly up at us. It was my first earthquake, and I assume a relatively minor one, but the hotel was already so rundown, we really could not tell if it had sustained any further damage.

Early the next morning, after buying supplies, we went—with some slight trepidation—to meet our new travel partner. In the light of day, in a strange and faraway city, it suddenly seemed bizarre, if not downright foolhardy, to be embarking upon such a venture with someone we had never met in person. We really knew next to nothing about Steve except that he wrote highly entertaining emails. We did know, however, that a poor traveling companion can ruin a holiday, and on a serious expedition an unreliable teammate can put your life at risk. Perhaps it was lack of sleep, but a sense of foreboding got hold of me as I walked into the arrivals hall to greet a man I had never before seen.

In baggage claim I noticed a long and narrow hard shell case, locked with steel clamps, and standing on its end. I knew Steve was bringing a magnetometer with him, and that peculiar case could only contain one thing. Eventually a broad-shouldered and youthful-looking man in mirrored sunglasses walked up to claim it. I enjoyed the luxury of a few anonymous moments in which to study our new comrade.

Steve was six feet three and built like an armored car. He wore a bright yellow t-shirt, olive green cargo pants, a white ten-gallon cowboy hat, and looked extraordinarily out of place towering over the petite Chileans, dressed as they were, simply and in white cottons. His face was roundish, jovial, with a wide forehead and suntan. He scooped up all his gear in thick brawny arms and carried it in a haphazard, nonchalant, almost jolly manner across the terminal floor, careening around with an expectant smile on his face, looking for me, and nearly knocking over a gaggle of tourists as he swung the magnetometer case behind him.

He appeared cheerful and confident, and just a little goofy. I liked him immediately and I decided he would likely make an excellent teammate. If we happened to get stuck in the desert, he could probably drag the truck out all by himself.

SEVEN

DESERT PAVEMENT: HARD ROAD TO IMILAC

I think I should have stayed with the car
"If you break down stay with your car"
Was that a bone bleaching in the heat ray?
Was that a road sign pointing back the other way?
I think I'll just rest over here for a minute
Let's see which way
Is that truckstop?
I passed the last truckstop
Where's my guitar?

From "Last Truckstop"
By Geoffrey Notkin and Anne Husick

THERE WOULD BE PLENTY OF TIME in which to get to know Steve. Chile is a vast country, stretching from near the Antarctic Circle in the south, past the Tropic of Capricorn in the north. It is made up of wildly differing landscapes: vineyards, deserts, salt flats, snow-capped volcanoes, immense deserted beaches, rocky islands populated by flocks of giant seabirds, and all of it joined by one road: Route 5, the Pan American Highway.

For thousands of miles this two-lane blacktop is the only artery for every bus, tractor and eighteen-wheeler that pounds through the ever-changing countryside. Chile's apocalyptic style of driving is well illustrated by roadside shrines—thousands of them—"like little white dog houses," Jackie remarked. Every one of those lonely temples is decorated with flowers, jewelry, Virgin Mary statues, and in one case, rather gruesomely, baby shoes, and each commemorates a fatal driving accident. You might think that these constant reminders of death would calm the ferocious drivers, but that is not the case. We were overtaken on winding roads, and around blind corners, by thundering buses and tractor-trailers on more than one occasion.

In hindsight it does seem audacious to have embarked upon such an expedition with someone we did not know well. The hardships of long journeys, desert camping, and scouring high-altitude desert wastes with a metal detector on your arm, day after day, can be taxing on your body, and on your friendships as well. Had our companion been a less affable one, the trip could quickly have turned into a nightmare. But luck was with us and Steve turned out to be as friendly and cheerful an expedition partner as one could have hoped for. No mishap or discomfort interfered with his perpetually sunny outlook.

[left] The Salar de Imilac is all that remains of an ancient lake. Receding waters have caused salts to crystalize into fantastic shapes.

53

As we headed north, Route 5 began its long slow climb to the high desert. We passed a beautiful vineyard and pulled the truck off to the side of the road for a closer look. I walked off alone through rows of lush grapes, perfectly aligned and staked, as if created by an artist. I heard a faint sound, and turned to see an elderly gentleman appear, magically, from the architecture of vines, his face lined from decades of sun and smiling. He spoke no English, and I very little Spanish, but we managed to communicate anyway. He explained that he built the vineyard with his own hands. I congratulated him on his marvelous creation and asked for permission to take some photographs. This unexpected chance visit by travelers from the far-off United States had brought the old man such genuine delight that he stood at the roadside and waved until our truck disappeared from view.

In the Southern Hemisphere, March is the beginning of fall. It was also, clearly, roadwork season. We were often diverted, sometimes waiting for long periods as heavy trucks crawled through one-way mountain passes. Our drive north should have taken two days, but it took four. And my guide book was hopelessly out of date when it came to hotel rates. Rooms listed at $4 and $5 per night were now $40 and $50. In 1997, Chile was a land discovering tourism for the first time, and making the most of it.

La Serena and Chañaral were the prettiest of towns, European Spanish in flavor, with their shady central squares and low whitewashed buildings; but many of the hotels we visited were sadly dilapidated and overpriced, so we spent several nights camping on lonely beaches and rocky hillsides. But there was one town we were not going to miss. In the small natural history museum in Copiapo, amid a dark and neglected display of local minerals was a glass case containing three remarkable Imilac meteorites—one of them weighing in at seventy pounds.

"That's what we're looking for," Steve said, as we pressed our noses against the dusty glass.

Nights in the high desert would be cold, and as we headed out of Copiapo, we became concerned about firewood. There are almost no trees in the north of Chile, and no firewood for sale. Fortunately for campers like us, it turned out that Route 5 was a 2,000-mile long national garbage dump. Discarded packing crates, beams, and other debris lined both sides of the road in such profusion that we could pull the truck over almost anywhere and collect armloads of dry wood in minutes. Our vehicle was so laden with the stuff that we looked like refugees, but the wood kept our metal detectors and other valuable equipment out of sight.

The Vaca Muerta (Dead Cow) strewnfield was our first hunting destination. The name could have come from an old western, and the photographs I'd seen of the site were one of the things that had made me want to go to Chile in the first place. Steve told me not to get too excited about Vaca Muerta. A scientific team from Scandinavia had been there several times in previous years and, according to Steve they had "Gone over the entire place with a toothbrush. There's nothing left."

But we had to see Vaca anyway. After days on the highway, we took the truck off road for the first time, sending a monumental cloud of sand and dust all the way to the horizon. Orange cone-shaped hillsides encircled us, like eroded pyramids pasted against the deep ocean blue of a cold and intimidating sky. We nosed the truck right to

[left] The author hunting in the Imilac strewnfield in the Atacama Desert, 1997.

the edge of a rocky promontory for a stupefying look across the rust and bronze-colored landscape. There was no tree, or house, fence post, or telegraph pole to disturb the endless view. We could have been the only people in the world.

Unfortunately, when we looked closely, there were plenty of signs to bring us back down to earth: Unfilled holes, jeep tracks, discarded batteries, even a pile of sifted meteorite dust. Little effort had been made by previous hunters to return Vaca to its original condition.

Near the northern end of the strewnfield is a skeleton, a ring of sun-bleached bones, supposedly the remains of the cow after which the site is named. We stopped to pay our respects. Steve also did a quick scan with his detector, and almost immediately it gave out a loud shriek. My heart jumped. Somebody had forgotten to search near the skeleton! Jackie and I rushed over to find a rusty horseshoe dangling from Steve's fingers.

"They even got the name of this place wrong!" he laughed. "It's not a cow. It's a dead horse." Years later, when we returned to Vaca to film an episode of *Meteorite Men*, we accidentally recreated this surprising find when Steve uncovered a second horse-shoe, still attached to a dessicated hoof.

Several meteorites were found during the 1990s among the light-colored sands of La Pampa—a roughly triangular desert area between the city of Antofagasta, the coastal town of Mejillones, and the ocean. We made the fifty-mile trip between Antofagasta and Mejillones four times, unable to find the track—clearly marked on our maps—that led into La Pampa. Long after sunset, tired and frustrated, our crew grudgingly agreed that the map was wrong, or the track did not exist, or both. We pulled off the main road and drove carefully into dark dunes, stopping eventually to make camp in a dry riverbed.

In Mejillones we purchased some pisco, which is a strong local grape brandy. I opened it as we started a campfire in our secluded hollow, ten feet below the surrounding desert floor. We sat on folding campstools, drinking pisco out of tin cups, eating smoky tortillas, and listening to a cassette of Brian Eno's ethereal *Apollo: Atmospheres and Soundtracks* float out of my tape deck, and blend with the magnificent black sky above us. Our spirits lifted. We were sure to find La Pampa the next day.

The best part of pitching a tent after dark is discovering where you are in the morning. We found ourselves on a sunbaked orange plain, with shimmering purple hills far to the west. It was a spectacular clear day, and Steve's GPS unit placed us only seven miles due east of La Pampa. After coffee, breakfast, and washing, we put our faith in the GPS and headed directly west, across the desert. We were low on supplies, so it was agreed that after a quick survey of the area we would return to Antofagasta for more provisions, then come back for a full day's searching.

But there was no clear route to La Pampa. We followed hard ridges of sandstone and quartz—like crocodile backs among the pale soft sand—zig-zagging for miles until we came upon a gently-sloping ridge. When we reached the summit, an extraordinary scene awaited us—a vast white sand bowl with steep sides, and a flat, undisturbed floor that stretched away into the far distance. Pock-marked by few stones, the ancient and featureless surface would be a perfect hunting ground for meteorites.

Steve volunteered to go down on foot, and report back to us by walkie-talkie. I watched through binoculars as he slid down the sand wall and tested the hard floor

[above] Surveying the Vaca Muerta strewnfield, Atacama Desert, 1997.

repeatedly with his walking stick. After the walkie-talkie crackled and Steve said: "It seems okay," I took the truck down with great care. When the Toyota's tires crunched onto the hard pan at the bottom of the basin, I increased speed slightly, we surged forward and bounced. I saw Steve waving happily from across the plain, and then the earth gave way. The truck made a horrible moaning sound, and sank down into a pool of fine sand. The engine stalled. We had fallen into an unseen hollow filled with wind-blown powder. I climbed out of the cab, and called Steve on the radio.

"You better get over here," I said.

The truck was in deep, with the rear axle completely buried. We took our heavy bags and equipment out of the back, and stacked them on the sand in a surrealistic montage of suitcases and metal detectors. As Steve and Jackie examined the truck, I took inventory of our supplies. We were in serious trouble.

There is no such thing as "a quick scout around" in the desert, and I—already a veteran of camping trips in the Sinai, the Negev, the Mohave, and elsewhere—should have known that. Any trip into the desert, no matter how short it might seem on a pleasant sunny morning, is a potentially deadly one. We had some water, and some juice, and some ice, but not nearly enough to sustain three people through a long-term digging operation in the hot sun. I took some of the ice cubes out of the cooler and put them in a jar to melt. I did not want Jackie and Steve to worry about the water situation, so I made the decision not to tell them.

"Here," I said. "Have some water. But let's go easy on it, just in case. And try to keep out of the sun. We'll find a way to get the truck out."

I estimated that we were at least twenty miles from the nearest road. We had driven a long way from last night's campsite, and it was already extremely hot. If we could not get the truck out within a few hours, we would have to walk out with whatever water we had left.

We pulled firewood and rubber mats from the vehicle and put them under the tires, but they gave no traction. We took inventory of all our gear, and it did not amount to much. What I remember most clearly, apart from absolute terror, was Jackie quietly and methodically emptying our purple kit bag, dragging it along the sand, and filling it with small pebbles in the hope that we could jam it under the wheels. She was a sophisticated woman—thoughtful and calm. She showed no annoyance or fear, even though her two scruffy companions had managed to sink their only lifeboat in an ocean of sand.

A few hundred yards from the beached truck, we discovered a half-buried stratum of limestone, packed with tiny fossil shells, something that I would have found fascinating under any other circumstances. We crawled under the Toyota to excavate mounds of sand from the axles, then used our entrenching tools to pry limestone slabs out of the desert floor, staggered back with them, and constructed a crazy paving ramp under the wheels. After much dizzying labor, we got the truck out and I drove it thirty feet before it sank into another pit. We dug the slabs out and started again. It took us four hours to escape.

I have never been so relieved to see a town. We walked through Antofagasta's central square in the cool evening, sat under palm trees and stared up at the clock tower— a miniature version of Big Ben given to the city by former British colonists. The hordes of black vultures that descended upon the square at sunset were a poignant reminder of what can go wrong in the desert.

Our next destination, Imilac, lay deep in the desert and there would be no supplies after Antofagasta. Finding jerry cans there was almost as hard as finding meteorites. We persevered, and eventually stacked the truck with wood, gasoline and water (we had over forty gallons this time, I was not taking any more chances), and finally turned away from the breezy coast towards the high desert.

We passed dune-covered mountains, where sheets of sand had been stripped from the desert floor and piled up by the relentless wind, and rolling granite hills burned through by ribbons of black basalt. Always, near the horizon—their distance impossible to guess—were the snow-capped peaks of the Andes.

In 1997 I was still working full time with Lach and Billy Ficca as a three-piece band. That spring we began recording our second album, *Blang!*, with talented producer Richard Barone, former lead singer of the successful '80s band The Bongos. Those few weeks in the studio were one of my happiest recording experiences, and I was irked that the Chile expedition schedule required that I leave the States before the final mixing sessions. It was the first of many instances in which I was forced to choose between rock 'n' roll and a meteorite expedition. I vividly remember driving along the white floor of an eerie, steep-sided canyon with a rough mix of the new album playing in the cassette deck. There were times during the expedition, lost on a barely-visible track or blasted by the wind on a rocky hilltop, when I wondered why on earth I agreed voluntarily to trek across the fiendish desert, instead of staying in the cushy New York recording studio to finish mixing the record with Lach, Billy, and Richard.

Once we left the Antofagasta road it was dirt track for hundreds of miles. We saw perhaps one vehicle every two days. At 7,000 feet Steve recognized the approach to Imilac, a forgotten roadside shrine, perhaps in honor of some long-gone prospector.

The sun was setting, and I could feel the cold night coming. Jackie and I hurried to set up our tent before dark, but Steve's detector was already strapped to his forearm.

"Come on, Geoff! Don't you want to find your first Imilac?"

I could not resist, so I broke out my Goldmaster and scrambled up the hillside after him. Within seconds my detector started buzzing. Steve was already down on his knees, poking around among the pointed stones.

"Here we go!" he shouted.

He held up a small impossibly twisted shard of orange metal, then he came over to me and pointed out the piece that my detector had already spotted.

"They're not easy to see," he smiled.

As daylight vanished, Jackie took a photo of us with our very first finds as a hunting team. The pieces were small, but they were Imilacs. We were ecstatic.

And then, without warning, the wind came.

Inside our steamer trunk was a watertight plastic jar. I rummaged among canned food and entrenching tools until I found the container, and threw in my new Imilacs as the winds rushed down the curved and barren hills surrounding us. We pounded eleven sturdy pegs into the desert pavement to anchor our tent against the gathering gale. I drove the truck to the windward side, so close that one mirror pushed into the tent's fabric. We tied the tent struts to the truck, and then inched the steamer trunk—laden with enough canned goods to sustain three hungry people for ten days—inside.

Within a few minutes darkness had entirely hidden the bright hilltops, and with a steel flashlight under my arm, I scrabbled around the windy scarps in search of twenty and thirty-pound rocks, which I lugged back, dropping one atop each tent peg. Even so, it seemed that our shelter might snap its tethers and scamper across the curved valley below us, covering in moments the mile or so that separated us from the Salar de Imilac—a round desert of salt crystals still glowing faintly in the night.

Jackie and I huddled in the blackness, our tent whipping and fluttering in the tempest as if a Titan crouched outside and pounded relentlessly upon us. Through the fabric, we could see a faint light—a lantern from Steve's one-man tent braced inside a slight hollow—and imagined him inside, examining some hefty reference work on meteorites. We did not know if we would even still be there in the morning, but Steve was calmly planning the next day's strategy.

Exhausted, Jackie and I fell asleep amid the howling and shrieking; but all through the night I continued to wake, startled, zipped up tight in my sleeping bag, and gasping in the cold thin air.

In the morning there was utter silence.

The sun rose exactly twelve hours after it had set, coloring the coarse, rock-covered hills with an alien beauty that left me feeling displaced and wondrous. No bird or insect, car, airplane, breath of wind, or sound of any kind disturbed this place in which no one lived—until a clattering noise rolled down from behind our tent.

"Good morning, Compadre. Bwaaynoze deeyoze sen-yooore!" boomed across the valley and Steve—in his baggy jeans—shuffled past us, barely awake, metal detector in hand, into the mouth of the desert.

Jackie and I moved slowly. Our camping stove hissed in an effort to make coffee. I dug five pits in the unforgiving ground, and erected our sunshade. I hammered the poles in deep, piled a mound of stones around each, and secured them with eight guylines.

We moved our gasoline cans out of the sun and each hissed unpleasantly as I removed the caps to relieve pressure. I unfolded our campstools, and over breakfast examined our finds from the previous evening. The Imilacs were marvelous twisted and tortured bits of cosmic wreckage: orange, brown, yellow, and white, just like the hills in which they had been buried. Under the shade, commanding an expansive view across the Atacama, the desert suddenly seemed less hostile. As the sun cleared the mountains to the east, it cast broken shadows, many miles long, up towards us. We watched them shorten and disappear in less time than it took to drink a mug of coffee. Palpably, like a rip tide moving over sand flats, the heat of the day rose up out of the basin below and dropped solidly upon us. And then a sudden gust of wind arrived, plucked our sunshade instantly from the ground and whipped it two hundred yards down the slope, leaving us blinking and blinded in the glare.

Each day we rose earlier, so that we might benefit from the gentle hours either side of dawn. Those were the best times for hunting. As we grew familiar with the terrain, we split up, each of us drawn to a different place. In those early hours I could read in the sand a palimpsest—an old map of footprints left by the prospectors that had been

[above] The author and Steve Arnold with our very first joint meteorite finds. Imilac, Chile, 1997.
[following page] Our isolated campsite in the Imilac strewnfield.

there before. With no recorded rainfall, tracks made years before by other visitors were still faintly visible when the sun was low enough. I followed those footprints, looking for islands of undisturbed pavement, and in those islands—sometimes—my Goldmaster would shriek, and a brightly-colored ball of jagged metal would leap happily onto my magnet.

Hours went by, locked into a kind of floating silence. I sang imaginary songs, recited nonsensical rhymes, predicted where my detector would sing next, drank water, dug, and baked in the sun. We wore gloves, bandannas, hats and high boots, even though the heat could be overpowering. For a week after, I carried a narrow red ring of sunburn around one wrist to show where my glove and sleeve had not quite met.

And always, just at the edge of hearing, floated a curious buzzing: the faint chuckling of metal detectors far away, behind hills and valleys, their sound carried an absurd distance in the motionless air.

One morning, Steve's enthusiasm got the better of him, and he disappeared into the wilderness before I was even up. Hours passed. Eventually, I untied our truck from the tent, and took the battered Toyota down into the soft sand to look for him. With every turn of the wheel I was afraid I would once again get stuck. On a hilltop of hardpan, from which the wind had removed every whisper of sand, I could just see Steve far below me—a tiny grain against the landscape. I parked in a hopefully safe spot, took my detector and a spare canteen, and began the long walk down.

When I reached him, his skin was the color of fresh radishes. I gave him the spare canteen and urged him to come back under the shade.

"No, look what I've found," he said.

He led me across a dry sculpted riverbed to a small and perfect crater, the size of a washbasin. "Somebody beat us to it," he said. We skimmed the area with our detectors, finding several ejected fragments around the empty pit. Steve had covered an enormous amount of ground, finding one good piece above 100 grams about every five hours: one in the dry gully; one under the tracks of some long-gone 4WD truck.

Each day carries a visual bookmark in my memory. There was the day that Steve found a 260-gram piece buried in the flats below us; the day a lonely bird—stretched and sinewy like an American roadrunner—visited us, hopping lightly across the hot rocks; the day we saw the bright speck of another vehicle moving fast across the horizon; the day we drove to the springs, where 43-degree water poured from a rusty and abandoned pipe. Jackie and I hoisted the pipe atop our truck, and I plunged my head under it. I was instantly carried back to my youth as I experienced a sharp pain in the base of my skull—just as a little boy might, after too quickly eating his summer ice cream—but at the spring I felt that same pain of sudden temperature change throughout my entire body.

Each evening we made dinner, cleaned up, consumed a quick cocktail during the brief calm of sunset, rushed to get into our tent before the winds came, only to then sit and stare at each other and comment that it was barely 7:15 p.m. We were trapped for the next twelve hours. Our tape player broke, all jammed up with fine sand from La Pampa. Hypnotized by boredom, we invented a game called Rorschach Meteorites. We took turns holding Imilacs in front of a candle, and challenged our comrades to guess what we saw within each abstract silhouette.

Every night seemed colder than the last. My evening ritual involved dressing in long

johns, a t-shirt, sweat shirt and pants, then blue jeans, a heavy weather parka, woolen cap, and finally zipping myself up to my nose in a cold-weather sleeping bag. Still I shivered and pulled thin air into my lungs with difficulty. But each evening we also placed more meteorites in our container, now half full, beside my army cot.

I slept so little the fourth night at Imilac that I feared I was suffering from altitude sickness. I consulted our First Aid manual: "Exertion at, or prolonged exposure to high altitude may cause altitude sickness. Symptoms include: Dizziness, fatigue, shortness of breath, loss of appetite, irritability, difficulty in sleeping or performing simple tasks." Concerned, I read this out loud to Jackie and Steve over breakfast.

"I think you have all of those," Steve laughed. I laughed too, and we all felt better.

Yes, we were finding meteorites, but for every good one there were hundreds of little scraps ("two-pea pieces," Jackie called them) which clamored just as loudly for attention from the Goldmaster's speaker.

We washed out at Vaca Muerta, were stranded at La Pampa, and made moderate finds at Imilac. We hoped that Monturaqui, our final destination—a remote and rarely visited 100,000 year-old meteorite crater on the far side of the salar—would be our greatest success. After my 1994 visit to Meteor Crater with its fences and guards and regulations, I daydreamed of wandering unfettered across the floor of a different crater, untouched by civilization and commerce.

During our last night at Imilac I sat up on my army cot, and shook Jackie awake. "What is it, what's wrong?" she asked.

"Listen," I said. "Listen. There's no wind."

It was around two in the morning, but we clambered out of our tent, and into the clear night. We made a fire from the scrap wood we brought with us from the real world, and drank grape brandy from tin cups. The sky was perfectly clear and black, the Milky Way an incandescent sash, spray painted above. As if to taunt us, a brilliant blue and white fireball arced overhead, showering sparks and burning fragments into the night. I knew, intellectually, that it was probably a hundred miles away. But it had seemed—as they always do—to have crashed just beyond the nearest hillock. In the morning, knowing it was fruitless, I took my binoculars and climbed the highest point to scan the surrounding land for a non-existent crater.

Perhaps I had a mild case of sunstroke, or perhaps it was the altitude. I felt strange and uneasy. I was both relieved and saddened to leave Imilac; relieved to reach lower altitude and breathe real air, but I also felt incomplete, as if we were abandoning our home before completing our work there. I was certain that more pieces, big pieces, awaited us somewhere beneath the hardpan. We journeyed all that way, to that fabulous and frightening place, took what we wanted, and left nothing in return. I tried to explain this to my bewildered comrades as we drove north along nearly invisible dirt tracks.

"We'll stop again on the way back from Monturaqui," Steve said. "For another day, maybe."

"Yes," Jackie replied. "We could stack up the leftover firewood and leave a note for the next people." It was a sweet idea and I thought such a gesture might make me feel better. The disappointment of not making a big find, after all the expense and hard-ship, was heavy upon me, and upon the others, too, I was certain.

In a fairy tale landscape of boulders and dunes, we drove past plants so strange that we had to pause and look, even in the perilous soft sand that tried to envelop us whenever we stopped moving. Darwin had come this way more than a hundred years earlier. "It is almost a pity to see the sun shining constantly over so useless a country," he wrote. Chile was barren, but also magnificent. I thought Darwin's words a little harsh. He must have seen, and been intrigued by, the same pincushion cactus plants that we did—solitary islands of life, the size of Volkswagen Bugs, slumped beside the track like sullen and waterlogged camels.

Steve knew where Monturaqui was, vaguely.

"Only a couple of hours drive," he estimated.

We had with us a photograph of the crater from an old reference work. Behind the crater were easily recognizable twin mountain peaks. We also had the latitude and longitude, but after three days of searching, we could not find it. Our maps were infuriatingly contradictory. Some showed a road running immediately adjacent to the crater, where there was no road. We found other actual roads that were not on the map; some led over the side of precipices or to puzzling tiny oases where llamas and alpacas lazed under the unexpected shade of scrawny trees.

We drove for hundreds of miles, across the vast Salar de Atacama with its sharp and hellish crags of salt, and all the way around the upland area containing those two volcanic peaks, which we could clearly see from the road. But always, the GPS unit pointed us across impassable, steep-walled canyons.

We headed north and stayed a night in the ancient adobe town of San Pedro de Atacama where a crooked restaurant owner overcharged us, then called in the heavily-armed local police after I disputed the bill. Surrounded by jackbooted thugs, all with hands on their guns, it suddenly became obvious that paying an inflated bill was better than spending the rest of 1997 in a Chilean prison.

We had been in the wild for more than two weeks, and with our departure date looming, we chose a different route back to Imilac. A route that appeared as a major road on our maps was now a shambles of rock and trenches—the handiwork of an unreported flash flood. Some of the washouts were so deep we had to get out and walk them first to make sure the truck could pass. We were delayed again. Another day slipped by as we checked maps and gently rumbled the truck over one obstacle after another.

We never did make it back to Imilac on that trip. Dizzy, fatigued, sunburned, scratched, covered in dust and cuts, with ripped clothes and torn fingernails, and without the large find I coveted, I promised myself, as we began the arduous drive back to Santiago, that I would never, ever, as long as I lived, return to the Atacama.

In the years that followed I often dreamed of Imilac at night, and the disappointment of not being able to experience the isolated splendor of Monturaqui Crater haunted me for over a decade. I ordered a large custom photographic print from my best snapshot of the Imilac strewnfield. I hung it in my apartment and stared at it daily. I memorized every crease in every hillside. I knew the color of the stones and the smell of the thin air. It was a horrible and terrifying place. The grandeur and emptiness of the landscape made me feel temporary and worthless, like a trespasser in a timeless place. No, I misremember. Surely, it was a beautiful and magical place.

"If only I'd thought to look on that one hillside," I said to myself at night, over and over, as I perched at the perimeter of sleep. And some damnable and reckless part of me still wanted to go back.

EIGHT

INTERLUDE AT THE SMITHSONIAN

I'm watching the setting sun
It's important to set the sun down easy
It's fragile and might crack open
Spilling liquid waves of heat
Down the plastic suburban streets
Killing quickly each one it meets
The setting sun will burn your feet
On Alien Street

From "Alien Street"
By Lach

THROUGH ALL THE HARDSHIP AND DANGER of the Chile expedition, Jackie remained calm, thoughtful, and resourceful. She mastered our portable gasoline camp stove, quickly learned how to use a sophisticated metal detector, and was brave enough to try steamed abalone—which looked like small waterlogged brains—in the port city of Antofagasta.

I remember pulling the Toyota truck over so she could collect colorful pieces of malachite—a bright green mineral associated with copper deposits—which had been dumped by the side of a desolate dirt highway; probably waste from one of the big Atacama mines. We were, at that moment, almost exactly on the Tropic of Capricorn. Far to our east stood the magnificent Andes Mountains, snow-capped titans soaring into the blue air. With nothing between us and them to measure the expanse of desert floor, they seemed almost within walking distance. Actually, they sat more than a hundred miles away, rearing up above the horizon, oblivious to the curvature of the earth which would have rendered smaller masses invisible.

Our home-bound flight put down at John F. Kennedy International Airport in New York, and we walked down a long jetway, meticulously clean, and decorated with flags of all the world's nations, except probably Libya. We passed the Chilean flag and I could see those faraway mountains, and the alpacas, and the bright red chilies drying in the clear sun, and the pisco, and our lonely desert campsite. I was absolutely certain I would never see Chile again. A customs officer looked at my passport, smiled, and said: "Welcome home, Mr. Notkin."

Jackie later told me that she had never been so relieved to return to the United States and fought an overwhelming urge to get down on her hands and knees and kiss the floor of the customs hall. We stayed together for several more years, but Jackie never again went meteorite hunting. Chile was enough for her.

I returned to my apartment and unpacked meteorites and rocks, heavily-worn maps, and the ever-useful *Latin American Spanish Phrasebook*, which I kept as a souvenir. I carefully examined the Imilac meteorites I had plucked from the desert floor. The relentless Atacama wind had long ago sandblasted away many of their olivine crystals, leaving twisted metallic skeletons colored ochre, peach, and crimson by their long desert sojourn. They were beautiful, but they were also small, and I was disappointed. Steve found the largest piece on the expedition and it weighed 260 grams. At today's prices it would be worth about $2,000. Steve had been doing this for years, and he kept telling me how incredibly lucky we were to have recovered any meteorites at all, but I wanted to find a big one.

We did find meteorites, hundreds of them, and in a joke ceremony which has now been repeated many times to honor new finders, Steve welcomed me into the Brotherhood of Meteorite Hunters. It was not nearly enough.

I put my best Imilacs on display, and sorted the rest by size. They live in glass specimen jars in my collection room, except for the very small ones which fill a ceramic llama bowl that I bought in San Pedro de Atacama.

I kept in touch with Steve by phone and email. Meteorite hunting was Steve's profession, and after selling all of his finds—except for one that he kept because it looked exactly like a crab—he had barely broken even on the gruelling three-week venture. No more meteorite expeditions were planned.

Some months later, I took a short vacation to Washington, D.C. I explored numerous museums along the Mall, but the National Museum of Natural History— part of the Smithsonian Institution—held treasures beyond any expectations. The meteorite exhibit reminded me of my childhood visits to the Geological Museum in London, but the display at the National Museum was larger and much more comprehensive. Scores of the world's finest meteorite specimens were suspended beautifully in bright wall-sized enclosures, while massive irons lay in the center of the room.

That same day, Dr. Timothy McCoy, curator of the meteorite collection, happened to be giving a public lecture about the theories of pallasite formation. It seemed peculiarly coincidental after my recent pallasite-hunting adventure, so I took a seat.

During the talk, one of Dr. McCoy's associates passed around a meteorite specimen from the Smithsonian's collection, so novices in the audience could have the chance to hold a space rock. It was an Australian iron meteorite, a Henbury. It weighed about 1,500 grams and was covered with intriguing surface features. I was seated at the back of the auditorium and was, therefore, the very last person to get hold of the iron, which came sealed up in an air-tight plastic baggie. The meteorites I had found thus far were from very old falls, altered by explosive fragmentation, and then weathered by wind, sand, and water. This was different.

The blood-red, hand-sized alien, bore stark witness to its inferno-like journey through incandescent air. The heat generated by its passage turned the iron's surface momentarily to liquid metal. Traveling at thousands of miles per hour, the burning mass shrieked through Earth's upper atmosphere, brutally forcing a column of compressed air ahead of it, until atmospheric pressure slowed it, up there in the thin, freezing air. It fell, cooling almost instantly, its molten, flowing surface solidifying into rivulets of tiny thumbprints—known as regmaglypts—as it plummeted, spinning, to the surface of the earth seven miles below.

Legends about a "fire devil" suggest that ancient Aborigines may have witnessed the Henbury fireballs and subsequent impacts. The iron I was holding in a plastic bag, then lay in the Outback for thousands of years, alongside many others from the same fall, slowly acquiring the dazzling red hue of the harsh desert that surrounded it.

I stared at that meteorite intently. I thought it the single most amazing thing I had ever seen. A good five minutes must have passed, and I was still holding on to it, entranced. Dr. McCoy's associate watched me—a bit nervously, I think. He did not take his eyes off me for a second. Eventually, the gentleman came over and took the Henbury out of my hands—kindly and with a nice smile—and said, jokingly: "I thought you were going to run out of here with that."

After the talk I introduced myself to Dr. McCoy. He was gracious and cordial, and most interested to learn that I had recently returned from Imilac. I would have the pleasure of meeting and working with many top meteorite academics in the coming years, but I always remembered that first, friendly reception I received from him.

As soon as I returned home, I started searching on the internet for Henbury meteorites. The iron that so hypnotized me at the National Museum was exactly the kind of meteorite I wanted to find. It was unique and awe inspiring, and entirely unlike anything that could have been created on our planet.

In 1997 the web was in its infancy. There was no Google or MSN.com; but, to my great surprise, there actually were a few people selling meteorites online. At that moment I fully and clearly realized that a subculture of meteorite collectors existed in the world. It was not just Steve and me and a few academics. There were other people like us out there, and I just knew I was going to meet all of them, sooner or later.

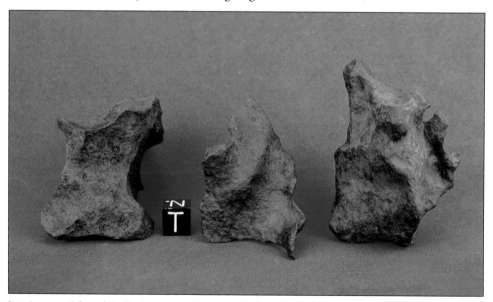

[previous page] One of the Henbury meteorite craters, Northern Territories, Australia.
[above] Three examples of the Henbury iron meteorite. Note the twisted, angular shapes, consistent with meteorites blasted out of craters. The attractive, bronze-orange natural patina has been acquired as a result of thousand of years of exposure in the Australian desert.

69

None of the fledgling online meteorite businesses were offering Henburys at that time, but there were Gibeons for sale from the Namib Desert, and Canyon Diablos from Meteor Crater, and stone meteorites with matte black fusion crust. I started buying.

At about the same time I discovered an independent science magazine, *Meteorite*, out of Auckland, New Zealand. I subscribed immediately, then wrote to the editor and publisher, Dr. Joel Schiff, and told him of our recent expedition across the Atacama. I asked if he might be interested in receiving a submission. A reply came back in short order: "Yes, of course, we'd love to have it."

I set about writing my first meteorite adventure article. It was published in May of 1998, commencing a long and happy association with the magazine.

When I become interested in something, I immerse myself in it absolutely and completely, and learn everything I can about that subject. This had already happened to me with fossils, model rockets, steam engines, science fiction, and punk rock, among other things. This time, however, I had been accosted so savagely by my newest passion that I could barely think of anything else. Family and friends were already somewhat accustomed to my eccentric behavior, but even they became alarmed when I took to tearing across dangerous deserts in the company of complete strangers, in a truck full of metal detectors and magnets.

Meteorites are bigger than I am. They are bigger than all of us. They are older than the Earth, and some are older than our solar system. They have spent millions of years traveling through unknown parts of space, being bathed in cosmic rays and frozen almost to absolute zero. By the most amazing coincidence, during their celestial wanderings, a few happen to cross paths with our planet, and we are a pretty small target out there in the perpetual night. Some of them bounce back into space, never to be seen again; some burn up completely in Earth's atmosphere; others fall into oceans or dense jungle where they will not be found. A very few are seen to fall by fortunate observers. Some of those falls are recovered, studied, photographed, and placed reverently in museum cabinets and collection cases.

Even though I had once dreamed of becoming an astronaut, I came to the realization early on that I would never really make it into space. So, instead, I would find a way for space to come to me. Meteorites are mementos of other worlds, far away, and long gone. They connect us to the arcane processes that created the universe. They were here before us, and they will still be here long after we are gone. For now, while we are here and alive, when I hold a meteorite, I gain the faintest shadow of understanding about where I might fit into the overwhelming complexity of the cosmos; I can almost feel the heartbeat of space and time.

As a species, we may never fully understand the fabric of space, but meteorites are as important a beacon as we are likely to find in this lifetime. Like the sound of the ocean in a seashell, meteorites carry within them a faint murmur of infinity.

The winter of 1997 was a long and cold one on the East Coast. It would also be the last time I saw my adored mother, who had been such a force in my developing love of science and adventure. She came to the States to visit me, that November, and I remember a lovely dinner at a small restaurant in Hoboken, NJ, the night before she flew back to England.

She passed away very suddenly at the age of 72. I flew home immediately for the funeral, and cut long-stemmed yellow daffodils from her beloved Surrey garden. I went, alone, to the funeral home and put them beside her open coffin, along with candles, and one of our fossil finds from the old quarry, to keep her company in the night.

She did not live to see my science articles in print, or my books, or my television shows, and she would have loved every part of it. I have always felt cheated by that because there would have been no grand adventures if Mom had not taken a little boy to the Geological Museum back in 1968.

Mom would have been angry with me if I mourned for too long and wasted time; so as that wet and dreary winter dragged on I set about devising new plans. I came across an article describing an international gem and mineral show that took place every February in Arizona. My previous two visits to the Grand Canyon State had each been remarkable in their own way, but I had yet to see the odd little city of Tucson. Its annual gem show was reported to be *the* place to buy meteorites.

I called Steve. It was the first time we had spoken since South America.

"Steve, I'm thinking about going to that rock and fossil show in Tucson in February. Are you interested?"

"Yeah, I've kinda always wanted to go an' check that out. My friend Blaine Reed, the meteorite dealer, sets up there every year. You need to meet him."

"Well, I think we should go. My birthday is in February and I'm going to buy myself a nice present."

"Really? My birthday is in February, too," Steve replied. "What day?"

"February the first."

"*Get out of here*! February the first is my birthday, too."

And so we planned our first trip to the world's greatest rock, fossil, gem, and meteorite show. Steve and I were to meet up in Texas, do some hunting at the Odessa meteorite crater, and then drive west into Arizona.

Nothing in my life would ever be the same again.

NINE

A GIRL NAMED ODESSA

You can try to reach an aftermath
Change your fate, to hell with that
You will reach your peak beyond the path
But still what kills your dreams?
You can touch someone and miss the feeling
Try to catch the past
'Cos you're living in an undecided dream

From "Undecided Dream"
By Chris Gibson

PERFECT SQUARES OF LIGHT-COLORED GROUND scattered across the grassy flatlands; a country-sized patchwork of yellow and green. They appeared as plots of graded earth, ready for development. Hundreds became thousands, and I wondered what major construction project was underway east of the Midland/Odessa airport.

As my plane descended almost imperceptibly against a featureless horizon, I made out a speck at the center of one of those squares, and then another. Were they water tanks, or piles of cinder blocks? We came closer and I realized that the structures were not growing up from the ground, but rather digging down into it. Oil wells, or "pump jacks" as the locals call them, are powered by electricity or sometimes—in what almost seems a perpetual motion machine—natural gas that comes as a by-product of oil production. It was my first ever sight of Texas. Oil country.

The lady at the car rental desk immediately wanted to know all about me, and what I thought of Texas. With little time to form an opinion, so far, I assured her I was very impressed by the number of pump jacks you could see from the airplane.

"Ya'll here to see the meteor crater?" she beamed, speaking in a wide sunny accent, and winking. She handed me a map. "Ah'd sure be happy to tell ya'll how to get there, 'though there sure ain't much to see now."

She shook her head sadly, as if recalling the crater's original appearance say, 20,000 years ago. "It's mostways filled in now, but folks still go."

Everyone I spoke to in Odessa: the car rental lady, the motel clerk, the librarian, a dapper businessman, knew about the crater. Most of them had a tale about it, and everyone was more than happy to tell me their life story.

I sped along Interstate 20, too excited even to stop and check in at my motel.

[facing page] Meteorite hunting pioneer, James Pliska, at the Odessa Crater, 1998.

It was early February and already warm. The land was flat as a windowpane and the color of faded army pants.

"The crater isn't easy to find," a friend advised me before I left New York, so I drove slowly. After leaving the highway and passing a line of dusky railroad cars that appeared to have been waiting there since Frontier days, I got lost. The featureless panorama loped non-stop to the horizon in every direction, with only pump jacks and the occasional grain silo to remind me that I was supposedly in a modern world built by human people. I turned off the motor and watched a dry wind hack tumbleweeds around in the void. Meteorites usually live in the empty places, and it suddenly dawned upon me that I was spending a lot of time in those places. It did not feel like home, but it did feel bracing. I did not care if I was lost. I was in Texas for the first time!

I got back in gear and motored up and down dirt roads, plastering bitter dust onto my rental car. I turned on the radio and settled on a country music station—there was only country music and talk radio, but then I barely consider talk radio to be radio. After a time, I was startled to see a green highway-style sign that read "Meteor Crater" staggering out of the distance. For a moment I thought I must have taken a wrong turn, and ended up back in northern Arizona, but there were about a thousand too many oil wells for it to be anywhere other than West Texas.

Bemused and slightly annoyed that this crater had the same silly error attached to it as its big brother near Winslow, I pulled up in a deserted car park. I found a display board, some booklets, a picnic table, and a path that led down into the shallow but clearly visible feature.

There was not a soul anywhere in sight. Blissfully alone, I walked with solemn purpose to the very center, and stared in wonder at sarcophagus-sized limestone slabs thrown up by the fury of impact. Heaps of plum-sized fossil shells, which I took to be the Cretaceous bivalve *Gryphea mucronata*, littered the floor. Off to one side I could see the sealed mining shaft, a relic of the failed 1940s attempt to find a giant buried iron; beside it an exploratory trench which, surprisingly, yielded not a visitor from outer space but a fossil mammoth.

In terms of size, the Odessa Crater is not nearly as impressive as its grander namesake in Arizona. It is, however, one of the very few places on earth where the wandering cosmological pilgrim can contemplate the processes of the universe while standing in the middle of an impact site.

The crater is 650 feet across at its widest point and only about ten feet deep. That is considerably more than three times the diameter of Barnum and Bailey's biggest-ever traveling circus tent. Erosion has worn away most of the rim, but it is one of only two large craters in the United States where meteorites have been recovered—Arizona's Meteor Crater being the other. There are numerous other impact structures in America, and many are much larger, such as Beaverhead, Montana, and Kentland, Indiana. The events that shaped those great scars in the earth took place tens of millions of years ago. The iron-rich meteorites that created them have long since wasted away in our moist atmosphere. All that remains are geological clues in the form of impactites: shattered and melted terrestrial rocks deformed by ancient impacts.

I made a slow and contemplative lap around the crater rim, skirting scrub brush and tumbleweeds, alert for the Texas-sized rattlesnakes and sidewinders who doubtless made their homes there. I found a few small meteorite fragments near the crater and as

I sealed them up in a plastic bag, I thought of the pioneer hunters working out on the plains in decades gone by, with their bulky army surplus equipment and tried to imagine what it would be like to dig up a really big iron meteorite.

I did not have to tax my imagination too hard as I had an appointment with one of the original hunters the following day. Before leaving home I took out a classified ad in the *Odessa American*, the local paper, which carries on its cover a very imposing bald eagle clutching, with considerable fervor, at the Stars and Stripes. "Science writer," read my ad, "Researching history of Odessa Crater, wishes to view or purchase meteorite specimens and interview meteorite hunters." I thought it a ridiculous long shot, but received several replies within just a few days.

My second day in Texas started early, with a visit to the Ector County Library. I had forty-eight hours to myself, time enough for interviews and scallywagging, before Steve arrived by car and we headed out for Tucson. As I walked into the peaceful, low-lit room, almost the first thing I noticed was a glass display case and I rushed directly to it, much as a stray cat runs to a saucer of milk. Several Odessa irons sat quietly in the cabinet. Nice specimens, several pounds each, with pointed "feet" that made them resemble metallic piggy banks; they were sadly neglected. Every piece was rusting, and scores of tiny flakes had fallen to the bottom of the cabinet.

I mentioned, respectfully, to the librarian that their meteorite specimens were in need of some curation and, by the way, did they have any historical material about the crater?

My discussion was overheard by a tall and imposing Texan gentleman who courteously introduced himself as Jack Walker. Like everyone else in Ector County, Mr. Walker had his own personal anecdotes about the crater. As a Boy Scout, he had camped in it a number of times and later, as a teenager, crept into the abandoned mine and recklessly climbed down the 160-foot shaft in complete darkness.

"But Tom Rodman really is the man to talk to about it," he suggested.

Everyone was extremely gracious, as is typical of Texans. Telephone directories were produced, Mr. Rodman's number was located, and I was soon on my way, leaving Mr. Walker with a wistful smile on his face remembering, no doubt, his bold teenage escapades.

Without Tom Rodman, a local attorney and member of the Meteoritical Society, there would probably be no Odessa Crater today, lying as it does, in the middle of active oil fields. Fascinated by the place as a boy, in later life Mr. Rodman became its champion.

"I always knew the crater was out there," he told me, "But I didn't know there were any meteorites in it until a guy came down and without permission dug up a bunch. We took half of what he had, and let him keep the other half. We built a little museum on the site, but vandalism got so bad we had to close it down."

In the 1950s Mr. Rodman formed the Odessa Meteorite Society in an attempt to generate interest in the landmark. Many years later, the National Park Service allocated funds for the crater's preservation, and it is now designated as a National Natural Landmark. Today there is a beautiful new museum beside the crater, with a fine meteorite collection. Many of their pieces were donated by meteorite enthusiasts, including me. Visitors are still likely to see Mr. Rodman making one of his regular stops, perhaps to drop off informational brochures, pick up some wind-blown trash, or just spend a little time at the unique place he has spent most of his life protecting.

On my next stop I parked on a pretty suburban street, in front of a wooden house surrounded by trees and shrubs. A broad and powerful man with brilliant white hair and a thick beard, dressed in a red lumberjack shirt and black suspenders opened the door. In his late seventies, Jim Pliska still looked as if he could pull a hundred-pound iron from the ground with no trouble at all.

[above] Historic Odessa iron meteorites collected during the 1940s.

Jim invited me into his study, where I was greeted by a kaleidoscopic collection of meteorites, arrowheads, rocks, fossils, vintage bottles, Civil War belt buckles, badges and harnesses—all of it found by Jim, his son James Jr., and their hunting partners. Before I could fully appreciate the scope of this vast collection, we were back in the car and heading for the crater, accompanied by Jim's son.

Jim was full of stories, but most of all he wanted to personally show me the location of his biggest finds. It was a hot and sunny morning, and cane in hand, Jim walked us slowly along the network of paths that crisscross the crater field.

"Back in the '60s and '70s, a friend that I used to hunt with and me, got permission to hunt from the rancher that owns this land. Sometimes we'd be huntin' and he'd come out in his truck. He'd see it was us, and stop and talk a while. One time he saw someone else come in and start huntin' while we were talking. He pulled out his big 30-30 rifle and started shooting. 'Get off my land or I'll kill ya!' he yelled." Jim paused, then pointed at the rim with his stick. "We found a big concentration over there; a hundred-pound one over there."

A local folk tale has it that during the 1880s a runaway girl, Odessa Brockett, was taken in and cared for by workers on the Texas and Pacific Railroad. Enamored by the young woman, they named their camp after her, and the name stuck. Another less romantic explanation claims that the "future great city of West Texas" was named after the Ukrainian city of Odessa. In any case, there is no doubt that at the end of the same decade, Jim's father arrived in Ector County from Czechoslovakia. An entrepreneur and adventurer, Mr. Pliska, Sr. built and flew the very first airplane in Texas in 1910. James followed his father into the exciting new world of aviation, and became an accomplished airman.

During World War II, Jim, a recognized expert on the B-17 heavy bomber and a savvy pilot, was considered too valuable an asset to risk on combat missions, so the Air Force gave him a critically important task: pairing pilots and co-pilots for the air war in Europe. Because of the extreme stress that pilot and co-pilot teams were likely to face on combat tours, it was vital that they were compatible and could work together under fire.

"We had special B-17s," Jim told me. "We stripped everything out of them, no guns, no bombs, no unnecessary equipment. We'd fill 'em up with gas and I'd fly with these guys non-stop around the country. I'd do my best to teach 'em everything they'd need to know out there. We'd give 'em all kinds of problems and see if they could fly together okay. You didn't want a pilot and co-pilot fighting with each other over Berlin. If they passed the test, they'd ship off together to Europe and start flying missions into Germany."

Jim's military career did not end with the Nazi surrender. He headed east and was one of the first Americans to set foot in Japan after the surrender. He helped rescue and evacuate U.S. prisoners of war, and showed me a Japanese naval flag—its red sun rays still bright more than forty years later—which he liberated from a captured enemy warship.

Returning home after the war, Jim bought an army surplus mine detector and began exploring the remains of Frontier-Era camps, forts and wagon trails. There were no regulations about treasure hunting in those days, and Jim was almost certainly the first person to visit scores of historic sites with a metal detector. Native American artifacts and relics from the Civil War and the Mexican-American War were abundant.

Jim amassed an extraordinary collection. Then a friend mentioned something about iron meteorites up at the old crater.

Early detectors were primitive and Jim's son told me just how difficult it was to use them.

"I used to hunt with Dad all the time. The Metrotech was my first detector. It looked like a coffee can with a handle, and a tube running down to the loop. It didn't have a speaker and you had to hook it up to an earphone. We had to figure out a way to hunt those meteorites, because there was so much iron in the ground, the detector would go off all the time. This was before discriminators, and we had to put it on the mineral setting. When it passed over a meteorite, it would null out, and make no sound. Then we knew we had something. When we first started hunting, we would find big chunks that were deeper; and the more we hunted around, the smaller the pieces got. One of the first I ever found was a forty-pounder. I found it as a teenager. It barely fit in a shoebox once the encrustations had come off. Dad wanted $90 a pound for it, but we never could find anyone that would pay that much 'cos they didn't know what it was. In the end Dad traded it for something. He was always trading."

In the 1960s, Jim moved up to more sophisticated equipment and started looking for Odessa irons with modern commercial detectors.

"I tried every one on the market but they didn't work. And then I happened to meet Mr. White of White's Detectors, because he had a big dealership out here. I told him his detectors didn't work. 'Well, give me a piece of that damn meteorite,' White said, 'And I'll make something that *will* work.' And he did. Most of what I found was with a White's detector. I probably found about a short ton. Some of it I traded. Some

[above] Pump jack near the Odessa Crater, Texas.

I sold to museums here, and in Germany, and Japan."

"No, I don't hunt at the crater anymore." There was the answer to the question I'd been dying to ask all day. "There's not much of anything left."

I felt a real connection to this man who led such an extraordinary life. He was one of the first people to hunt meteorites with a portable metal detector, and, as such, became a trailblazer for the rest of us. And yet his story remained untold. I had never read anything about him; never heard mention of him in any book or article. It was only because of my ad in the *Odessa American* that I was lucky enough to meet him—a genuine meteorite pioneer.

Jim sold off the bulk of his meteorite finds during the intervening years, but held on to a few favorites. I bought a beautiful 2.6-kilogram specimen from him, shaped like the African continent and it is still a favorite personal collection piece. As I prepared to leave, he handed me something else.

"Here, I want you to have this."

It was another iron, a smaller one, but a complete individual cut in half to show its inner structure.

Meteorite individuals are pieces that have travelled through the atmosphere on their own, with their structural integrity intact, sometimes acquiring attractive, sculptural features like regmaglypts. Fragments, also known as shrapnel because of their similarity to bomb case debris, are more angular and are created by explosive disintegration in the atmosphere or upon impact. Individuals are more highly prized by collectors, and I have always treasured the golf ball-sized iron that Jim gave me.

Inspired by my interview, I could not resist another drive out to the crater. As the sun set, pulling long angular shadows from the pump jacks, I moved slowly through the underbrush, far from the rim, with my Goldmaster detector in hand. There were plenty of nails and barbed wire scraps, and I found a couple more small meteorite fragments. Under the final wisps of daylight I got a deep reading, faint but unmistakable. I dug down a few inches and the signal was just that little bit stronger. More digging, and by then the detector was putting out a sharp whine. Thinking of those big buried irons, and of James Pliska's comment that if there were any more out there, "they'd be real deep," I dug frantically. My shovel nicked something metallic, and suddenly there were rusty iron flakes filling the bottom of my hole. My heart pounded as I dug around the iron. I was incredulous. In just one day I had found a meteorite that all the old-timers had missed! I brushed away more loose dirt and uncovered a fine example of that long smooth tubular kind of meteorite that is unique to Odessa—a decaying metal pipe from an old pump jack.

It is the classic Odessa prospector's joke, and no meteorite hunter's trip to the crater would be complete without falling for it once.

A few weeks later, James Pliska's wife telephoned to tell me he had passed away. I was shocked and almost dropped the phone. My intention was to visit with Jim again as soon as possible and do some real hunting with him, but now that would never happen. I felt an immediate bond of friendship with this powerful yet gentle man, as a result of the afternoon spent in Odessa. He was one of the most remarkable people I ever met and I felt fortunate indeed to have been able to hear his life story in person. Jim was one of the very first modern meteorite hunters and I was quite sure we would never see his like again.

TEN

TUCSON ROCKS

And my sweet Pistols are still a secret
Punk was a ribbon some careless girl wore
Nobody sings about their true lovers
No, everyone just crowds
For another drink at the bar

From "Questions"
By Lach

WHEN I RETURNED TO MY DUSTY MOTEL ROOM outside of Odessa, with a few small iron meteorites in my pocket and the memory of a very big and very rusty buried pipe clearly in my mind, I found the door to my room open.

Steve Arnold had arrived. After somehow convincing the day manager that it was okay to give him a key to my room, he proceeded to litter both beds with field equipment, reference books, treasure maps, plastic baggies, tools, an armored briefcase and hundreds of small meteorite specimens of almost every type and locality known to science.

"Howdy, pardner," he beamed, as he lumbered off one of the beds, knocking a metal detector onto the floor. "Good ta see you again. Didja find anything?"

"Just a couple of small ones," I said, and showed him the little iron fragments I had collected near the crater.

"Cool beans."

Steve is an Interstate man. Given the choice between flying to a destination or driving, he will always choose the Interstate. The previous day he set out from Tulsa, Oklahoma, stopping at one casino for each reservation he passed through on the way. A skilled blackjack player, he was now several hundred dollars ahead and ready to buy me dinner.

"I've got some things to show you," he said, hefting his bullet-proof steel case and lurching out the motel door.

"Hey, have you got your key?" I yelled after him.

"Oh no, probably not. Can you bring yours?"

I thought back to the last time I had seen Steve when we parted company in South America after our three-week Atacama odyssey. Steve found the best and largest Imilac pallasites and I convinced him to let me keep one. All the others would go to a meteorite

81

dealer back in the States for cutting and selling. I thought I should preserve one of his finds in my personal collection. When I looked at it on my desk it would remind me of our faraway desert camp, perched on a barren orange hillside, and the way Steve would shuffle out of his tent each morning, bleary-eyed and wild-haired, and trudge directly to the strewnfield in his yellow overalls before breakfast or bathroom.

I developed this desire to acquire Steve's finest Imilac suddenly and inconveniently after Steve's bags had already gone through airport security. Somehow, knowing absolutely no Spanish except for "compadre," "hasta la vista baby," and "no problemo dude," Steve managed to persuade the guards to let him go get one suitcase and come back through the security checkpoint. On a row of metal chairs in the international departure lounge, and in front of many puzzled travelers, we spread out the best Imilac meteorites, agreed on a price for my favorite one, and went our separate ways.

Nearly a year had elapsed since the South American trip and I was about to learn an intriguing thing about Steve. Each time I saw him, he would be driving a different vehicle and using a different metal detector. Every beaten-up car in which he appeared suffered from some unusual defect: reverse gear did not work or the back doors were broken and remained permanently locked. One year he showed up in a camper van with a 300-pound block of shiny, black volcanic obsidian on the floor. Another time he made a magnificent entrance in a canary-yellow Hummer, and another time in a station wagon stacked literally to the ceiling with his mobile office: printer, fax machine, filing cabinets, packing material, and hundreds of meteorite specimens.

In 1998 he was slowly working to death a large, blue and gray Dodge van which very nearly scraped the tarmac as it pottered along the highway. Inside were four pool table-sized slabs of poor-quality petrified wood, each weighing several hundred pounds. They were not at all attractive, and had been stacked uneasily against one side of the van's interior, making it list heavily to starboard, much like a damaged warship skulking back to port.

[above] A Sikhote-Alin iron meteorite that fell in eastern Siberia in 1947.

"Whaddya think they're worth?" Steve beamed, clearly delighted with his not-very-impressive acquisitions. I doubted he could find a gullible individual foolish enough to part with even $40 for the whole lot, so I lied and said I really had no idea.

"I got the whole bunch for fifty bucks in a garage sale in Oklahoma City," he explained. "I figure no place better to sell them than the gem show. They'll make great tabletops!"

Here was another fact I was to learn about Steve: there would always be something—or some things—related to the meteorite business inside his vehicle at any given time. They might be rocks, metal detectors, maps, books, notes, cardboard cut outs, giant slabs of petrified wood, or all of the above. They would, definitely, be in random heaps scattered around the vehicle. Every minute of the day, and most of the night as well, Steve would be thinking about how best to maximize his profit on these items. There was never a time without a plan, a scheme, a brainstorm or new venture, half-formed idea, fully-formed idea, possible sale or complicated trade, morse-coding its way through a brain that managed to discern business opportunities no other person ever noticed.

We climbed into the van that leaned uncomfortably on its right-side tires and drove into town where we consumed the first of many on-the-road dinners at Denny's. I am not particularly a fan of Denny's, or any chain restaurant for that matter, but that diner serves a most valuable purpose for us. Steve is as voracious a meat eater as I have ever encountered. He will typically start with a double order of chicken wings, followed by a steak or a burger, with meatballs or a chili dog on the side. I am a strict vegetarian and will not even allow bacon bits on my salad. At Denny's Steve can get his buffalo wings and steaks and burgers and extra super-giant industrial family-size Pepsis, and I can enjoy a veggie burger with a couple of glasses of white wine. What more could a pair of meteorite hunters want?

In 1998, Steve was the only other "meteorite person" I knew. I was, therefore, starved for conversation on my favorite topic and when we sat down in our quiet and spacious booth in Denny's, and Steve unlocked his steel case, it was as if a dam had been opened.

In those days, Steve was permanently joined to his bullet-proof briefcase. Large enough to hold a pair of typewriters, it sported two big locking clamps on the front; and when he walked around with it, he looked like a hit man. From inside the case Steve produced a kaleidoscopic assortment of meteorites of every size, shape and origin. Some were in bags, others were in display oxes and some just floated around loose in the case, like small asteroids in the void. I was still learning about the business and bursting with questions.

"Where did this one come from? What's the story behind this old handwritten label? Is this piece for sale, and how much is it?"

A long time passed before I even looked at the menu.

One piece intrigued me above all the others: black and silver, very heavy, and about the size of a chair from a doll's house, it had been hammered by the elements into the shape of an elephant. I found it captivating. Steve said it was a Sikhote-Alin meteorite, just one of thousands of delicately-shaped individual irons that had been part of a terrifying shower in Siberia during the winter of 1947. That fall was the largest meteoric event witnessed in modern times, and had it occurred over a city, hundreds, or maybe thousands of people would have been killed or injured.

We went through every piece in the case, one by one. With our table covered by strange rocks, boxes, labels, and small portable scales for weighing specimens, it must have looked to our bemused waitress as if we were making a drug deal rather than examining fragments of the cosmos. Hours passed and I devoured every scrap of information Steve cared to pass on.

In the morning we set out for Arizona. It was the first visit to the gem show for both of us, and the city of Tucson for that matter. We stopped in El Paso to buy cowboy boots. To a resident of the crowded East Coast, in love with the Southwest, it just seemed a given that if one were on a mission to acquire cowboy boots then El Paso, Texas, was the place to do it. As we headed west towards the Arizona border, we passed through Texas Canyon, a startling alien landscape where car-sized boulders are piled on top of each other in a vista that looked as if it had been designed by Dr. Seuss.

"So, Geoff. What's on your shopping list?"

"Well, Brenham," I answered without hesitating. "I need a piece of Brenham." A rare type of stony-iron meteorite, loaded with green crystals it is a pallasite—the same kind of meteorite we found at Imilac.

The first finds were made in the 1800s by farmers, and in the 1930s, H.H. Nininger found numerous round, tangerine-sized corroded pallasites in a crater-like depression in Brenham, Kansas, and coined the term meteorode. They looked like big chestnuts on the outside but were packed with olivine crystals on the inside.

"We should hunt at Brenham some day," I said wistfully, as cacti and boulders flitted by.

"I've been up there," Steve answered. "Talked to that guy who owns the supposed crater. He wouldn't let me hunt there, but I'll give it another try one of these days."

We crossed the state line on Interstate 10. Snow covered the East Coast, but in southern Arizona the evening air felt warm and full of life.

Some miles north of Benson, the highway loped up over a ridge and with the sun setting across a great basin, I experienced my first view of Tucson. As we wound our way down into the dusty twilight, toward twinkling lights far off in the desert, I could never have guessed the leading role that city would play in my life during the years ahead.

After living in London, Boston, and New York, Tucson will always be, for me, a small city. I find it one of the most fascinating places on Earth: part Mexican barrio, part Wild West frontier settlement, part wealthy retirement community, part avant-garde arts center. It feels like a small town, yet half a million people live within the city limits. Every November Tucsonans close down one of their main streets for the All Soul's Procession. They dress up as ghosts, dragons, giant puppets, and deceased relatives, in whimsical handmade costumes, and bound through the city pounding on drums and pulling burning cauldrons. Onlookers shake their heads and say: "Only in Tucson."

I knew none of this as we rolled into town that first time. Initially, Tucson seemed much like other Southwestern cities I had visited: spread out, wide streets, one-story adobe-buildings, few trees, lots of cacti. Then there were all those gem show tents—big white carnival tents which, in fact, did not remind me of any other Southwestern city, or any other city at all when I stopped to think about it. We passed one tent after another, most of them with forklift trucks whizzing in and out at top speed, depositing wooden crates in teetering stacks along the side of the road.

Interstate 10 cuts right through downtown Tucson, and from the overpass, in the approaching darkness, we were greeted by a parade of brilliantly illuminated motels jammed to overflowing with banners, flags, signs, display tables full of rocks, dinosaur skeletons, cars, trucks, buyers, sellers, tourists, prospectors, all rushing around like possessed people beside the highway in a whirlwind carnival of commerce, and all of it to do with rocks, fossils, minerals, and meteorites.

I suppose I expected that all the natural history dealers would be set up in one organized location—a convention center, perhaps—where they kept sensible business hours like a normal trade show. But, just like the town itself, nothing about the Tucson gem and mineral show is normal.

It all started pretty small, back in 1955, with a free exhibition put together at a local school by the Tucson Gem and Mineral Society. In later years the event moved to a spot in Tucson's Rodeo Grounds, and eventually grew into the largest and most amazing natural history display the world has ever seen. The Tucson Convention and Visitors' Bureau puts the annual number of attendees at more than 50,000 and that is a big influx for a small city.

The show takes over the entire town and you either love it or hate it. It is impossible to get a hotel room or a rental car and the most frequently heard comment among locals during February would be: "Well, it *is* the Gem Show." Such an observation might be used to explain the relentless traffic, the lack of parking, the overcrowded post offices, the strange blend of international characters on every street corner, and that every popular restaurant is packed to capacity.

During a three-week period from late January to mid-February, fossil dealers from England, moldavite miners from the Czech Republic, meteorite hunters from Russia, France, and South America, diggers of Australian opals and every other imaginable kind of natural history entrepreneur occupy many of Tucson's hotels. And they take all the rooms. Hotel furniture is removed and replaced with glass display cabinets and expensive lighting, and suites and queen rooms and even ordinary twins at the Holiday Inn are converted into temporary showrooms. A friendly, slightly dizzying, circus-like atmosphere envelops the town, especially at sunset when vendors open a bottle of wine after a long day of answering endless questions about what they sell and where they found it.

Most of the sellers are hands-on people. They find their own material in the wilderness and are experts at what they do. In one room at the InnSuites, I met the world champion gold prospector and held a nugget the size of an Idaho potato that was worth fifty thousand bucks. Next door was a room with blacked-out windows where I spoke to a man who sells florescent minerals, the beauty of which can only be appreciated when viewed under an ultraviolet light. Next to him, we met a French explorer who spends months alone, each year, collecting treasures in the Sahara Desert. One door down from him resided a character who offered the world's biggest fossil shark teeth, plucked from the bottom of a river in South Carolina. And those were just the first four rooms out of hundreds.

Everyone ran around like crazy for three weeks, buying, selling, trading, making under-the-table deals, catching up on the latest gossip about who found what, and still trying to fit in a little sleep after partying in the hotel bar until closing time.

It was exhausting, bewildering, and overwhelming. Nobody seemed to quite know what was really going on. It was also—easily—one of the most exciting things I had ever been part of. These were most definitely my kind of people.

That first night we went straight to the Ramada Inn, a faded but charming 1950s motel with swaying palm trees towering over a grassy lawn. It was dark when we arrived. A floodlit twenty foot-high steel sculpture of the dinosaur *Tyrannosaurus rex* dominated the courtyard, and some wag had suspended two large grapefruits between his thighs, making for a very amusing and certainly politically incorrect spectacle.

Colorful, sloppily-dressed, generally unshaven vendors sat in deck chairs smoking cigars, gulping wine and chuckling over the day's events. I heard British, French, Russian, Arabic and other accents I did not recognize. They were all rockheads, all from different cultures, yes; but there together in that one kooky hotel, with the same mission: buying and selling natural treasures, and I immediately felt completely and entirely at home.

When Steve first decided to become a meteorite hunter, his mentor was a jovial, thirty-something expert on cosmic rubble named Blaine Reed. Tall and slender with straight sandy hair, blue jeans, delicate silver-framed glasses and a smart leather jacket, in 1998 he was probably one of only three people on the planet making a living entirely from the buying and selling of rocks from outer space. When Steve and I walked into Blaine's room for the first time, he was propped up on the queen-size bed, next to his identical twin Blake, both of them dressed in matching clothing. They greeted Steve with big smiles and ordered us to help ourselves to beer. There were several large coolers in the room completely filled with cans and bottles.

Blaine conducted all business from his bed in the Ramada, and I discovered that everyone involved in meteorites in any way at all went to see him. The Reeds' room existed at the nexus of the meteorite world, and if someone had a question about identifying a rare type of space rock, or needed a valuation on something, or some personal advice, or a cold beer, or even just somewhere to hang out at 11:30 p.m. on a Wednesday night, Blaine was the man to see. Business was done in that room pretty much non-stop from about 9 a.m. until 1 a.m. every day for almost three weeks, with serious parties starting most nights at official closing time which was 6 p.m. Business continued during the parties. People brought meteorites for Blaine to see, deals were done, money changed hands, and all the while, charming mild-mannered and brilliant Blake Reed sat on the same bed designing, building, and playing with complicated electronic gadgets like satellite monitoring equipment and geiger-counters.

Every flat surface in the Reeds' room, including most of the bed, had meteorites on it: dinner plate-sized polished slices; ginger-colored specimens from Russia with nearly unpronounceable names; a dark and regmaglypted iron monster from Argentina sat on the floor, and a tabletop display case was filled with the rare and expensive. The only other time I had seen so many meteorites in one place was at the National Museum in D.C., and this felt so much more exciting because every one of them was for sale.

Steve wandered among the display, pointing at one specimen after another and saying, mostly to himself, "That's mine. That's mine. That's one of mine."

"What do you mean?" I asked him. "Do you have some of these on consignment with Blaine?"

"No, they're all meteorites I found and sold to Blaine."

At that moment I fully grasped that being a meteorite hunter was not just something that Steve did; it's who he was.

The Reed twins and I took an instantaneous and permanent liking to each other. They had a generous nature and an irreverent sense of humor and loved English TV, especially *Monty Python's Flying Circus*. I was delighted when—in my best British public school accent—I quoted some dialog from a favorite sketch, and they howled with laughter and insisted that I continue with the entire routine. For years after, whenever I arrived in Tucson for the show, the first thing out of Blake's mouth was: "Geoff, do the *Python* thing!"

There always seemed to be an excessive amount of merriment spilling out of the Reeds' room into the grassy courtyard beyond and, after Steve, Blaine and Blake were the first meteorite professionals I came to know as friends.

Steve and I spent the next few days wandering the show, meeting meteorite hunters, dealers and collectors, but every night we returned to the Reed's room for more beers, entertainment, and camaraderie.

I had been charged with one special task that first year. My Chinese doctor, Master Nan Lu, an eminent martial arts expert, author, and highly respected traditional medicine practitioner in New York, knew all about the Tucson show and asked me to bring him back a meteorite. "Meteorites have special energy," he instructed me. "If I had enough money, I would make a bed completely out of meteorites and sleep in it every night." He was quite serious and, actually, it did not sound like that bad of an idea.

I selected an apple-sized Nantan, certain that it would make an appropriate gift. Nantan irons from Guangxi Province in China are believed to be the remnants of a spectacular fireball witnessed in 1516, making it one of Earth's oldest known meteorites. Master Lu was delighted with his present, and kept it at his office at the Taoist Healing Center in downtown New York City.

At the time, I was unaware of the fact that Nantans have a reputation for being a horrible investment; over time pieces begin flaking off, and sometimes specimens will disintegrate completely. Several years later, after I was no longer in his care, and fearing the worst, I checked back with Master Lu to see how his Nantan was holding up. I had great admiration for my former doctor and hated to think I might have given him a gift which later fell apart.

"It's fantastic!" he exclaimed. "This meteorite has so much energy it comes out from inside and the meteorite breaks up into many pieces. It is unbelievable."

The old iron had literally exploded into scores of fragments and now sat in a pile on Master Lu's desk. He was thrilled with this development. I refrained from saying anything about how Nantans are awful rusters and prone to falling apart if you look at them in a funny way. I did not want to ruin his fascination over the meteorite's demise. Anyway, who am I to contradict a sagacious Chinese master who holds four advanced degrees? Maybe there was indeed cosmic energy in that particular Nantan just desperate to get out into the world of humans. It is a much more inspiring explanation than the mean and relentless processes of terrestrial decomposition.

I was wrong about something else too. On the last day of the show Steve pocketed five hundred bucks in cash for those ugly slabs of petrified something. We then drove north of Tucson for half an hour, to a new destination, in order to learn the secret of an amazing meteorite discovery, with a wad of twenty dollar bills stuffed into the van's ashtray.

Steve always kept his road money in the ashtray.

ELEVEN

DESERT PIRATES

Don't tell me what I can't do
You've still not seen my best
Jump your ass in the ring
And that will be your test

From "Tight Genes"
By Krista Khrome

THE SLOPES ARE LIKE MONSTROUS EELS half buried in the sand. Intervening gullies are choked with silt and pebbles from centuries of flash floods. The sky is crystal blue over rolling sun-blasted hills dotted with twisted Joshua trees. Steep-sided washes that run parallel to each other for miles and miles are covered with a hard, dense desert pavement, almost exactly the same color as the Gold Basin meteorites that lie within.

In Mohave County, a sparsely populated and largely forgotten corner of northwestern Arizona, lie the remnants of a great meteorite fall. About 15,000 years ago, an asteroid exploded in the low atmosphere, east of present-day Las Vegas, and showered the picturesque concave valley between Garnet and Senator Mountains with thousands of angular fragments. The silent field of ancient extraterrestrial stones survived the last Ice Age and a millennia of desert sunblasting before being recognized by an amateur Arizona gold hunter named Jim Kriegh. The meteorite was named Gold Basin after the valley in which it was found, and unofficially dubbed the world's first fossil meteorite strewnfield.

When an official announcement of Jim's Gold Basin find made the news, Steve and I were already on our way to Tucson for the gem show. Dr. Joel Schiff, editor of *Meteorite,* was about to publish my first science article about the Chile adventure and I decided to be bold. I tracked down Jim Kriegh's phone number and called him from a gas station payphone somewhere in the Texas flatlands. I introduced myself as "a writer from *Meteorite* magazine," said I would be in Tucson for the gem show and asked if I could do an interview with him. He agreed, and on a bright and sunny morning at the end of the 1998 gem show, Steve and I arrived in the town of Oro Valley. Under the shade of mighty pine trees, we were welcomed to a secluded ranch house by Jim Kriegh, and his vivacious neighbor and prospecting partner, Twink Monrad. That meeting would be the start of two long and important friendships, and a catalyst for many future adventures.

Evidence of Jim's former career as a University of Arizona civil engineering professor was everywhere: bookcases crammed with textbooks, articles and scholarly publications. Among them, a shelf full of meteorite books by H.H. Nininger and others. It was immediately obvious to me that this clear-eyed and vigorous man in his late sixties had not settled quietly into retirement but had, rather, reinvented himself as a meteorite hunter.

We examined some of the stone meteorites Jim had found. They did not jump out at you and it was little wonder that it had taken 15,000 years for somebody to realize what they were. Caramel colored and weathered, they looked just about the same as any other desert-varnished rock, but when I picked one up it, was heavier than it should have been, and—when you looked very carefully—was punctuated with minute, shiny pinheads of other-worldly metal.

Gold nuggets first tempted Jim Kriegh up to Mohave County, and the unexpected discovery of meteorites kept taking him back. He and Twink made the 800-mile round trip from Tucson almost every month for several years.

Gold Basin is peppered with "hot rocks"—worthless terrestrial stones with enough metallic content to set off a detector. When gold prospectors pull up a hot rock, courtesy dictates that they leave it on the surface, so the next guy does not waste his time digging it up all over again.

"We found some meteorites sitting right up on top," Jim told me. "Put aside next to holes that old prospectors had dug looking for gold. They thought they were ordinary hot rocks."

They were also sure to tell us about the many fruitless hours spent searching through harsh terrain with nothing to show for it.

[previous page] My friend and mentor, Professor Jim Kriegh, shows off a new find at Gold Basin.
[above] Detail of a 197.9-gram Gold Basin stone meteorite found by Jim. Although it may look much like a terrestrial rock, close examination reveals remnant fusion crust and nickel-iron flecks.

As Steve and I prepared to depart—eager to experience Gold Basin for ourselves—Jim presented us each with a stone from his personal collection. He also pulled out one of his detectors and showed us how best to calibrate it in order to distinguish the elusive space travelers from terrestrial rocks.

We drove hard all day, passing gorges, red sandstone cliffs, and crags of volcanic rock that gave suddenly onto fields of saguaro cactus, their arms pointing at crisp desert skies. Exhilarating as the scenery was, it held little interest for us. In our minds we were already digging into the floor of Gold Basin.

"Get a move on, people!" Steve yelled once, in an exaggerated hillbilly accent, as a sluggish motorist slowed us down to a crawl. "Don't ya know there's 'meters' waiting for us?"

Kingman is the only sizeable town near Gold Basin. We arrived there well past dark; but after stopping for supplies, we pressed on for one more hour. We pulled off Route 93 and crept along a deserted road, past a billboard that advertised "Your own Arizona ranch for only $79 a month!" and arrived in a sandblasted trailer park outpost named Dolan Springs, consisting of a dilapidated gas station, a general store and a crooked and dimly-lit motel. Perhaps presentable in the '50s, the crumbling motel appeared desperately seedy now—even to the two of us, dressed as we were in army boots and faded t-shirts—but we had driven nearly 400 miles, and any kind of bed would be agreeable.

Steve kept the motor running while I went to see about rooms.

A stooped and crusty old man peered suspiciously at me from inside, refusing to open up, no matter how many times I rang the bell.

"What's going on?" Steve yelled from the car.

"I don't know. There's a creepy-looking guy in there. I can see him but he won't come to the door."

Steve lumbered out of the car and pounded repeatedly on the locked office door with his toaster-sized fist until we heard a far-off voice cackle: "No rooms!"

We looked at each other, wearily, then crossed the road to the general store in search of help. A frail weatherbeaten woman, as thin as a piece of kelp, hovered behind the counter like a desert wraith.

"Is there another motel in town?" I asked. I pointed out through the swinging saloon-style doors. "That one is full."

"Which one?"

I gave her a puzzled look. "That one there. Right across the street." I pointed again, out into the night.

"Oh, you can't stay there. The people . . . they, you know . . . the people that stay there, stay there *all* the time."

Steve nodded at me knowingly, and whispered, "Prospectors." I assumed she was taking about criminals or drug addicts, not prospectors, but was not about to debate the point just then.

"Is there anywhere else to stay around here?"

"Not this side of Kingman."

"Nothing north of here?"

"I think there's a place all the way up there by the lake."

"Is that far?"

"It's pretty far."

"Do you have a phone number for that place?"

"No."

"Well, do you at least know the name of the place?"

"No idea."

And so it was that we drove all the way back to Kingman, where Steve consumed a very large steak, and I drank a very large Tennessee whisky before disappearing into sleep.

Monday greeted us sunny but cold. "High of only 48 degrees," the Weather Channel warned. We crossed a wide alluvial plain, and wound along dirt roads through low hills dotted with Joshua trees—angular and awkward like stunted monkeys. The valley of Gold Basin is really a plain, a beautiful olive and ochre pebble-covered plain that slopes ever so gently toward jagged aquamarine mountains. It is an ancient and undisturbed landscape stippled with tumbleweeds and hardy cacti. If a herd of dinosaurs ambled across your field of view, they would fit in so perfectly you would not even look twice.

I remembered Jim showing me a topo map, and pointing to the very spot we were now passing. "We found meteorites on both sides of the road, here and here," he told us. So we pulled over, assembled our detectors, and as if by silent agreement, Steve took the south side while I headed into a broad gully to the north.

Almost immediately I heard a strong beep from my detector. "Oh it can't be that easy," I thought. I dug down an inch or two and found a muddy ball that leapt onto my magnet. I was about to yell out, "I've already got one!" when I noticed the quartz crystals, and there are no quartz crystals in meteorites. I filled in my small hole and tried again. In no time I had found enough meteor-wrongs to build an impressive rock garden. My substantial collection of other discoveries included rifle and shotgun cartridges, barbed wire, nails, lead slugs, and one of those keys for opening sardine cans.

We continued well past sunset, trying several different locations, but finding nothing of value. At last we called it a day.

The next morning we tried a new area, and as I searched, it was hard to imagine that a crowd of rockhounds would one day soon descend upon Gold Basin in search of their own space rocks. Our sole companion on that clear and silent morning was a stealthy one whom we knew only by the marks of her passing—mountain lion tracks, recently imprinted in damp sand, elegantly followed the line of a riverbed, reminding us how far we were from civilization.

After an unsatisfying lunch of dry roasted peanuts, bread, and energy bars, we drove south along steep dirt tracks, miles from anywhere.

Rounding a low hill, we came upon a most unexpected sight. Off to our left and nearly hidden in a gully down below was a gang of prospectors sweating over a dry sluice. We could have been transported back in time a hundred years. Maybe we had been. Five bearded and burly men hastily shovelled dirt and rocks into a device that looked much like a portable cement mixer, and hand cranked it in an attempt to separate out any gold that might or not be in there. Wearing red bandannas, dusty cowboy hats, and leather vests they were as scary a bunch of ruffians as I had seen in many years—an unsettling blend of frontier desperados and Blackbeard's pirates.

"Hey, look over there! Let's go talk to those guys," Steve boomed, and brought the car to a jarring halt on a ridge overlooking their gold claim.

"I don't think that's a good idea, Steve." I shook my head emphatically. "They don't look like they want company."

Steve was already out of the car and bounding over towards them like a big, friendly Labrador. I followed, warily.

"Hi, guys!" Steve roared, waving and smiling. "How's it going?"

The gold diggers stopped shoveling grime into their cement mixer and looked up menacingly, in much the same way that an alligator's head slowly rises out of a swamp. One of them threw his shovel on the ground.

"Didja find anything?" Steve asked, beaming.

The diggers stood still and said nothing. I was not sure if they would gun Steve down where he stood or grab him and throw him into a crevasse to die later.

"Didja find any gold?"

They turned, and looked at each with poker faces. Two of them shook their heads, and one made a growling sound which eventually resolved into something that sounded a bit like: "Not much."

"We're looking for meteorites," Steve said, and pulled Jim's little Gold Basin gift out of his shirt pocket. "Look, here's one."

The head pirate plucked the stone out of Steve's hand and held it up close to his black eyes, squinting in the sunlight.

"This a meater-ite?"

"Yeah, a real meteorite. Cool huh?"

The pirate sneered and put the stone back in Steve's hand. "So that's what them things is."

"You've seen them around here?" Steve asked.

"Yeah. I seen hundreds. I just throw 'em away. Some of 'em this big." With both hands, the pirate made an imaginary shape the size of a microwave.

"Really! Do you remember where you threw them?"

"Yeah, away!"

Steve is a big guy but two of these characters were considerably bigger than him. They moved in and formed a semicircle around us.

"Well, Steve, let's let these gentlemen get back to work. I can see they're very busy."

I sensed inordinate hostility coming our way and it would be very easy to lose a couple of bodies out there in Mohave County.

I put my hand on Steve's arm and started moving him back to the car, quickly, but hoping it did not look too much like I was about to bolt.

"Okay, goodbye gentlemen. Thanks. Sorry to have interrupted your day," I said, in as friendly a tone as I could manage.

We were halfway to the car before Steve turned and ran back.

"Hey, guys, if you find any more of those big meteorites, give me a call. They're worth a lot of money." He gave every one of the pirates a business card.

We got in the car and drove off. My heart was pounding. I looked discretely out of the back window. As we rose over the next hill I could, for a moment, see the five of them down there in the gully, standing in a circle, staring at Steve's cards as if in a trance. The Five Horsemen of the Apocalypse.

"Nice guys," Steve smiled, and nodded happily. "I wonder if they'll find any more Gold Basins."

The car left a trail of fine dust in the air behind us. Maybe there were some tiny gold flecks mixed in with it.

We stopped randomly when we thought, or more likely just guessed, we were at a good spot. Mercifully, we did not run into any more prospector pirates. Again we toiled away past sunset, half-filling a bucket with worthless hot rocks almost identical in appearance to the meteorites Jim had given us. Ours were not real meteorites, but we put them in the bucket anyway, just to feel that we were finding *something*, I suppose.

A typical stone meteorite contains between 20 and 30% nickel-iron, compared with 50% in pallasites and over 90% in iron meteorites. When a metal detector passes over a stone meteorite, the audio signal is quieter and gentler than the sharp tone we were accustomed to hearing at Imilac. Imagine hiding those weak audio signals in a dry desert full of hot rocks, that sound almost exactly the same as stone meteorites, and you have Gold Basin. It was my first attempt at hunting for stones. It was hard, and it was a failure.

I kept in touch with Jim and Twink, and a year later they asked if we would like to return to Gold Basin, but this time join them at their private campsite—an invitation as exciting as it was unusual. Meteorite hunters are protective of their secret locations and their personal hunting methods; few are generous and trusting enough to bring company.

I flew to Albuquerque in early February, 1999, where Steve picked me up in an unfamiliar but similarly battered van. After driving across much of New Mexico and Arizona, we left paved roads beyond Dolan Springs and headed cautiously onto rough trails suitable only for mules and the hardiest of 4WD vehicles. A grand old wooden sign, perched among sage brush and peppered with bullet holes, but otherwise reminiscent of the rustic plaques that welcome travelers to America's National Forests, proudly announced that we were entering Gold Basin. It seemed oddly out of place, since there was no actual road there, or buildings, or even any trees for that matter. I wondered who went to the trouble of making that sign, trucking it all the way out there, and setting it up as if to proclaim a future town would rise on the spot—a town that never arrived.

Steve's beaten-up van seemed to sag in the middle and scrape its bottom along the pebbly tracks. We made rather slow progress, lurching over shoebox-sized rocks and dry stream beds—all of them hungry for our muffler and exhaust pipe. Jim and Twink set out for Gold Basin a few days ahead of us and furnished us with detailed directions, but there were few landmarks in the strewnfield, and we managed to miss all of them. We looked in vain for the "old placer mine"—supposedly right beside the track we were on—where Nineteenth Century prospectors washed gold particles out of surface sand and grit. We also missed the "sign that's fallen under a bush," and several other markers which turned out to be less obvious than anticipated.

A few times Steve stopped, and I walked on ahead, pacing the roughest stretches on foot to make sure the tired old van could handle it. It took us 45 minutes to traverse three puny miles, never certain that we were even going in the right direction. One nearly invisible turnoff looked much like another, and what I imagined to be the placer diggings turned out to be animal burrows. We were about to turn around and start from the beginning again when I saw a flash of white from the top of a steep hill—a splendid RV glittering in the sun.

We came to a stop in a cloud of dust and got out to look for our hosts. There was nobody in sight. Nothing moved for miles.

After some time a young couple appeared over a ridge and trudged slowly toward us, eyes always on the ground, watching for rattlesnakes. The metal detectors and rock hammers they carried made it clear we were all there for the same purpose.

"You must be Geoff and Steve." Suzanne, attractive, with long blonde hair, slightly tomboyish, and with an unmistakable air of determination and no-nonsense about her, and her boyfriend John, introduced themselves. Friendly and welcoming, they were also decidedly serious—kitted out in army gear with hiking boots, shovels, backpacks, wraparound sunglasses and canteens. Suzanne would go on to become Director of Operations for my company, Aerolite Meteorites, and the location photographer for *Meteorite Men*, but such things were still more than a decade in the future.

"Jim and Twink went in to town to fix a flat," John told us. "Get your gear together and we'll take you hunting with us." We piled into Suzanne's pickup truck and in no time were off bumping along rickety roads. We parked upon a flat plateau, covered with brush, and crisscrossed by gullies with almost vertical sides.

Correctly calibrating metal detectors, so they can see into the ground while ignoring mineralized soil is difficult and takes practice and patience. As a musician I was, of course, smugly confident that my trained ears could by now immediately tell the difference between the sound of terrestrial hot rocks and the real thing.

John reached into his pocket and pulled out a bronze-colored stone, the size of a golf ball. "Here, try this. It's a meteorite. I found it this morning."

He threw the stone on the ground. My detector produced a modest hum as I swung over it.

"Okay, now try this." John rummaged around in a random pile of stones and came up with an earth rock that he dropped at my feet. I swung the detector over that, and it delivered an identical hum.

"Hear the difference?" he asked.

I tried both stones again. And then another time, and then about forty more times, straining to find some note or timbre that felt different. Even Mozart could not have told those two tones apart.

"Yes, I guess I hear a slight difference in the tone," I lied.

John laughed. "The point is, you have to dig up a whole lot of hot rocks before you find a meteorite."

After a few hours, Jim materialized in the distance. He presented a rather unique appearance in the field: colorful plaid shirt; black headphones clamped around a round, narrow-brimmed white hat; fawn-colored leather work gloves; the control box of his detector suspended around his neck with webbing straps. And always circling happily nearby, Jim's German shepherd Christie. With a wry smile he claimed that, when she was in the mood, Christie helped ferret out buried meteorites.

Six people hunted, each with their own detector, for several hours. John found a small piece, and Twink found three. As the sun began to set, turning the sage and Joshua trees orange, Steve let out a whoop. He held up 60-gram fragment, found only fifty yards from the road. Thin and flat, heavy for its size and colored like a pancake, it looked like something from a suburban garden, but was truly a fragment of another world.

Steve and I each set up a small tent, near the RV. I put together my collapsible army cot, and after a long day of travel and hunting, fell sound asleep under the stars and Joshua trees.

At 6:45 a.m. I crawled out of my tent to watch the sunrise. I could find no natural wood, but dead cactus limbs burn well. I built a small fire and brewed some English tea. Jim had cautioned me about rattlesnakes so I put on gloves and, before picking anything up, poked it repeatedly with a stick. We traveled a long way to hunt and every hour of daylight seemed precious. I had no intention of wasting time on elaborate meals so I quickly prepared my typical campsite breakfast: two cans of French-cut green beans in a tin bowl, with salsa and lemon juice for flavor, all warmed up on the fire for a few minutes.

That February was the beginning of Jim and Twink's third year hunting at Gold Basin. "It's getting harder and harder to find anything," Jim told me later, as we careened along dimly-lit trails, my head banging against the roof of his truck. "But we're definitely going to find some today. Don't you worry."

His confidence was inspiring, but as my forehead slammed once more into the headrest of the passenger seat in front of me, all I could think about was the mound of hot rocks I collected the previous day.

[above] The author taking a breather under a very grand Joshua tree. Gold Basin, Arizona, 1999.

A year had passed since Jim went public with his discovery, and things were very different at Gold Basin now. Always willing to share the wealth, Jim replied to all inquiries about how to find meteorites, giving advice and tips. Many would-be meteorite hunters made their first find at Gold Basin, thanks to him. The desert which Steve and I enjoyed in solitude the previous year was now in the midst of a relentless search. I noticed footprints, partially filled dig holes, and vehicle tracks almost everywhere. Off on a ridge there appeared to be three mobile homes.

"Jim, are there actually people living out here?"

"Yes," he replied, a degree of disapproval clear in his voice. "Some people, prospectors, maybe, heard there were meteorites here and just moved on in."

I imagined weatherbeaten rockheads out there hunting all day, every day, until the very last meteorite was pulled from the ground.

"Well, I guess we better get on with it then." I smiled.

Jim unrolled his map, upon which two years' worth of finds were scrupulously recorded. He examined it for some long minutes, in silence. "I think this area is good." He pointed at a spot marked by a flurry of contour lines, indicating steep-sided gullies, and also speckled with red dots, added in by hand—a record of find locations. It was a real treasure map and we were headed for White Elephant Wash.

The higher ground in Gold Basin is capped by desert pavement, with a bronze patina so colorful it could have been airbrushed on. Below, the ground is softer, and it is easy to dig through. I attached a powerful magnet to my digging tool to test all the meteorites I planned on finding, but the only thing it stuck to that morning was a buckle on my Swiss army surplus camouflage jacket. I determined to dig up every single target my metal detector found for me. Eventually, through sheer weight of numbers, I had to find something.

"You should just follow Twink," Jim laughed. "She has some kind of sense about where they are." I tried that for a while, but after putting my detector down and scraping through dirt several times, my comrades were now fixtures in the middle distance.

On a gentle slope, where the ground was soft and the color of buttermilk, my detector picked up a few small targets. I dug down five or six inches and pulled out several dust-covered hot rocks. One of them miraculously jumped onto my magnet. I looked at it very closely and told myself it was just a lump of iron or some other as-yet-unknown type of hot rock which is magnetic, but still not a meteorite. I unhooked my canteen and washed off the dirt with some overpriced European spring water that I usually reserved only for drinking. The rock appeared brown and speckled, like old leather, and on its surface, glinting in the sun were tiny metal flakes.

I saw Jim, methodically working his way along a ridge, and hiked over to him, clutching my rock, and expecting the worst. He looked at the stone for a moment, wiped a little more dirt off and pronounced: "Yes, that's a meteorite. No question about it. It even has some fusion crust on it."

There is a great feeling of joy, for a moment, in succeeding in doing something difficult, perhaps nearly impossible, something that most people will never accomplish. In my hand was a small piece of a lost world; a memento from the Asteroid Belt that found its way through the darkness of space, all the way to Earth, and fell onto the sands of Mohave County long before the place had a name or was disturbed by humans.

After dinner, all the hunters built a roaring campfire of dry cactus parts. I poured whisky into tin cups and we sat up late into the night, laughing and recounting tales of earlier adventures. An occasional meteor streaked across the clear sky, reminding us why we were out there.

The previous day's long hunt conspired with late night whiskies and, never being much of a morning person anyway, I overslept. At 7 a.m., Jim yelled outside my tent, impatient to get hunting.

"Come on! We're burning daylight."

There would be no time for breakfast. Groggy, and moving as quickly as possible, I threw some canned food into my pack, checked my water and—a little wobbly—shoe-horned myself and my gear into the back seat of Jim's truck.

We drove far out across the basin to a new location. The land felt different: the wash backs were narrow and lay close together, like parallel fingers on a long hand, covered with cactus and brush that cast cool, elegant morning shadows.

After half an hour my detector briefly produced a slightly different sound, and I wondered if my ears were finally getting attuned. On the surface and fitted perfectly into the jigsaw puzzle of natural pavement sat an exquisite golden meteorite. This one was not caked with dirt like my previous find. It was rounded and tapered, like the nose of an airship and clearly showed patches of black fusion crust. It seemed very different from the other Gold Basin finds. Jim told me that whenever I found a meteorite, I should search the immediate area, as they seem to fall in clusters. I carefully covered the surrounding quarter acre and found a normal-looking meteorite fragment sitting beside an old miner's burrow.

Our group was widely scattered and, with nobody around to share in my excitement, I set myself atop a hill, under a particularly grand Joshua tree, took off my sweaty hat and bandanna, granted myself a few minutes to appreciate the wonderful view, and enjoyed a sumptuous lunch. There is nothing like a can of garbanzo beans and a couple of stale rice cakes to celebrate a meteorite discovery.

There are documented examples of erratic meteorites being found in existing strewnfields. In such cases, hunters have searched so thoroughly for examples of a recognized meteorite in a known area that—completely by accident—they discover an entirely different meteorite that fell in the same zone, but at a different time.

The golden stone I found embedded in desert pavement is likely such a discovery. It is heavier than it should be, and different in appearance from the others. Only slightly weathered by the elements, it tells the story of a landing on our planet much more recent than the Gold Basin meteorites.

An enthusiastic academic once tried to coax me into handing it over for slicing and scrutiny in the lab, but it is too lovely for such a fate. While the study of new meteorite finds is vitally important, occasionally beauty must win out over science. My little stone will not share its secrets. It remains in a special place in my glass cabinet, un-named and unclassified, but whole and complete—just as it fell, alone and unnoticed somewhere in the unrecorded history of Gold Basin.

TWELVE

MOTHER RUSSIA

I've travelled many roads
And I've played so many shows
Kissed all kinds of toads
'Til I hit the mother load
I've danced at every party
On every floor
On a moonbeam, baby
Let's party some more

From "Every Party"
By Anne Husick

MY FATHER'S MOTHER, Sasha Margolin Notkin, was born into a Russian peasant family during the first few years of the Twentieth Century. She survived the 1905 Revolution and the October Revolution of 1917. In the early 1920s as a lone teenager, she traveled to Riga on the Baltic Sea, the capital of Latvia, boarded a ship bound for North America and arrived in New York City via Ellis Island. She lived to be 94 and remembered, with great precision, her early years in Russia.

I once sat her down, encouraged her to drink a couple of beers, which she secretly loved, and asked her detailed questions about her youth. I discretely recorded the conversation on a miniature tape recorder. What an extraordinary opportunity to speak with someone who lived through both Russian Revolutions. It felt like time travel.

When I asked how the 1917 revolution affected her and her hard-working rural farming family—exactly the kind of people the revolution was supposed to help—she said: "The Bolshevik soldiers came on horses and took away our cow."

Growing up, I knew we had relatives in Russia and during the Cold War years my grandmother made several trips behind the Iron Curtain to see them. When I was about ten, she revealed that a cousin of mine, of similar age, wanted to be a biologist but could not afford a microscope. After some soul searching, I agreed to send mine by way of Sasha on her next visit. It was only a beginner's level microscope, the kind a student might use in high school in America, but its arrival in Russia caused great celebration among the family. I received a heartfelt thank you note, beautifully and carefully handwritten in Russian.

At my British school all students were required to study a minimum three languages. French and Latin were, of course, compulsory. The third was an elective and

[facing page] The mighty Roy Gallant, with translator, and Chief of Staff, Katya Rossovskaya, at Popigai Crater base camp, 1999.

that was about the only thing we ever got to choose for ourselves. Most took German or Spanish and a very few—only seven boys out of 860—picked Russian. I did it mostly to be contrary but also partly because I believed, even back then in the midst of the Cold War, that I would, myself, one day make the journey to Mother Russia.

Such dreams were largely forgotten twenty-three years later, during the spring of 1999. *Meteorite* magazine had just published my fifth article, and *Rock & Gem* magazine selected my story about hunting for fossil ammonites in England, titled "Chambers Fit for a Queen," for a full-color feature. The $300 check for that piece made for a welcome bonus, but science writing was not likely to be paying the bills any time soon, and neither was meteorite hunting. After all the hardship I endured in making those early finds, there was no chance I would consider parting with them for ordinary money. As time went on, Steve teased me that I kept every single meteorite I ever found.

"Geoff will never sell any of his meteorites," he would tell fellow enthusiasts, laughing. "He'd rather starve."

In 1998 I moved into a third-floor apartment in an old brownstone in downtown Jersey City, just a few minutes' walk from the Hudson River, and directly across from the World Trade Center. My graphic design work continued, barely, to pay the bills. A lucrative short-term contract arrived from New York's famous department store, Macy's, and was about to put me firmly in the black for the first time in several years. For some months, I worked there as a consulting art director and oversaw a major nationwide design job. I worked twelve hours a day, six days a week; when the paycheck arrived at the end of the project, there was enough to pay off my credit cards, as well as the rent, the utility bills, put a few dollars in the bank and still, maybe, have enough left over to buy a new meteorite or two.

At just about that time, an unexpected email arrived from my publisher, Dr. Joel Schiff, of *Meteorite,* magazine asking if I might have any interest in accompanying fellow author Professor Roy Gallant on an expedition to Siberia, there to explore a 35.7 million-year-old meteorite crater full of micro diamonds.

Roy was one of my favorite writers. A chronicle of his journey to the mysterious Russian impact site, Tunguska, appeared on the cover of the first issue of *Meteorite*. His articles appeared in print regularly after that—each more exciting than the last—and I soaked up every one. Like me, Roy was drawn to the adventurous side of meteorites, and he ranged across the wilds of the former Soviet Union looking for them.

An astronomer, planetarium director, prolific science author, and specialist in Russian impact sites, Roy was often described in print as "The Indiana Jones of Astronomy." He spent three years devising a bold plan to reach Popigai, a vast meteorite crater at the northern edge of Siberia, 100 kilometers in diameter, and so remote the only way to get there was by ex-army helicopter. Since the helicopter would have to make four round-trips to carry all the necessary gear—at $800 per hour—Roy hoped a couple of adventurers might be willing to chip in for a seat on that chopper. He asked if Joel knew anyone who might be interested, and to my great good fortune, Joel said: "I know just the person."

I could pay off all my bills, or blow everything on a grand Russian adventure beside my favorite author. There really was no decision to be made. I thanked Macy's for making it all possible and asked Joel to tell Roy I was in.

Since I had made a rash decision to depart for one of most hard-to-get-to places on the globe, with a team of strangers, it seemed only fair to authorize another trip to my favorite camping store and treat myself to absolutely anything I wanted.

Campmor is staffed entirely by hardcore campers. The employees have a serene yet focused look that can only be acquired by spending solid months each year contemplating the redwood forests, or perhaps meditating, alone, deep in South American jungles. The men all have beards and wear expensive hi-tech sandals made out of some kind of space-age plastic. The women are extremely fit and sinewy and look as if they run a marathon each morning on the way to work. I imagine them to all be vegans and to subsist largely on trail mix and eucalyptus leaves. The Campmor staff know everything there is to know about camping, and camping gear, and I have always been somewhat in awe of them. During previous visits, when I asked a question about a piece of equipment, and intimated that I might not want to spend too much money on it, a staff member would wave, slightly disdainfully, at a cheap pair of hiking boots as if to say: "Well, a part-timer such as yourself would only require *this* type of footwear." Not in a rude or mocking manner, it was just clear that I was not anywhere near their league.

On my visit that June, I respectfully approached one of the equipment gurus and asked his opinion about purchasing a new extreme cold weather sleeping bag. He rubbed his auburn beard and asked where I would be using it.

"Well, I'm headed for Siberia."

"Siberia? Dude, that's intense! Jobey, could you come over here, please. This customer is going for it all the way, man—Siberia." He winked at me privately, and wisely, as Jobey floated over in his plastic sandals.

"Jobey is our top man when it comes to Polar-type gear. He'll take care of you from here, bro."

We laid all kinds of fancy sleeping bags on the floor, tried them out, tested the zippers, crunched them up into tiny waterproof carryalls—"See, sir, this unit can compact to approximately 1/40th of its original volume"—and the other staff members stood around grinning and nodding their heads in silent, considered approval. It actually was pretty intense. Once I made my selection they all wished me well, said they sure hoped they too could make it to Siberia one day, and made me promise to come back and let them know how I, and the sleeping bag, made out. I finally felt like a real adventurer.

I have always been a great fan of 1970s spy movies, the super-complicated Cold War-era dramas with their sleeper agents, double agents, and double-double crosses. In order to visit Russia, and in particular the Tamyr Peninsula which was our ultimate destination, I needed to be "invited," and that sounded very much like a plot twist from one of those spy movies.

The invitations were one of the reasons that Roy and his Krasnojarsk-based translator and "Chief of Staff," as he liked to call Katya, spent three years organizing the Popigai expedition. They had to come from a person in some senior position of authority—a scribbled note from one of our meteorite-hunting pals just would not do. Although relations between Russia and the United States were reasonably good in the late 1990s, we would still be a band of men and women traveling by helicopter, armed and with plenty of heavy equipment, in an area that was so far off the grid that it made the Moscow officials a little nervous.

This issue was further complicated by the diamonds.

Russian geologists discovered industrial-grade diamonds in the bleak tundra wilderness of Tamyr—truckloads of them. They were no good for jewelry but were of considerable use to the war effort during the 1940s. Although more than a half century had elapsed since then, and the mining operations were long gone, Popigai was still considered a top-secret resource and some Moscow officials were uneasy at the idea of American geologists and impact specialists skulking around their disused 100-kilometer wide diamond mine. As such, the invitations were required, and they all had to be approved by the KGB. When my approved application did arrive in the mail, with that blue KGB rubber stamp on it, I wanted to frame it and put it on my wall; alas, the original had to be surrendered when I deplaned in Moscow.

We were all responsible for our own flights to Russia and were to rendezvous at Moscow's Sheremetyevo airport on the morning of Friday, July 2, 1999. After weeks of planning and preparation, the excitement of the coming venture was gloomily replaced by trepidation. I felt almost certain I would not return from Siberia. Something was going to go wrong out there on the tundra, and I would never again see my little 1890s Greek Revival apartment in downtown Jersey City. I felt not so much fear, as foreboding. I scrambled to get a will drawn up and called my close friend Anne Husick for advice.

"Geoff, you're just feeling uneasy because you're going somewhere strange, with a group of people you don't know. It'll be fine. But listen to me, I have two pieces of advice for you. One: you're *going to Russia*. Things are going to be very different. Don't get aggravated or impatient, just enjoy it for what it is. You're always going to look back on this as one of the great adventures of your life. And two—take a chill pill."

I got a ride to the Port Authority bus terminal, and took the express bus to John F. Kennedy International Airport. I boarded an Aeroflot Airbus 300. The plane was only about half full and I found a row with two empty seats. The stewardesses were serious and businesslike in their blue uniforms.

The intercom crackled into life, and a short message was delivered in Russian. I recognized a number of words.

This is it. I'm really going to Russia. There's no backing out now.

"Hello, thiz iz Keptin," the intercom crackled again. "Velcom in Aeroflot flights to Saint Peeterzboorg and to Moskva. In event of emergency oxygen mesk drop from ceiling of errcreft. If you are treveling with small cheeldren, please put on your mesk foorst, then put on your cheeldren."

I laughed to myself, but the pilot's English was much better than my Russian.

The first glimpse of my ancestral homeland came in the form of tankers, hazy in the distance, floating serenely in the Finnish Bay, off St. Petersburg. After a short stop there, our plane continued on to Moscow.

The ramshackle outfit that operated a pair of Mi-8 army surplus helicopters out of the crumbling Arctic Circle outpost known as Khatanga wanted to be paid in cash. American dollars cash, and four round-trips into one of the world's largest impact structures at $800/hour translates into a lot of bank notes. We were each instructed to bring our share, along with additional money for food, transport, extra equipment,

[facing page] Footprints of tiny birds, inside the Popigai meteorite crater.

[above] Exploring caves along the Yenisei River in Siberia, by hydrofoil.

expedition staff, and souvenirs. By telephone from his home in Maine, Roy told me to carry at least $3,000 in cash, so I brought $4,000. He was very emphatic about one thing: "Whatever you do, when you arrive in Moscow, tell them truthfully how much money you're carrying."

"Really? Is that safe?"

"Geoffrey, they don't care how much money you bring *into* the country, they just want to make sure you don't leave holding more than you arrived with."

In Russia, customs and immigration are handled largely by the military. A young soldier, tall and stern in his perfect uniform, with a large pistol at his waist housed in an antique leather holster, handed me a lengthy form to fill out. Everything was in Russian. I asked if anyone spoke English and he shook his head. Evidently, he exaggerated a little, but only a little. After some back-and-forth and some sign language, he pointed to a line and said "Nem." Another was for "Edress in Russia," and another for "How much dollars you kerry." I wrote $4,000 and when the soldier looked at my completed form, he was visibly startled. He looked me up and down. I had an awful feeling he was going to tell me to hand over the money, or at least some of it, but in the end he nodded his head angrily and I went on through.

Much later on I learned that the average salary for a respected university professor was about $35 a month.

My journal entry for July 1 reads:

My gear: blue jeans, hiking boots, ranger vest. Small camo shoulder bag with books, passport and important papers; blue backpack with food and cameras; large duffel bag with everything else.

Everything else included a sleeping bag, tent, rock hammer and chisel, emergency first aid kit, a tiny inflatable sleeping pad, two sunshowers, notebook, specimen bags, spare batteries and film, my favorite camping knife which I bought in Flagstaff, Arizona, a couple of flashlights, and enough clothes and energy bars to last a rockhound for two weeks on the tundra.

I was the first of our party to arrive in Moscow. I do not sleep well on airplanes, had therefore been up all night and had forty $100 bills rolled up in the breast pocket of my ranger vest. I told my barber to cut my hair "real short and spiky" before I left, figuring it would be easier to deal with. I did not look like a local, but with all my army surplus gear, I did not look much like a tourist either.

There were no chairs or benches in the terminal so I put my kit bag on the floor, next to a wall, and sat down on it. I tried to look nonchalant and completely at ease but did not pull that off too well, as taxi drivers constantly implored me to ride with them for "very chip price." One of them turned out to be surprisingly helpful and said: "If you vait for Delta flight from US of A, iz on other size of beelding." I was waiting for the Delta flight, so I said: "Spasiba bolshoi" (A big thank you), which suddenly surfaced in my memory from those dull language classes in English school, and started dragging my gear across the terminal.

Almost immediately, an elegant woman in her early thirties approached me. Dressed in red and black with smart leather boots and lush auburn hair tied behind her head, she put out her hand, and said: "You just have to be Geoffrey Notkin." Recognized by an imposing redhead at the Moscow airport, I felt immediately at home in my own personal spy drama, and happily shook hands with Ekaterina "Katya" Rossovskaya.

Dr. Keenan Lee, arrived half an hour later, all the way from Colorado. I took an immediate liking to him. A bearded, thoughtful, soft-spoken career geologist who perpetually sported an Australian style bush hat, he had been to Siberia before and was eager to return.

The 1999 Popigai Expedition would consist of eighteen people: nine Russians and nine Americans. In addition to Roy, Keenan, and myself the American contingent would include Jonathan Gallant, Roy's son who had spent several years working in Russia; Dr. Jared Morrow, a vigorous young paleontologist; and Professor John Warme, an impact researcher, both from the Colorado School of Mines. Rusty Johnson, jovial, broad-shouldered, and part Cherokee, proudly announced that as Roy's stockbroker he and his teenage son, Travis, had come along on the expedition "to protect our investment." Dr. Kenton Stewart, a limnologist from Buffalo, New York, eager to investigate the uncontaminated freshwater life in frigid Siberian rivers, rounded out the Western half of the team. We would meet our remaining Russian comrades later, in Krasnojarsk.

Katya helped us cram our bags and ourselves into tiny Moscow taxis, smaller than a Volkswagen Bug. She gave explicit instructions to the driver in such a commanding and authoritative manner that I expected him to salute when she was done. She handed me a piece of paper with an address and phone number written in delicate cursive script. "This is just in case." And then she whispered in my ear: "Pay the driver exactly $50, U.S. No more. Valentin will meet you at the apartment."

The first thing I noticed about the airport highway was how old most of the vehicles were. Almost everything looked as if it had been on the road since the 1950s or '60s and there were also plenty of retrofitted World War II-era trucks hard at work.

As we approached Moscow proper, a striking modern sculpture came into view. Painted crimson, the building-sized monument stretched away on both sides of the road and looked like giant anti-tank obstacles. I asked our driver what they were.

"Iz var memorial. This iz area in which ve turn German army bek from Moskva. They came that close."

A memory of the war lingers—and memories of Stalin, and the *gulags*. The Russian people have suffered pretty much continuously for a hundred years and yet there is a kindness about them, and a quiet resignation as if to say: "Well, that's just the way it is, and we keep on doing the best we can."

Hundreds of beautiful silver birch trees lined the highway on both sides. We passed a shiny, modern gas station. I was surprised. It seemed like something you might see in Monterrey or San Diego. Everywhere I looked, there was work going on. Things being built; trucks carrying wood, metal, and equipment. Somehow I expected Russia to be all in ruins and in the grip of despair, but commerce and construction went on briskly at every turn: street markets, colorful billboards, people buying, selling and trading, and even a few new, expensive cars. I saw a sprawling, resolute country, desperately trying to survive the legacy of communism.

The taxi driver stopped and pulled in behind a drab high-rise apartment complex. Perhaps twenty stories tall, it was modernist architecture at its worst, the kind of color-less inner-city housing one might expect to see boarded up in the New York Bronx. But I soon learned that this was one of Moscow's most desirable neighborhoods, consisting of—by Russian standards anyway—luxurious apartments reserved for accomplished intellectuals, university professors and scientists.

Outside in the parking area sat a parade of odd structures, constructed from sheets of corrugated iron. They were in the shape of a bucket or helmet; larger than a dog's kennel, but smaller than a tool shed. Each had a simple handle bolted on one end. I puzzled over them for a while and eventually realized that they were makeshift shelters—lightweight, movable garages—designed to be lifted up by hand when the contents needed for transport. Each miniature tin hut had, nestled within it, a miniature Russian car. They were sad little structures, but no doubt vital in allowing a treasured 1960's Lada to survive one more brutal winter.

Valentin came out to meet us. He was a stocky, kindly man with thin, dark hair, blue eyes and a melancholy smile. He insisted on carrying our bags and ushered us into the rickety elevator. Valentin Tsvetkov is an eminent Russian astronomer, and an inter-nationally-recognized expert on iron meteorites. He helped map the 100-plus craters of the Sikhote-Alin strewnfield in eastern Siberia, and is a friend of Roy's. As we had a twelve-hour layover before our next flight to Krasnojarsk, the capital of Siberia, Valentin and his family kindly offered to host us for the day.

The Tsvetkovs considered themselves a lucky family and were grateful for their warm and cozy apartment, which provided a sharp contrast to the building that housed it. The largest room doubled as dining room and Valentin's study and library. A grand bookcase, neatly filled with textbooks and scientific papers, many of them about meteorites, took up one whole wall. On a large wooden table, covered with a white tablecloth, Valentin proudly displayed part of his meteorite collection. He showed us a fabulous array of Sikhote-Alin iron meteorites from the witnessed Siberian fall of 1947. They had been melted into amazing shapes, and showed the most detailed surface features: small pits, flow lines, ridges and channels—all caused by flight through Earth's atmosphere. Valentin found every one of those marvelous pieces himself, while mapping the strewnfield.

I took a shower and changed into my favorite pair of desert-yellow shorts. I had been awake for over twenty-four hours and Valentin's wife gently persuaded me to lie down for a while. As I dozed, the rest of our contingent arrived, in ones and twos, in taxis. Laughter from the next room woke me. I splashed some water on my face and walked into the Tsvetkovs' living room, now full of unfamiliar faces. All of the Americans were there, except for Roy; his flight had been slightly delayed in Germany.

Meeting a hero for the first time is a confusing experience. We feel as if we already know the person because of a strong familiarity with his or her work; but, in truth, we do not know him at all. We have no true experience of his physical presence or personality and no idea where he fits in the real world. There is always the possibility of disappointment in the actual person.

When Roy Gallant did walk into Valentin's apartment, he was, at once, entirely as I had imagined him to be. He appeared as a professional adventurer should—with great style. Dressed for the desert, he wore a sand-colored long sleeved shirt with narrow button-down collars, and a field vest loaded with zippered pockets. A wide-brimmed expedition hat, military style knee-length shorts, and lace-up hiking boots completed the picture. He strode into that room and placed a pair of matching leather bags on the floor. They were, of course, rugged, expensive-looking bags with heavy buckles: the kind of gear I imagined Lawrence of Arabia would have traveled with.

In his early seventies, Roy was still a powerful man. Sturdy and regal, with a wide smile and a twinkle in his eye, he made his way around the crowded apartment, shaking hands and introducing himself. He was charming, gracious, engaging, and perfectly spoken, his voice carrying the hint of a British accent. He reminded me of Richard Burton, not only in physical appearance but also by his aura of complete confidence and determination. Here was a man who had never met the river he could not cross.

Roy and Katya were close friends. A veteran of several previous Gallant expeditions, Katya's respect for, and loyalty to, Roy could be seen from across the room. She stood by his side as he spoke with each team member in turn. I thought I was the only one of the crew who did not know Roy personally, but several of us were meeting him for the first time.

Finally, Roy walked across the room, took my hand, and with a Theodore Roosevelt smile said: "Geoffrey Notkin. Welcome to Russia!"

"It's a privilege to be here, Roy, meeting one of my favorite writers. Thank you so much for inviting me."

"Well, thank you for being here, my dear boy," he beamed.

We chatted for some minutes, and then he excused himself. One of the other team members—also a newbie—sidled up to me and asked: "So, Geoff, how many expeditions have you and Roy been on together so far?"

"Oh, this is my first one."

"Really?" He seemed amazed. "You're both dressed exactly alike, and so I just assumed you were old friends."

I looked down at my boots, and British Army desert shorts, and the rest of my gear, and realized that Roy and I could almost have been twins.

THIRTEEN

CRATER AT THE EDGE OF THE WORLD

It's quiet now and I have a chance to think
The sun sets in the biggest sky I have ever seen
I'm far away and I don't know how I'll make it
'Til it's time to go . . .

I'm not sure I understand the meaning of this yet
Time will pass but I know that
I never will forget
All these strange days

From "Strange Days"
By Anne Husick

FOLLOWING A DELIGHTFUL VISIT with the Tsvetkov family, the American contingent, together with Katya, traveled to Domodedovo Airport where we boarded the largest civil aircraft I have ever seen, en route to Krasnojarsk, the capitol of Siberia.

Domestic airline travel in Russia is unlike anything else in the modern world. We walked out onto the tarmac at Domodedovo, under expansive wings with jet engines running, in the dead of night, carrying all of our own luggage and climbed through a door to the airplane's lower deck. We stowed our bags in racks and angled up a cramped stairwell to the passenger deck. There were no seat assignments and a churlish free-for-all ensued as passengers pushed and elbowed their way to the front of the plane. I assumed every seat would end up being taken—hence the melee—but much later I realized the flight was only half full, so I moved to the rear of the jet and enjoyed a row of four seats to myself. I am not clear why the passengers felt it was so important to sit close to the cockpit.

As is typical almost everywhere, smoking was not allowed onboard especially not in the toilets, but throughout the flight young Russian men constantly walked to the back of the plane, went into the lavatories, lit cigarettes, and stood there leaning punkishly against the rear cubicle walls, with the bathroom doors open, as if that somehow made it okay.

Krasnojarsk is an enticing river city, founded in 1628 by a regiment of 150 Cossacks. We were treated to a private tour of the geological institute, enjoyed a cruise up the Yenisei River on a marvelous white hydrofoil that looked like something out of *Thunderbirds* and passed the site where, in 1772, the German zoologist and botanist Simon Peter Pallas identified a strange iron meteorite full of green crystals. Today, all pallasites carry his name. After our boat trip, things started to go wrong.

Our permits were already approved, the helicopter company had been paid a deposit, and various officials were given a little something extra, to help things move along. Evidently, we had neglected to pay a suitable "consultation" fee to a local political boss with the unfortunate name of Fokkin. He wanted a substantial payoff and threatened to interfere with our existing travel arrangements. Katya called the governor, and other calls were placed to various big wheels in Moscow, and at the American embassy. It looked as if we may have come all that way for nothing. Our group passed a few tense days in Krasnojarsk waiting for news and then, mysteriously, Fokkin disappeared. We were warned that he may have sabotaged our deal with the helicopter outfit in the northern outpost of Khatanga, where we were headed, but we decided to continue with the existing plan anyway.

From Krasnojarsk, we took an aging four-engine propellor plane to the military air base in Norilsk in northern Siberia, for refuelling. Similar in appearance to an American DC-6, our aircraft surprisingly lacked any overhead storage bins. The pilot and co-pilot stepped in first, bolted the cockpit door, and then the solitary flight attendant stacked all of our carryon bags against that door. In the event of an emergency, I thought, our flight crew would have little chance of escaping.

As we touched down, I noticed an army vehicle speeding along the runway beside us. Once we came to a stop, two tall and very imposing Russian officers with bright red bands around their caps, and antique bolt-action rifles boarded our plane and confiscated all of our passports. A couple of our team members were rattled by this, but I found it very exciting and slipped back into my imaginary spy movie. We were herded out of the plane, with our luggage, and left to stand on the windy runway, under guard. One of our team produced a camera and starting taking photos of military jets, slumbering in the distance.

[previous page] Our helicopter prepares to depart from the Khatanga outpost, for Popigai.
[above] A massive slab of impact breccia inside the Popigai Crater.

112

"Are you mad?" I asked. "You can't take photos at a Russian air base."

"Just relax. The Cold War is over. They don't care about things like that anymore." He continued snapping away for another thirty seconds until one of the Russian officers came over and barked at him, while making an "I'll cut your throat" gesture.

After some time, our passports were returned and we were herded aboard the small plane, once again. I became concerned when the engines failed to start. Watching from my small and scratched window, I observed an odd vehicle approach, towing a decrepit device that looked much like an oversized transformer. Cables and clips appeared and were attached to the starboard engines. Right there, with everybody watching, they jump-started our plane on the runway.

Khatanga is as devastated and forlorn an outpost of doom as I ever hope to encounter. It once served as the supply and transport hub for industrial diamond mining at the Popigai Crater, but such industry ceased long ago and Khatanga had nearly become a ghost town. Winter lows register so frighteningly far down on the thermometer, it is necessary to keep all heating and electrical conduits above ground, and insulated with wood, blankets and old rags, as best they can manage. As such, the ugly pipes and flues that are typically hidden within buildings elsewhere in the world, snaked and staggered from one collapsing structure to another, in a spiderweb of despair.

In Khatanga we met our Russian science colleagues and support staff—nine in all—making our party sixteen men and two women; eighteen specks of warmth almost invisible in the endless tundra. Notable among the team was Valery Kirichenko, senior geologist of the Krasnojarsk region and a veteran of mining operations inside the crater. As a young man, Valery worked with miners in their relentless search for diamonds, and he had yearned for decades to return.

That evening—before retiring to a pre-fabricated one-story building where I spent a fitful night on an army cot, fully dressed inside my sleeping bag—I took an evening walk with the charismatic John Warme. Well, I say it was evening, but in Siberia in July the sun never sets, so who could really tell? We wandered along a cracked and crumbling road, past piles of forgotten wreckage, with grey skies covering the world of the north.

"Do you happen to know Matt Morgan?" he asked me, as I stared in puzzlement at the cab of a World War II cargo truck, just the cab, sitting on top of a pile of rusty pipes.

"I certainly do!"

Matt is one of my best friends, and a highly respected meteorite specialist.

"Oh, I thought you might. He's one of my students. He's working on his master's in geology."

Even in the most isolated corner of Siberia, the meteorite world remains a small one.

Prior to our much anticipated-departure the next day, our charming host in Khatanga, Michael Martyshkin, head of the Polar Exploration Group, threw us a lavish send off at the Carat Restaurant, a tidy and welcoming wood-walled establishment that boasted, in rather large colorful letters: "The World's Most Northerly Bar."

We filed in, all eighteen of us, at noon sharp. Each of our places presented a large, clean white plate, with a decent-sized glass of straight vodka sitting perfectly in the

[above] Our helicopter lifting off, after depositing us on the pebble island inside the Popigai Crater.
[facing page] Exploring the Mottled Cliffs, an impactite exposure that once formed the floor of the crater.

middle. Once everyone was seated Mr. Martyshkin, impeccably dressed in a suit and tie that added considerable class to the otherwise element-savaged town, proposed a toast to our successful expedition. Dr. Kenton Stewart, the resident limnologist was sitting next to me. A gentle and affable man who did not care for alcohol, he made an uncomfortable grimace and said, quietly enough so only I heard: "I'm not drinking this."

"Ken, it's an insult in Russia to refuse a drink with our host. Just knock it back, it'll be fine."

He declined emphatically to partake, so I downed mine, then switched glasses and quickly downed his as well. When I embarked upon this face-saving gesture, I did not realize there were to be multiple toasts. By the time we started loading the helicopter, I was as high as a satellite.

I vividly remember lying on my back on the damp runway, under the helicopter's nose and taking photographs of the rotors with my Nikon.

The Mi-8 is a medium-range helicopter, developed in the early 1960s, and has seen action all over the world, notably with the Russian military. Up to three tons of cargo can be loaded into the rear, via a large ramp. As I was a little woozy and completely focused, for some reason, on getting the perfect shot before takeoff, I was the last to board. Inside, there were no seats—just a bench along the starboard side—and our substantial pile of supplies were piled aft.

With no room available on the bench, I curled up with the tents and backpacks and prepared for my first flight in a bullish ex-army Russian chopper.

The pilot appeared and stood over me with his arms folded.

"You kennot seet here!"

"But there's no room on the bench, what else can I do?"

"No, you downt enderstand. Begs on cargo ramp. Sometimes, in flight, ramp open agzeedentalee and begs go fffzeeeeeet!" With his hands he made a motion demonstrating things falling quickly. "End you go fffzeeeeeet with begs. Understand?" I make gentle fun of our friends' accents with all due respect and affection; they made themselves understood well enough, and were only concerned for our safety.

"Yes," I replied. "Well, that seems a perfectly good reason for not sitting here."

I stood for most of the flight and even talked my way into the cockpit for a while which, with its big bulbous transparent nose made me feel as if I were flying over the tundra in a World War II bomber such as a B-17 or Lancaster—a pleasant daydream no doubt amplified by the six vodkas I downed, back at the Carat, in a selfless gesture of international goodwill. At some point, the co-pilot left the cockpit, made a circuit around the Mi-8, and casually opened up all the portholes—in a helicopter flying at 10,000 feet—as if it were the most normal of practices!

The Popigai Crater is so vast you cannot even tell you are inside. Roughly half the size of New Jersey, it is bisected by the Rossokha River, and if you stand anywhere remotely close to the center, the eroded crater walls are invisible due to the curvature of the earth. A small island, made of rounded stones, in the middle of the Rossokha, would be our home for several days.

The landing was just spectacular. Our pilot hovered over Pebble Island for some long seconds, then cut the power. We slammed into the rocky ground, hard. The back ramp went down so our gear could be unloaded and we climbed into the brisk Siberian sunshine. I was standing inside one of the world's largest meteorite craters, and I had never felt so far from civilization.

And then the mosquitos came.

Everyone has heard accounts of trips where people say: "There were a lot of bugs." They have no idea. Mosquitos descended upon us, instantaneously, in the hundreds and thousands. And they were big Siberian mosquitos, hungry for human blood— surely a treat they had, thus far, not encountered.

I doused myself with insect repellant, then rushed to pull on gloves, a wool skull cap, and a mosquito helmet. After that, the experience was only partially horrific. The angry little beasts clung to my helmet, day and night, trying to snare me with their probosci. To the great amusement of my teammates I had, very cleverly, brought along a fly swatter, and spent much of my spare time flattening bloodsucking mosquitos with it. The bugs were so aggressive they would bite clean through blue jeans, meaning we spent much of our time in Popigai wearing multiple layers.

The purpose of our visit, other than to bask in the magnificence of the nation-sized crater was to collect and study impactites. Meteorite impacts of sufficient size smash, pummel, and melt earthly rocks into new forms described as impact breccias. Although the intervening millions of years had long since caused the original meteorite to weather away, evidence of its handiwork lay everywhere. To me, impactites, with their multi-colored angular shards jammed together into a new matrix, are almost as fascinating as meteorites. They are silent witnesses to an ancient planet-altering event of literally cosmic proportions.

[previous page] A view across the river delta inside the Popigai Crater. [above] A polished slice of impact breccia from the Popigai Crater. Note the angular shards of varying rock types, shattered, and then cemented back together following the cataclysmic impact.

The finest impactite exposure in all of the dizzying expanse of the Popigai structure—the Mottled Cliffs—lived, conveniently, directly across from our quiet island. Along with all the other equipment loaded into the helicopter came two emergency life rafts and we used them, daily, to traverse the chilly waters of the Rossokha, so we might scramble enthusiastically over the piles of breccia that had once been the crater floor. The mind-bending fury of impact could easily be grasped by gazing upon the mishmash of rocks that were thrown high into the air before falling back upon themselves to form a mountain of checkered fragments. Some were the size of office buildings.

Our Russian comrades were extremely industrious and resourceful. Using a chainsaw they cut down pine trees and built a mess tent, tables, benches and, eventually, a formidable log raft that would carry our heavy equipment far down the Rossokha to the second base camp.

When, after four days, we bid farewell to the sweet little island, our expected journey time to the next site was four or five hours, but the water level that summer was unexpectedly low and we ran aground many times. The Americans, together with Valery and Katya went ahead in the life rafts. The log raft had been engineered to carry an overly large iron cooking pot, the 70-pound lead battery for our emergency radio, the chainsaw, and various other items that would have likely plummeted straight through the bottoms of our lightweight dinghies.

By mid-afternoon we were so far ahead of the log raft, we beached our craft on a bleak delta of stones, polished smooth by the river. We waited hours for the cargo raft to catch up. Katya went for a stroll and returned with a remarkable find: a fossilized mammoth tooth the size of a child's hand. Energized by this amazing discovery I set off, alone, in search of my own.

I strode across a field of perfect stones that seemed to stretch all the way to the sky. I felt certain I walked in an untouched zone that no human had ever traversed. Here and there rested pockets of fine white sand, tattooed by the delicate footprints of dainty birds. With no trees visible anywhere for miles, the birds made their nests among the rocks of the river delta. As I followed their footprints, taking photos, I was suddenly attacked by two small white birds which I took to be sandpipers. They did not actually strike me, but swooped aggressively at my head, repeatedly, and so close that I could see into their tiny pink throats as they snapped at me. I had, evidently, strayed too close to the one couple's ground nest and they were determined to scare me away. I found it a dazzling display of courage equivalent, say, to me attacking the Empire State Building. Anxious to both avoid stepping on any fragile eggs and getting pecked in the eye, I hurried back to the boats empty handed.

The Russians found the whole escapade hilarious: "Luke at D'Geoff! He is skeered by leetle Siberia boords!"

"Those birds are terrors! They dive-bombed me."

Valery was a bear of a man, and kind, but built like a concrete bunker. He was not intimidated by a few little water birds, and decided to go inspect their nests.

"I wouldn't recommend it," I called after him, as he marched deliberately out into the stone sea. "They're tough little guys," I added. "I wouldn't mess with them."

Within a few minutes he came jogging back towards us, with a squadron of sandpipers lunging at his head like miniature white demons. I will never forget the sight of such a big man being chased by such tiny and heroic creatures.

The cargo raft limped in by late afternoon and we set off, once again, down the slow-moving river. Many times, after getting snagged on pebbly shoals, we had to jump out in our thigh-high rubber boots and drag our craft into a marginally deeper channel. As we drifted hazily along I suddenly felt a sharp stinging sensation on my left wrist. I looked down to see eight or ten mosquitos feasting on a miniscule window of skin that appeared, momentarily, between the cuff of my jacket and my gloves. I brushed them off, tucked my shirt cuffs far down inside the gloves, and tried to ensure that no skin remained exposed, even for a moment.

Our second and final base camp took the welcome form of a splendid sand dune hulking out of the river. It even sported wispy dune grass, and I could almost have been back at the Cape Cod of my youth. We spent the next day examining other outcrops of breccia—wherever we might go, we were still within the massive expanse of the crater, and interesting features existed almost anywhere we cared to look.

On the morning of our sixth day inside the crater we broke camp, packed everything into our boats and ferried them across the river to a flat stony plain. The Mi-8 would not be able to land on Dune Island. We stacked bags and supplies, and the iron pot, and everything else into neat piles and awaited the arrival of the helicopter.

We waited for some time.

I took the opportunity to inspect a double-barreled 12-gauge shotgun that came along with us. "For protect against beers," one of the Russian crew said, laughing.

"Are those Siberian bears?"

"Yes!" He looked delighted and boomed with laughter. "Beeg Russian beers. They will like to eat you!"

I opened the old break-action weapon, which looked as if it had been around since the Crimean War, and peered inside. The shotgun was unloaded—so not much use in a sneak attack by "beers"—and the inside of the twin barrels were so very caked with rust and unidentifiable debris as to be utterly useless anyway. Fortunately, the largest wildlife we encountered on the entire expedition were some moderately fearsome-looking eels who skulked ominously in the dark river.

We waited some more for the helicopter and I started to remember the political boss, Fokkin, and his supposed threat to monkeywrench our travel plans. Stranding us in a forgotten meteorite crater at the edge of the world would be a great way to get rid of some troublesome Americans.

After several hours, Valery ordered his men to set up the emergency radio, and it was worth going all the way to Russia just to see that. Out came the chainsaw and down came three pine trees. They were fashioned into a skyscraping tripod and a wire was run up to the very top. The radio, bulky and green, and almost certainly of World War II vintage was connected to its 70-pound battery, and various other procedures and incantations ensued. I sat on a big rock and just hoped the venerable old box of wires and valves could murmur an audible signal as far as Khatanga.

After plenty of crackling and numerous attempts, a thin voice that sounded like a child speaking through a plastic cup, replied to us. Extreme bad weather at Khatanga had grounded all flights and we would have to set up camp again, and spend one more night at Popigai.

I congratulated Valery on his skilled assembly of the radio mast and his success in getting a message through to the far-off heliport.

"Yes, eets good. I just wish I think to call Khatanga before we take down all tents in kemp."

The next morning our brightly-painted helicopter showed up, and I unexpectedly encountered the strangest aural phenomenon. The sky was empty and silent and then I heard, quite clearly, the sound of distant engines. The noise faded and then reappeared several minutes later, somewhat louder. This happened over and over again, for perhaps ten minutes, and I thought I must be hallucinating, until the helicopter loudly burst into view only a few hundred meters away from us. My brother, Andrew, is a skilled airline pilot and explained I had not gone mad, but rather witnessed a most unusual event, peculiar to the Arctic. He was fascinated that I encountered the effect first hand and directed me to an article in the FAA *Aviation Weather* handbook which explained that engine sounds, and even people's voices can be carried over seemingly impossible distances, as a result of low-level inversion.

After one more night in Khatanga—which did not seem nearly as bad as the first one because they did have, in limited quantities, actual hot water—we started the long trek back. Perhaps due to the fact that their passenger planes sometimes require jump-starting on the runway, Aeroflot is extremely strict about baggage allowances. We were only allowed about 40 pounds per person and I learned during the outbound leg that carryon bags are weighed, as well as checked luggage.

Over dinner, during our last night in Khatanga, I gave my prized Estwing rock hammer—signed by every member of the team—to Valery as a thank you gift, and left other presents for all of the other members of the Russian crew.

Roy roared with laughter: "Nice try, Geoff, but you're still going to be overweight with all that breccia you collected."

He was correct, but I planned on outsmarting the Aeroflot airline officials when we arrived back at Norilsk. I stuffed all the pockets of my parka full of rocks, slung it over my arm in as nonchalant a manner as I could manage and walked—in only a slightly unsteady fashion—up to the counter.

"Poot all bags on scale, pliz," instructed a harsh-looking woman in army uniform, seated behind her faded, wooden check-in desk.

"End also poot coat and small beg, pliz."

The damage, in terms of extra pounds, was significant but not entirely my fault. Roy had a bag full of rocks, and Kenton had been collecting jars of river water for the duration. Three of the Russian team considered the terrifying Popigai eels to be a delicacy, and they caught a boat load of them during the final night by the river. Averaging four feet in length, the eels had now been dead for several days and—wrapped in an oily tarpaulin—were not smelling so good.

The lady officer looked almost as severe as the eels' pointed snouts, and informed Katya that we would have to pay however many tens of thousands of rubles in excess baggage fees. "Or," she lowered her voice to a husky whisper, "Xundred feefty in American dollarz kesh."

The "kesh" was handed over quickly, and discretely, and we were on our way.

Despite the mosquitos and the requisite payoffs to officials in a position of power, I fell in love with Russia. The memory that sticks with me most vividly is of our penultimate night in the crater, after that arduous 14-hour voyage on river rafts. I stood with a group of Russian scientists on an unknown sandy island at 4 a.m., drinking warm vodka out of tin cups; the ice that initially came out with us in a couple of coolers was, by then, long gone.

With the assistance of our long-suffering translator, Katya, we began exchanging jokes and communicating properly, at last, through the universal language of humor. Several of those men were important researchers during the Cold War era, but were, all through their lives, denied the luxury of international travel. They had never met an American before in person, and the discovery that surprised and astonished them the most was that we—we Americans—had a sense of humor!

We laughed long into what should have been the night, clinking metal cups together in the wind, and the wilds, and understanding at long last that Russians and Americans are not so different after all.

[previous page] Rafting on the Rossokha River. We experienced 24-hour daylight, and this photo was taken at about 2 a.m.

[right] Playing rock 'n' roll, in full mosquito gear, on a vintage Russian guitar inside the Popigai Crater.

FOURTEEN

FIELD OF DREAMS:
REDISCOVERING THE BRENHAM PALLASITE

I reset the mileage counter to zero
Outside the movie store
In old downtown J.C.
Rain filled every dirty, angry street
And they were almost as cold
As the heart I left behind

From "Five Highways Home"
By Geoffrey Notkin

FRESHLY PLOWED FIELDS stretch all the way to the horizon. Perfect parallel furrows race across the open ground moving closer, gently forced together by the relentless power of perspective. An owl hoots from tall trees to the south. The Kansas sky is a sharp acrylic blue, like a 1950s Formica kitchen table. A grain elevator, bright white and perched starkly at the edge of sight, is—apart from lonely telegraph poles—the only man-made object anywhere in the sweeping, rural panorama. This is Brenham.

In 2001 I explored the 367 million year-old Alamo impact breccia in Nevada with the U.S. Geological Survey, furthering my interest in impactites. Early in 2003, Steve and I rushed to Chicago, Illinois, along with our friend, John Sinclair—a meteorite dealer and gemologist from North Carolina—to search for fragments of the March 26 fireball and found many pieces of the freshly-fallen Park Forest meteorite. I also returned to Gold Basin with Jim and Twink, and participated in several other expeditions. I became great friends with Geoff Cintron, an aircraft engineer and meteorite dealer from Long Island, and we started working together at local gem and mineral shows. Meteorites were, slowly but undeniably, becoming my occupation as well as my passion.

In the fall of 2003, after twelve years together, Jackie and I went our separate ways. I had grown increasingly unhappy with the noise, crowds, and bustle of the New York area. Each February I visited Tucson for the big gem show, and gradually fell in love with that charming and odd small city in southern Arizona.

For some time I had been feeling guilty because my frequent excursions into the wilderness in search of space treasures were taking me away from my responsibilities with the band. Lach and Billy had no second profession, they were rock 'n' rollers through and through. I knew I was holding them back and so, on New Year's Eve at the Sidewalk Café on the corner of Avenue A and East Sixth Street in New York City, I said goodbye to Lach who had been a trusted friend, bandmate, confident, and inspiration for well over two decades.

"I never doubted for a moment that you would be hugely successful," I told him. "That's why I stayed for so many years. You are one of the best songwriters in the world and it's been an honor and a privilege to be your right-hand man, but the time has come for me to move on." Always supportive and understanding, even at times of personal loss, Lach saw my impending departure as a rite of passage. He predicted, in his oddly prescient and metaphysical manner, that I was starting a new and vital chapter of my life.

I sold my share of the condo that Jackie and I jointly owned in downtown Jersey City, New Jersey, and on January 3, 2004, at the age of 42, I put my cat, my best bass guitar, my computer, a few favorite meteorites and books in my car, and set off for Tucson to start over, yet again.

My friend Anne Husick, who spent years on the road as a touring musician, went along with me just for the adventure of it, and to offer moral support as I tried to put down new roots in the Southwest. We left the ice and snow of the East Coast and, a few days later, crossed the New Mexico/Arizona state line and pulled over at the first highway rest stop. A giant red, gold, and blue Arizona state flag fluttered in the cool sunlight and I paused to take a photograph of it. The desert that enthralled me as a child, and where I found my first meteorite, was now home.

The world of graphic design was very good to me, provided a decent living for many years, and funded many meteorite hunting expeditions, but the times were changing. With a new start and a new home, long dreamed of, comes a new outlook and determination. Meteorites were the beacon that illuminated my life, and shortly after arriving in my new adopted city, I registered Aerolite Meteorites as a business in the State of Arizona. I had been finding, buying, selling, and trading meteorites for a decade, and assisted many other meteorite collectors and dealers with their websites, photography, and promotion. The time for me to give up my other businesses and interests, and devote myself completely to working with rocks from space, had arrived.

A year later, I was sitting at my desk on a Tuesday morning, in October of 2005. At first it seemed much like any other Tuesday morning. I planned out my day's work, answered some emails and checked my messages. There was one from Steve Arnold. I saw Steve a month earlier at the Denver Gem and Mineral Show where he surprised everyone by strolling into the annual meteorite auction with his nine year-old daughter Kelsey in tow. On a whim Steve and Kelsey had jumped in their truck and driven the 850 miles from Arkansas to Denver, arriving just in time for the festivities.

Steve's message said it was "kind of an emergency," so I called immediately. As soon as he knew it was me, he launched into his story.

"After Denver, Kelsey and I drove back through Kansas and we thought we'd stop in Brenham and see the crater. I got to talking to a farmer who owns land near where Stockwell found the big Brenham back in 1947, and he gave me permission to hunt his property. So I went home, and came back and now I'm here in Brenham."

Steve was very calm on the phone, but I knew something had happened. I realized that it might actually be some "kind of an emergency" but probably not the bad kind.

"So . . . did you find anything."

"Yeah."

There was a pause. His voice got quiet, and he started whispering as if he had a great secret to share.

"I found the mother lode."

"What do you mean?"

"I found the main mass of Brenham."

"*The main mass* of Brenham? How is that possible!"

"I found it, seven feet underground. It's fourteen hundred pounds . . . and it's oriented."

There was another pause.

"Can I come up there?"

It is not easy to get a flight from Tucson to Wichita with no notice. The best my travel agent could manage was a hop to Phoenix, followed by a non-stop to Oklahoma City, arriving at 10:30 p.m. By the time I finished chatting up the charming Peruvian girl at the rental counter, received a complimentary upgrade to a luxury car, and found my way to the highway, it was already 11:30 p.m. My destination was Greensburg, a small town in Kiowa County, Kansas, a few miles from the Brenham strewnfield. Speeding north on I-35, the only car on an empty highway, I imagined what that farmer's field might look like, and what might lie beneath it.

I hoped to cover the 250 miles to Greensburg that night but after ninety minutes on the road I realized Kiowa County was still far away, and it had been too long a day. I overnighted in a small town named Blackwell, almost invisible in the flat, dark expanse where Oklahoma and Kansas meet.

The Brenham story goes that during the 1880s a pioneer farmer named Eliza Kimberly collected roughly one ton of rocks from around her family's homestead. Much to the irritation of her husband, she insisted that the dark, heavy stones were meteorites; her husband taunted her about it for years. Eliza was vindicated in 1890 when Professor Cragin, a geologist from Washburn University, verified that they were, in fact, meteorites and he purchased a number of specimens from her. Inspired by the cash they received, the Kimberlys became America's first meteorite-hunting family.

Seminal American meteoriticist H.H. Nininger carried out extensive work at Brenham during the 1930s. He recovered numerous pieces from the same strewnfield, and believed he identified an impact crater. Most parties now agree that the crater is more likely a buffalo wallow.

Brenham is one of the most interesting meteorites in the world. It can be described as transitional, in that some specimens show features of pallasites and are rich in olivine crystals, while others are siderites—nickel-iron masses with no crystals. All Brenham meteorites came from the same original parent body and fell at the same time but, in flight, they seem to have shattered along the points of least resistance, that being the boundaries where olivine-rich pockets adjoined wholly nickel-iron zones. In other words we have pieces that look different, and have a different composition, but all originated from the same mass within the Asteroid Belt.

In the late 1940s, H.O. Stockwell, an amateur geologist from Hutchinson, Kansas, found several massive Brenhams using a homemade metal detector, including a 1,000-pound pallasite. It now resides in the small museum in Greensburg and was, until October of 2005, the largest pallasite ever found in the United States. A few other

127

specimens were pulled out of the ground during the '60s and '70s, but popular belief held that, after nearly twelve decades of hunting, the Brenham strewnfield had no secrets left to reveal.

After receiving permission to hunt from a friendly landowner, Steve designed and built a revolutionary metal detector, and found a substantial iron meteorite on the first day.

Two weeks later he received an exceptionally strong signal. He dug down several feet before giving in and calling for a backhoe. At seven-and-a-half feet he found a pallasite weighing nearly three quarters of a ton. As the backhoe pulled it out and the big Brenham spun on its harness, the oriented face came into view. It had been lying, nose down, just as it had fallen thousands of years earlier.

After overnighting in Blackwell, I hit the road very early the next day, eager to see the big pallasite, but even more eager to get out in the field and see if it had any relatives buried nearby. Somewhere west of Wichita I saw a big billboard that said "Visit Dorothy's House," and then I called Steve on the cell phone. He was already out hunting, and sounding very happy.

"Sorry, I couldn't make it all the way last night, Steve. I should be there in about an hour and a half."

"Okay, pardner. Hey, listen, I got a strong signal this morning."

"Really? What do you think it is?"

"I think it's a meteorite. If you're good, I'll wait 'til you get here and you can dig it up. Oh, hey, when you go through Pratt, can you stop at the store and get me some envelopes? And we need a plastic trowel. And can you get me a burger? I forgot to have breakfast."

Steve's directions to the spot were the sort of directions you get used to following when you have been doing this kind of thing for a while.

"Go through Haviland a few miles, and then the road widens, and you have to turn there. It's just a dirt road. Go about a mile and half on the dirt road and there's another dirt road. Turn right there. Keep going until you see some trees and I'll be there."

After only two wrong turns I found the dirt road, and then the trees, and drove up a long winding path and there was a big yellow tractor under the trees, with Steve leaning against it, smiling, arms folded, as nonchalant as anything.

This was clearly Steve's base camp. Scattered around I saw a three-wheeled ATV, two metal detectors, a pile of recently-excavated rusty scrap iron about as tall as a hay bale, tools, some empty Gatorade bottles, and a weird wheeled contraption that looked like a cross between the Lunar Rover and the Wright Brothers' Flyer.

"Seems like ages since I saw you," he said.

"Yeah, I know, weeks at least. So . . . I guess you're pretty pleased with yourself?"

We ate quickly and then Steve asked if I wanted to go dig up a big meteorite. We clambered onto his ATV. I balanced, somewhat tenuously, with a long shovel in one hand and my Fisher 1266 metal detector in the other. Steve did a wheelie, stalled once, then lurched recklessly out of the trees and onto the vast expanse of furrowed fields.

There is a lot of dirt in Kansas. Rich farming dirt, and not many rocks. When they plow the fields, the furrows get deep, and you would think a powerful ATV could just go right through all of that but it doesn't. It bounced around, and my tailbone banged painfully on the metal rack behind me. I got tangled up in cables from the metal detector, and was sure Steve would flip the bike over, but then mercifully we shuddered to a stop next to a shovel sticking out of the ground.

I clambered awkwardly off the ATV and Steve unhooked a big metal C-clip, then pulled his contraption—which I immediately named the Meteorite Trolley—away from the motorcycle.

"You see those trees over there," he pointed to the southwest. "The so-called Haviland Crater is about a mile that way, behind those trees. That's where Nininger found his big haul. And this field right here," he pointed to a spot much closer, "is where Stockwell found the thousand-pounder. I found my big one over there."

"So we're right in the heart of it," I replied. "Right in the strewnfield."

"Yes we are."

Around Steve's neck there hung a black control box which looked much like a Philips cassette recorder from the early 1970s. It was a pulse induction metal detector—a high-end device designed and manufactured in Germany—expensive, deep seeking, and the first of its kind I had ever seen. He unplugged the headphones from it, wrapped a collection of wires and ropes around his forearm, yanked the trolley behind him, turned up the speaker volume on the box and said: "Watch this."

The trolley was one big portable metal detector. It had an oversize coil attached to it, connected to the control box by a long cable. Steve had designed and built the entire thing using his own imagination, and if you think that doesn't sound too hard, try constructing a versatile lightweight rolling vehicle the size of a large coffee table, tough enough to be towed behind a motorcycle across farm land for ten hours a day, and do it without using any metal. No screws, no wire, no washers, no ball bearings. Even one metallic component would cause continuous activation of the coil, rendering the detector useless.

As Steve pulled the trolley by hand, the control box started to whine. It gave out a long wailing sound, like an air raid siren; a clear strong signal that kept getting louder and louder and more and more high pitched, until I thought it could not possibly go on any longer without destroying the equipment. Steve stopped and let the thing just sit there, howling, above a deep target, invisible to all save itself. Pulse induction detectors. Impressive. Unlike most regular hand-helds they do not have to be moved over a target to generate an audio signal.

He handed me the shovel. "Wanna dig?"

"Yes, I do! I came to Kansas to dig. My father is on vacation at an opera festival in Europe, so I think I should be doing something entirely different. I came to Kansas to dig in the dirt."

Steve laughed. "At least one person in your family has his priorities straight."

The ground was soft and rich, and completely absent of indigenous rock. There are no rocks in Kansas, I thought to myself, only meteorites.

It was easy digging. Farmers turned that soil over twice a year for more than a century. It was good of Steve to have waited until I got there to pull up the target but, after seeing the pile of scrap iron at base camp, I refused to get excited. It was almost certainly another plow blade or wagon wheel. I have dug up so many non-meteoritic targets over the years I have learned, the hard way, to preempt the inevitable disappointment, even with a target that big and that deep.

[top] A place of wonder: the field in Brenham, Kansas that produced hundreds of pounds of meteorites for us.
[above] The 59-pound "Buffalo" Brenham siderite comes out of the ground, after a prolonged dig.

130

[top] Steve Arnold calibrates his high-tech metal detector while searching at Brenham.
[above] Brenham in late fall. Cold weather does not stop play.

131

By the time I was down several feet, I started trying to remember if I actually ever had excavated a bogus target from such a depth. Surely my hand-held detector could not read anything that deep. Which reminded me—dammit!—I forgot to run my Fisher over the spot before I started digging. That was exactly the kind of thing I wanted to know. Could my Fisher "see" a big target so far below ground?

Clink.

I was so lost in thought, so busy telling myself that the target was not going to be a meteorite that it took a metal-against-metal sound to bring me back down solidly to a muddy field in Kansas.

Steve stood there with his arms folded, smiling that big meteorite smile.

"Didja hear that? Now we wanna be kinda careful not to scratch it, if it's a meteorite." But he knew how excited I was now, so he added, "But, well, you know."

I quickly widened the hole and felt around at the bottom with my gloved hands.

"There's something here," I said. "Can you hand me that trowel."

I scooped out a couple of handfuls of soil, and suddenly there was a piece of metal blinking back at me in the sun, a rounded knob about the size of a child's thumb. It had a golden ochre patina to it—not rust, but a marvelous rich caramel coloring that could only be one thing.

Steve measured the depth and logged the GPS location. We both worked on enlarging the hole, so we could see the entire mass. We stopped several times to photograph it in situ.

"Okay, you wanna try and lift it out?"

I braced myself and lifted, and almost nothing happened.

"Wow, this a lot heavier than I thought it would be." I tried again and, with the faintest sigh, the pallasite slipped out of the clay cradle where it had rested for centuries.

"It must weigh 75 pounds!"

With some effort I lifted it up and dumped it next to the hole.

There it was, a real meteorite from outer space, a pallasite, a classic American find from a venerable strewnfield hunted by Nininger himself. It was so big we could barely lift it. I sat in the dirt staring at all those green and brown crystals sparkling in the Kansas sun.

Steve went back to check the pile of dirt with one of our smaller detectors, and he instantly got multiple targets.

"Hey, look at this." He held up a small 50-gram Brenham nugget—almost an exact miniature reproduction of the monster we just pulled out of the mud.

After all those years, Steve's relentless enthusiasm for meteorites had not mellowed in the slightest. He lay right down in that pile of dirt and sifted through it with child-like delight, producing another twenty or so fragments. By chance, I found the best of the lot: a 47-gram twisted metallic sculpture of exquisite beauty, which we later named "The Camel" after its animal-like character.

The next day, we went to see the new main mass of Brenham.

We drove miles down empty dirt roads, and met the landowner, Allen Binford, in front of a capacious steel building. Trucks and farm equipment of all sorts lay parked around it. Allen was a likeable man: broad shouldered, rugged, and with no time for nonsense. He received a generous share of proceeds from all the meteorites found on his land. Allen pounded me on the shoulder and told me to "be sure and find another one of those big ones."

Even sitting on a broken forklift palette on the floor of a Kansas barn, the big meteorite remained dignified. Three feet across, rounded on top like the nose of the space shuttle, its surface mottled caramel and chocolate; it was stunning. A three-quarter-ton nose cone, packed with semi-precious gemstones—the largest oriented pallasite in the history of the world, and Steve found it, all by himself, out in a muddy field in Kansas.

Anyone other than Steve would have been satisfied with that, but we were out in the field again first thing the next day. There had to be more meteorites out there waiting.

We ran into trouble immediately. The ATV had a flat and we had to make a 52-mile round trip to the town of Pratt to get it fixed. It was extremely cold, below freezing, so we bought extra cold weather gear. We got the ATV going, and then a key strut on the Meteorite Trolley snapped. We worked late into the night, in front of the headlights of my rental car, to repair it. We lost a full day's hunting.

The morning of Monday, October 24, started out chilly. We stopped briefly in Greensburg to get some spare parts for the trolley. News travels fast in small town America, and someone called out to Steve: "Hey! I heard a rumor you found a big one!"

"A rumor . . . in *this* town?" Steve replied dryly, and left it at that.

We fell easily into an efficient system. I stood off to one side holding my Fisher detector, a shovel, a magnet and other assorted digging equipment as Steve tore up and down on the motorcycle, with the trolley bouncing behind, gridding the field.

I stood there for a long time, and it was cold.

When the ATV stopped, it meant Steve had a good signal. He marked the approximate spot and moved on. I would hike over, pinpoint the target with my hand held, and dig it up. Usually I found it with ease, and usually that would be a bad sign. The Brenhams are deep and if the 10-inch coil on my Fisher returned a signal, it was likely a shallow target. We excavated an antique pitchfork, a hammer, some vintage horseshoes, a wagon wheel, and many other arcane and unidentifiable metal implements, and added them to the ever-growing pile of scrap at base camp.

Steve motored up the ridge of a low hill. It was a fine sight: the bike and trailer moving along the crest, almost in silhouette, with a clear blue sky behind. I thought what a perfect spot it would be to make another discovery—it was all so very scenic. I decided to walk that way and was perhaps thirty feet from the ATV when Steve stopped and turned the engine off. I gave him a hand unhitching the trolley and we rolled it back and forth, a couple of times, over the target. It was pretty strong—a long clear howl.

"Well, I'm going to keep going," he said. He reattached the trolley, and went bouncing off across the wide brown fields again.

I turned on my Fisher, put the sensitivity to maximum and scanned the roughly sixty-square foot zone. I did get a signal. It was very weak, and it covered a large area. It was so gentle an undulation in the detector's tone that I would not have bothered with such a target if the big coil had not spotted it first. I dug another deep hole.

Nineteen inches down, a small caramel-colored face appeared out of the sand and dirt. I jumped into the hole and brushed some of the soil away with my hands. It was another pallasite, sitting there, quietly, patiently, in the ground, at the top of a sunny, windy, lonely ridge in rural Kansas, waiting for me to find it. With great care I dug all around, slowly and carefully exposing its surface with the plastic trowel.

A couple of times Steve roared up to check on how it was going.

"Come back in ten minutes," I said.

I was the first human ever to have seen this visitor from deep space and I had an overwhelming desire to unearth it alone: carefully, delicately, thoughtfully. It was egg shaped and larger than a football; its surface chestnut and bronze, and checkered with dark crystals. I scooped every bit of soil away, gently lifted it up, and placed it beside the man-made crater I had excavated.

A slight breeze blew across the fields. The day had warmed up nicely. I sat down on the ridge, with my hand on the pallasite and looked out across the farmlands. We just sat there for a while, the two of us. The old meteorite was seeing sunshine for the first time in two thousand years, and I wanted to remember that moment forever.

Later, Steve returned to see what we found.

"What'cha got there, pardner?"

"A pallasite," I said. "A lovely pallasite. The two of us are just sitting here enjoying the moment."

"Well, take as many moments as you like." He smiled, fired up the ATV, and hurtled off across the fields once more with that crazy plastic trolley trundling and lurching along after him.

We could have strapped the new find to back of the ATV, but I carried it myself, respectfully and with both hands, all the way back to base camp. I put it on a towel in the passenger seat of my car, and we drove back to the hotel. It weighed a little over 28 pounds. We washed it in the tub with distilled water, carefully pulling off the mud and dirt to reveal all its unearthly beauty.

We found a 59-pound siderite the next day, sculpted by forces unknown into the shape of a buffalo. We zeroed in on another big target, but left it waiting in the ground because our good friend Dr. Art Ehlmann was on his way up from the Monnig Meteorite Gallery in Texas, and we wanted him to experience the joy of digging a Brenham for himself. He and Steve excavated the iron weighing more than 100 pounds. After a distinguished career in meteorite research and curation, it was Dr. Ehlmann's first find, and he later joked that he only dug up the really big meteorites.

I wrote a press release about the giant pallasite and sent it out to television stations. I received a call back in less than five minutes, and we scheduled the first of many interviews with Steve for that evening. Steve's find was featured on every TV network in the country and in hundreds of newspapers around the world.

Steve bought a little fallen-down house in Greensburg and acquired leases to the surrounding properties. It was the start of the biggest and best hunt of our careers.

[facing page] Detail of a prepared slice taken from one of our Brenham pallasite finds. Note the abundant green olivine crystals, also known as the gemstone peridot.

FIFTEEN

FOUR NETWORKS

Saxophones blew smoke rings
Of blue gasoline
And martinis were served up
By science fiction magazines

From "Gasoline Blue"
By Lach

IN 1996 I APPEARED BRIEFLY in a superb *Arena* television documentary for the BBC about Art Spiegelman's *Maus*, a celebrated book on which I worked as a production assistant. I also had a non-speaking part as a young French painter in the first episode of A&E's enjoyable series *The Impressionists*, but my very first television appearance took place in 1975 on London's *10 O'Clock News* when I was accidentally caught by a news team while bunking off from school, aged fourteen. When I returned home that evening, my mother asked me several times how school had been. I gave her some typically trite answer along the lines of "Boring, as usual," and when she asked me, flat out, to confirm that I did actually go to school that day I lied and said: "Of course."

"Then how do you explain being at Paddington Station with all those football hooligans in the middle of the afternoon?"

An ITV film crew covering a story about soccer fans torching a passenger train—a train that I unfortunately happened to be on at the time—caught me on tape fleeing from the station and I was, evidently, very clearly visible, front and center, on the national news. It was not the finest start to my television career but it did prove conclusively that lying to your mother is always a bad idea.

All through the 1990s I considered most of American television to be a wasteland of annoying commercials and cheap programming. It is my understanding that the initial idea behind cable television was to provide original, quality entertainment in exchange for a subscription fee. What consumers ended up receiving for that fee was, for the most part, a hundred additional channels of annoying commercials and more cheap programming. I remember being on the road with Steve, staying in a crummy

[left] Steve Arnold and the author, immediately after excavating
a large Brenham pallasite, while filming *The Best Places to Find Cash & Treasures*.

motel somewhere, watching a numbing reality show on A&E and saying: "Hey Steve, remember when A&E used to stand for Arts and Entertainment?" He found that very amusing and often repeated it back to me in later years.

There were exceptions, of course, but, in my view, not enough to justify $80 or $100 a month in bills. Why should I pay money to watch bad commercials? I grew up with the BBC and their elegant documentary shows such as *Horizon* and *Chronicle* had set the bar too high. American reality programs featuring sappy teenagers forced to live together in fake houses with the cameras rolling, and endlessly spouting vapid dialog along the lines of: "And she was like 'okay, whatever,' so I was like 'yeah, whatever,'" were so odious to me that I disengaged from the source completely, gave up cable, and did not watch television at all for about ten years. When I returned the box to the office of my local provider, a terse lady asked me why I wanted to cancel my service.

"Because your programming is useless." She looked extremely offended, so I followed up with: "Well, you did ask. Nothing personal, I'm just giving you an honest answer."

I love movies so, when I was in the mood, I rented DVDs instead. I also did a lot of reading.

Early in 2006 and not long after returning from my very first Brenham expedition with Steve, I received a call from Indigo Productions in San Francisco asking if I would be willing to assist with a Travel Channel program about meteorites. I had avoided commercial television for so long, I did not even know what the Travel Channel was.

The researcher explained that Indigo was in the process of developing a new series,

[above] Becky Worley and the author, with one of our Glorieta Mountain meteorites from *The Best Places to Find Cash & Treasures.*

The Best Places to Find Cash & Treasures, with former CNN host Becky Worley, and they were very excited at the idea of doing an episode about how to find meteorites. They wanted me to pretty much guarantee we were going to be able to produce a find on camera. Had I been asked such at thing at any other period in my life I probably would have said it was not possible, but, at that very moment, Steve was still digging in a field in Kansas.

Television is expensive and complicated to make, and film crews always seem to be on a very tight schedule. There never is quite enough time to get all those shots they want. We were given only three days to film the entire half-hour episode and, shortly before we began shooting, Indigo Films called back and advised me that they now, in fact, wanted to film at *two* locations, and did I think we could find meteorites at both? I made some calls and quickly put together a team that included my great friends Sonny Clary, Ruben Garcia, and Mike Miller, all of whom had experience hunting for meteorites at a notoriously difficult and mountainous site near Glorieta, New Mexico. I told Indigo I had called in the best hunters I knew and we would do our best to deliver at both sites.

Sonny and I met up in Wichita and drove to Kiowa County in western Kansas, where Steve was waiting for us. After one day of filming in Kansas, the crew would travel to New Mexico for the second segment. The plan had always been for Steve and me to appear only in the Brenham segment, while the rest of the guys would guest in the New Mexico segment. Sonny came along to observe at Brenham, and I offered to tag along and advise at Glorieta, mostly because I was dying to hunt at that famous site with a team of experts who knew the area. All I really wanted out of the whole thing was to come home with a little Glorieta Mountain meteorite in my pocket.

The very first time Steve and I ever filmed a meteorite hunt together was a glorious sunny morning in April of 2006. Becky drove across the wide, empty field in a black Kia, pulled up alongside us, wearing an almost fluorescently-bright green shirt, and delivered her introductory monologue through a rolled-down window. That first shot of the day was, surprisingly enough, also the opening shot of the episode. As we would later discover, television episodes are usually not made exactly in order.

Becky is a beautiful and elegant woman, with long blonde hair, and I thought to myself: "She's not going to much care for getting down in the dirt with us." I could not have been more wrong. From the outset, she wanted to try everything: drive the ATVs that dragged Steve's giant metal detector, learn how to use our hand-held detectors and, eventually, dig in the mud.

Steve and I each had an ATV. His towed the big detector and I drove close by, like a chase plane, keeping an eye out for plant stalks and other debris that might damage the big sled. To my considerable annoyance, I soon realized that the camera crew were focusing entirely on Steve. Becky directed all of her questions toward him and it seemed as if I was not to be included at all in the action. I kept trying to manoeuver my ATV into the frame, and the camera crew kept turning away. Brenham is Steve's site and it is completely understandable that they wanted to focus on him. I had, however, flown all the way out from Tucson, put the hunting teams together, and liaised with the production company from the very beginning. I was not about to poodle around in the distance, on my own, on a forgotten and unrecorded mission of solitude. I was there to be part of a TV show about meteorites.

When Steve located our first target with the big coil, he shut down the quad's engine, and the camera crew rushed over to detail his every move.

"Hey!" I yelled out. "This is my part."

I stopped my quad and walked briskly to them with my smaller Fisher 1266 detector in hand. "This device," pointing to Steve's oversize detector, "picks up large buried targets. The detector's signal is an electromagnetic field that decays quickly over distance. Therefore, the larger the coil, the deeper it can 'see' into the ground. This little unit," I held up my 1266, "is for pinpointing, so we don't have to dig up the entire field. Pinpointing. That's my department."

I sort of shouldered my way into the heart of the action and added: "Okay, everyone?"

The cameramen looked at me, and then at the director, Chris Leavell, and they all nodded in a somewhat surprised, but not unfriendly manner, as if to say: "Oh, look, it can talk."

I suppose you could say that moment was the very beginning of a four-year friendly contest in which Steve and I vied for air time. Teamed up with a co-host as amusing and energetic as Steve, with his one-liners, his excellent comedic timing, and his great ability for physical humor (wrecking expensive equipment, and so forth), I quickly learned that I had to stay on my best game, at all times, just to keep up with him.

Steve and I already shared plenty of experience at Brenham and had pulled several large masses from the ground using only shovels. I like to think I am rather skilled at pinpointing, so when Chris asked us how long it would take to excavate the buried target, I brashly said: "Oh, about half an hour."

An hour later we were still digging.

We put down a narrow three-foot test hole and missed the target completely. The same went for our second and third test holes, and I could tell the crew was getting nervous. With only a single shoot day at Brenham, we could not afford to waste time on difficult targets. At that point Becky took a shovel, jumped into the hole and started digging like a crazy person. After an hour and a half of sustained effort, the three of us had excavated a hole large enough to hold a couple of toddlers' swimming pools, but no rocks were forthcoming. Fearing we were about to lose the entire day puttering about in a futile manner with shovels, Chris called in the backhoe and—in no time—a lovely pallasite weighing ninety pounds emerged from the ground. We named it "The Becky Stone" in honor of our host. We found a second mass, of similar size, that same afternoon and everyone was rather stunned by our success. In our very first TV outing we managed to deliver meteorites specifically to order: on time and on target. It would not always be quite so easy.

Steve remained in Kansas to continue his work while Sonny and I hit the road for the nearly 500-mile drive to New Mexico. The crew were to travel by plane and meet us in Santa Fe.

As Sonny and I motored through the charming old Route 66 towns of Tucumcari and Santa Rosa with their wide streets and shimmering, faded neon motels, our friend Ruben Garcia, who would later appear with us in *Meteorite Men*, was already on the ground near Glorieta.

Producing a television show about meteorites is very different from organizing a meteorite hunting expedition for fun or profit. Location releases granting us permission to film on private properties must be secured, as do agreements from anyone who might appear on the program. In Kansas it was simple. Steve already had solid relationships with local landowners and we knew exactly where we wanted to hunt. At Glorieta we knew approximately where meteorites might be found, but securing permission to work and film at those sites could be problematic. Ruben is a dashing and charismatic Mexican-American man, with a boyish charm and a friendly disarming manner, so we sent him out to deal with the locals.

Becky, Chris, the crew, and some of the meteorite hunting team met for dinner in a quaint Santa Fe restaurant. The meal was scheduled for 8 p.m., and when Ruben finally arrived closer to 9 p.m., the production assistant who had been assigned to go with him on a land permissions scout was as white as a hotel pillowcase. Ruben was laughing and smiling, as usual, but I could tell he was a little shaken.

"We drove up to this one house, right in the strewnfield, after dark, and rang the bell," he reported. "There was a lot of noise and banging inside and then the porch light went on. The door opened and out comes this guy, roaring drunk and waving a big handgun in our faces. He was screaming at us and said he'd kill us if we didn't get off his property."

And then added: "And this poor guy," pointing at the young production assistant, "it's his first day on the job!" The P.A. was new to the company and had just flown out that morning from Los Angeles, specifically for the Glorieta shoot. So, his very first experience in location filming involved being driven around dark canyons with the exuberant Ruben Garcia, and threatened by a lunatic hillbilly with a .357 magnum.

The next day, Ruben, Chris, and I headed back out to try our luck. A narrow and tree-shrouded lane wound down to the site that most interested us, and we had to open and pass through a wire gate with a sign that said something like: "Trespassers will be shot and buried in the woods with no questions asked." Welcome to New Mexico.

At the first of several houses situated in promising locations, we were met by a small man with a wide smile and an odd little green canvas cap perched on his balding head. After explaining that we were making a television documentary about meteorites, he jumped right in: "I know all about you TV people, you're all just made of money!" He offered to let us film on his tiny quarter-acre property for the sum of $10,000 per day. We moved on, eventually finding a welcoming landowner who not only allowed us to film there, but invited us back several times in later years. I found my first Glorieta Mountain pallasite that day, under a little bush, on camera, with Becky by my side. Glorieta is a beautiful meteorite: toffee-colored, showing patches of blue-grey fusion crust, and decorated with pockets of yellow and green crystals. The first example was discovered in 1884, only nineteen years after the end of the Civil War, and a significant battle from that era was fought in and around the strewnfield. We uncovered numerous Civil War bullets and artifacts, and I found it fascinating that they lay buried at almost the precise depth of the Glorieta meteorites. I have often wondered if the thunder of incoming meteorites, which were surely seen or heard by locals at the time, were mistaken for military cannon fire and never reported.

We found about twenty meteorites between us during the course of the day. At one point I was standing on a rocky promontory, with a cameraman directly behind me. Ruben toiled away about fifty feet below me at the bottom of a nearly vertical cliff face.

"Geoff!" he suddenly yelled, and looked up at me with his rakish enthusiasm and amazement. "I just found a beauty."

With the camera on him, he bounded straight up the cliff face, like some kind of mountain-bred ram, and appeared in front of me in mere seconds, with a glittering meteorite in his open palm.

"Wow, it *is* a beauty," I said.

And then the cameraman said: "Damn!"

"What happened?" I asked.

"Oh, my tape ran out just as he came up the cliff. That was an amazing shot. Can you do it again?"

"Seriously?" Ruben asked.

So he climbed back down the cliff, with some difficulty and re-enacted the entire thing. Despite Ruben's efforts the shot did not make it into the final cut. It is not an easy thing to try and recapture the genuine delight and excitement of a meteorite find for the camera.

My screen time had already been allocated for the Kansas segment, so I did not bother shaving on the morning of the New Mexico filming day, since I was there to hunt on my own and not appear on camera. Early that morning, Chris took me aside and said: "Look, Geoff, you were really good on camera in Kansas, and we'd like you to appear in this segment too. Actually, if you could kind of lead the action, that would be great."

When the episode went to post-production, the order of the hunts was reversed: The Glorieta segment in which we found numerous small meteorites was used to open the show, and the Brenham hunt, where we made two very large finds, worked well for the ending. When I watch that episode of *Cash & Treasures*, I always find it amusing that I start off scruffy and with a two-day beard in New Mexico, but end up clean shaven and bright eyed in Kansas.

The "Meteorites" episode of *Cash & Treasures* was our very first foray into space rock television, and we were later told that it was the most popular episode of the entire series.

Much later, I became involved in an amusing incident with Travel Channel. Becky maintained an engaging blog about her adventures while filming the series, and wrote a lovely passage about us: "I've met some great people during the filming of *Cash & Treasures*, but two of my all-time favorites were Steve Arnold and Geoff Notkin. We got to know each other while digging for meteorites in Kansas. I'd dig for treasure with those guys any day of the week." I thought it so gracious I put it on one of my websites. Shortly thereafter, I received a curt email from Travel Channel's legal department ordering me to remove the quote, and claiming that I was "using copyrighted material without permission."

I wrote back immediately and said something along the lines of "(A) I am a writer and publisher and I know something about copyright law. There is usually nothing wrong with reproducing a brief quote from copyrighted material, so long as proper attribution is cited, and (B) You definitely cannot stop me from using a quote that is specifically *about me!*" The legal department apologized, and grudgingly agreed that it was, in fact, okay for me to reproduce the quote, provided I put a tiny "© by The Travel Channel" notice at the bottom of the page. This incident had nothing at all to

[top] Steve's Hummer heads out across the Brenham strewnfield, along with the metal detector sled, while filming the *Wired Science* pilot. [above] The 50-pound "Wired Siderite" iron, at the bottom of its dig hole.

[top] The author, Steve Arnold, and the 1,430-pound Brenham, filming the *Wired Science* pilot.
[above] Steve Arnold, director Sean Dash, and the author with our *Cosmic Collisions* find.

do with Becky. She was a delight to work with, and we stay in touch from time to time.

It seems that once you open the door to television, the offers just keep on coming.

In January of 2007 *Wired* magazine published a lengthy article entitled "The Meteor Farmer," by science writer Ben Paynter. The piece was a detailed examination of Steve, and his work in Kansas. Soon after, we were contacted by the producers of *Wired Science*, one of three entries in a contest run by PBS to generate a new and cutting-edge tech series for television. They wanted to film with Steve in Kansas. Since were so successful during the *Cash & Treasures* hunt, I offered to join in. As is typical of many production companies, they made sighing noises on the phone and said: "Well, money is very tight and we really don't have the budget to fly you out for the shoot."

I had been reading *Wired* for years, was a great fan of PBS, and was not about to miss out on another televised meteorite hunt, so I flew out to Kansas and rented a car at my own expense.

Our director, an accomplished professional, had worked in television for some time. An older man, he did not seem much interested in the actual hunt. We spent most of our shoot day sitting in a diner in Greensburg, Kansas, while he interviewed farmers. It was all extremely boring. I got quite agitated and pulled a 1-kilogram iron meteorite out of my bag and passed it around for the crew to examine. Everyone was fascinated and asked over and over: "Is it really from outer space!?" The meteorite toured the diner and the mood of everyone present began to change. The cameramen appeared restless and I went to speak with the director who appeared to transmit, to me at least, the impression of not really wanting to be there. In later years I would learn how exhausting it is to relentlessly make television programs, thereby understanding why some take a laid-back approach. But, in 2007 with the idea of working in television still new and exciting, I felt impatient for action.

"Why are we in this diner when we're supposed to be looking for meteorites?" I asked.

"It's getting late in the day and you're not really going to find anything, are you?"

Steve had been working continuously at Brenham for months, and successfully recovered several large meteorites in addition to the 1,430-pound monster. Eager though he was to continue digging, as soon as he received news about the *Wired Science* pilot, he stopped excavating targets and, instead, began marking them with orange construction flags.

"We have thirteen targets in the ground, all in one field, just a few miles away! At least one of them is going to be a meteorite."

"Are you certain about that? If we go to the trouble of driving all the way up there, are you definitely going to find something?"

I argued with him for a while and then Qynne, Steve's wife, walked over. Qynne is a polite and courteous lady with great charm, but she also has a resolute and determined manner. I cannot think of a time during the past fifteen years when somebody has successfully tried to bend her will.

"Why don't you just let the guys do what they do?" she said to the director, most delicately but also, somehow, in a way that made it seem as if a building-sized pile of steel girders loomed in the distance and could possibly fall this way if her instructions were not followed.

Suddenly, miraculously, and with surprising speed, the entire group packed up, left the diner and followed Steve's canary-yellow Hummer into the strewnfield.

The sun already sat low in the sky. At best we had two or three hours of daylight left; without the targets marked earlier by Steve, we would not have sufficient time to find anything on camera. We corralled our vehicles out there on the plains, like steel wagons in the brisk wind. The director climbed out of his rental car, bundled up in a parka and not looking, in any way, pleased.

"Where are those marked targets you told me about?"

"Steve!" I yelled. "Where are those thirteen target flags?"

Steve turned around, squinted, turned around some more, in his finest little-lost-boy way, and finally said: "Umm, they're gone."

To this day we have no idea what happened. The landowner swears he did not remove them, and why would he? Perhaps a mischievous kid crept into the field and stole them for a lark. Maybe aliens were to blame. We shall never know, but the director's I-told-you-so grimace was now clearly focused on me.

"Steve! Let's get the big rig hooked up to the ATV and find those missing targets. What's your best guess as to where they were?"

"Well, gee. I was working close to those trees, so they should be somewhere between them and the trucks."

Rapidly, because daylight was disappearing and because I made a promise that we would find something, we got the detector prepared and Steve started blasting across the several acres that lay between our vehicles and the stand of trees. Within twenty minutes we had a good, solid target: loud and probably deep. Steve and I debated whether we should scout for some of the other twelve or just dig up the single one we had. With time running out we broke out the shovels.

Adam Rogers, the celebrated editor of *Wired* magazine, was hosting the show and I enjoyed his sophisticated and witty presence. He also pitched in to help us dig. After about thirty minutes of effort, and in-between deep breaths, he jokingly asked if, assuming we found a real meteorite, he would get a third of it.

Without missing a beat Steve replied: "You get a third of the enjoyment."

An unexpected dust storm sprang up and peppered us with dirt as we tried to find the buried object. The director remained somewhat skeptical and asked, a number of times, if we were really sure there was "something down there."

Shortly before we lost the last of the afternoon's light, one of our shovels hit something hard, about three feet down. We carefully uncovered a wonderfully shaped meteorite that weighed exactly fifty pounds. It was a Brenham alright, but a siderite rather than a pallasite—a rare individual composed entirely of iron, with no olivine crystals present.

Wired Science won the PBS pilot contest and became a television series. Our segment on meteorites was seen a second time when it was re-cut into the first episode of the first season. Some weeks later, Steve went back to the site and reacquired the other twelve targets he marked prior to our shoot day. Every last one of them was a meteorwrong—man-made trash.

As a little boy, one of my great delights was reading through copies of *National Geographic* magazine that my mother collected during the 1950s. The accounts of archeological expeditions, and blue-tinged images of sunken ship excavations filled me with wonder and a hunger for adventures of my own. In the fall of 2007, therefore, when we received an invitation to film a segment for a National Geographic Television episode called "Naked Earth: Our Atmosphere," I could not have been more excited if a meteorite had just landed in my own garden.

The production company was from England and—being unfamiliar with the American holiday calendar—informed us they could only film with us during the third week of November. Not wanting to go immediately back to Brenham for yet another shoot, we teamed up with our friend McCartney Taylor, a meteorite enthusiast from Austin who had been inspired by Steve's techniques and started working at the Deport iron meteorite strewnfield in Red River County, Texas. We managed to somehow convince "Mac" how exciting and rewarding it would be to appear on Nat Geo TV with us. He graciously cancelled his existing Thanksgiving plans and drove nearly 300 miles to the wet and muddy strewnfield to meet us.

Due to a now familiar tight shooting schedule, we were only allocated a day and half at the site. It would not nearly be enough. The area around Deport has been intensively farmed since the 1800s and the ground is packed with the discarded debris of cultivation. In one rather short and drizzly afternoon, we dug up 27 targets, and none were meteorites. Fortunately, I have a fine example of Deport in my reference collection and I brought it along for on-screen use as an example of what we were looking for.

During our lunch break on the second day, Steve, Mac, and I, along with our director and crew ate at a small local restaurant in the tiny town of Deport, population approximately 700. Unwilling to leave expensive high definition cameras in the trucks, the cameramen brought everything of value into the dining area and placed their equipment on the floor around us. A flirty and vivacious waitress bounced up to our rustic wooden table.

"Hi there! How ya'll doin' today?"

"Oh, very well, thank you," replied one of the crew, in a thick British accent.

"Aww, I just love yawr accent! Where're ya'll from?"

"Most of us are from England, some from the States."

"England! Gee whiz, I just love yawr accents."

She was very sweet and genuinely interested, and wanted to know what we were doing, "With all them cameras."

"We're filming a documentary about meteorites," I replied.

"Media-rights?"

"Yes, space rocks."

She chewed on her upper lip for a moment, and gazed up adoringly at the ceiling.

"Ya mean . . . like aliens?"

Most of the guys laughed but I assured her that, in a sense, we were, in fact, looking for aliens. I took the sample Deport meteorite, weighing about five pounds, out of my bag and placed it in her hand.

"Oh my lord! It's so heavy. Is this a real media-right . . . from spaaace?"

I told her it was and she stared at it in rapture for a moment, with her mouth slightly open, before slapping it back in my hand.

"Aww, you guys are jus' messing with me. I know ya'll are from *Candid Camera* or somethin' like thay-yat."

She was convinced that my entire explanation was some sort of jape or ruse we were playing on her, and went on to carefully inscribe our lunch requests in her order book.

Deport was our first televised failure—at least in terms of finding meteorites within a fixed number of hours—and "Naked Earth: Our Atmosphere," although a fascinating show, turned out to also be an unintentional slight against our friend Mac. After generously inviting us to hunt at his site, and working with us for several days on logistics and location permits, he was entirely cut from the broadcast episode. I started to grasp, clearly, and with some disappointment, that the minimal amount of time allocated for filming meteorite expeditions would likely always be at odds with the physical amount of time required to uncover that rarest of treasures—space rocks.

Almost a full year elapsed before our next broadcast adventure, but it was worth the wait. During the summer of 2008 Steve acquired the lease to an unhunted strip of land in the Brenham strewnfield. When Workaholic Productions contacted me and asked if we might be available to appear in a new three-part series, *Cosmic Collisions*, for Discovery Channel, we were all ready to go.

In September, I drove from Tucson to Denver in order to deliver a 200-pound iron meteorite to a customer. From there I crossed the plains of eastern Colorado and returned, once again, to the familiar fields of Brenham. Our director, Sean Dash, was an enthusiastic, animated man, and I hit if off with him immediately.

"What you guys do is amazing," he told me. "You should do a whole TV series about this!" Over a couple of cocktails in my hotel room, he went on to ask me about the chances of actually finding a real meteorite on camera.

"It's pretty simple really. The more time we have to hunt, the better our chances of finding something. We've never hunted this section of land before, and it's in a really good area."

I could see the excitement bubbling up inside Sean and felt that—for the first time—we were working with a director who was as smitten with the idea of finding visitors from space as we were.

Steve and I both brought our own 4WD pickup trucks for the *Cosmic Collisions* shoot. It was great fun blasting up and down straw-covered fields, with the big detector in tow, and a camera on a crane—or "jib" as it is called in the business—swooping overhead and capturing dramatic aerial shots of us in motion.

In documentary shows or reality programming that, in some way, involve a search for treasure or rare collectibles, or the chance to uncover unexpected wealth, there is sometimes a tendency to add in a little extra drama. If, for example, the host were to find a long-lost pot of gold beneath the rainbow in the first five minutes of a one-hour show, viewers might not hang around for the rest of the program preferring, instead, to flip channels or go out for some fast food. The writers and editors of *Cosmic Collisions* did not have to worry about such things.

The first day we hunted hard, in various areas of the newly-acquired land. We found a buried well cap and some rusty tools. The second day, we hunted hard, did some interviews and driving shots, and found some more tools and a very nice horse-shoe. On the third and final day we hunted hard, experienced some equipment problems, found a pair of pliers and an overly large spool of buried wire. As the sun began to sidle uncaringly into the western quarter of the sky I could feel the disappointment radiating from Sean. It was not a disappointment directed at us, or our efforts, but rather a growing realization that the odds are always against you in meteorite hunting, and we were about to enter our final hour of daylight.

Then the detector sled went over something shallow and sizable and let out a wail like a frightened coyote. Steve stopped his truck and leapt out.

"What do you think?" Sean asked, as he ran over, his eyes all lit up like fireflies.

"I don't know," I replied. "It's a strong target, but very shallow. The average depth of finds in this area is at least three feet. This sounds much closer to the surface. It's probably a well or a plow blade, or some other big piece of trash."

The crew hurried to set up the jib so they could capture the excavation from above, and Steve and I broke out smaller detectors to pinpoint our target. It was closer to the surface that it should have been and I was not overly optimistic.

The moment the cameras were rolling, we began shoveling away the dry and dusty soil and, at approximately 4 p.m. on September 19, 2008, after digging an unusually shallow hole, we uncovered a 50-pound oriented Brenham pallasite, covered in crystals and sparkling gently in the late afternoon sun.

The photograph of Sean, Steve, and me at the dig site, with our find, remains one of my favorite expedition pictures of all time. Somewhat sunburned, but joyous and victorious, we beat the odds, almost literally, at the last minute.

Cosmic Collisions turned out to be an excellent series, full of illuminating interviews and marvelous graphics and effects. Our segment is in the second episode and it has a grand, almost epic, cinematic feel that reminds me of the adventure films I adored as a child. The series repeats from time to time on Discovery Channel and is available for purchase on DVD from the Discovery Store.

And no, I do not get any residuals, and the only payment we received was some assistance with travel and accommodation expenses.

[above] Filming *Cosmic Collisions* in Brenham, Kansas.

SIXTEEN

A ROCK CALLED BUZZARD

Torch my bridges, build my walls
Ignore my honesty, bleed my pursuit
Diffuse my sincerity, fuel my integrity
Taste my compassion, free my soul

From "My Shoes"
By Krista Khrome

ONE OF THE STRANGER ASPECTS OF MY WORK with meteorites involves listening to eyewitness accounts of cataclysmic cosmic events that I, myself, have missed. When a bright fireball burns up the dark sky (and occasionally the daytime sky), the event is brief, shocking, unexpected, astonishing, and will almost certainly live in the viewer's memory for the remainder of his or her life. The excitement and wonder conveyed by the interviewee who has experienced one of these night-rending phenomena floods out relentlessly, like mineralized water from an Artesian well. "It was as bright as the sun!"; "The fireball traveled almost all the way across the sky, from there to there!"; and "Then it exploded like fireworks and the sound was like thunder!" are typical of the descriptions that have been related to me, suitably punctuated with wide-eyed amazement and the waving of arms.

These accounts are, nevertheless, genuinely exciting for me and they do become vital stepping stones along the road to recovery of fallen meteorites that caused the fireball, but—try as I might—I can never fully expunge a tinge of envy. I may be the one who finds the meteorite, but I was not the one who saw the fireball that shaped, melted, and burned it.

After decades of gazing into the night sky, I have, of course, seen fireballs myself, but none remotely as imposing as the one that split the chilly skies over Alberta and Saskatchewan on the night of November 20, 2008. The event took place at about 5:30 p.m. and was witnessed by hundreds of people. In fact, during my two trips to the site, which required staying in the neighboring town of Lloydminster, it seemed almost impossible to find someone who had *not* seen the magnificent meteor. While explaining to the receptionist at the Holiday Inn what we were doing, and why we had so much odd-looking equipment with us, she herself lit up like a diminutive shooting star and said: "Oh the fireball, eh? I was driving here to work the evening shift and I saw it from

151

my car. It traveled right across the sky. It was so bright it was like daytime, and all these burning pieces spiraled off, like a big sparkler." And there, again, came the envy.

The heat generated by the inferno of a large fireball—or bolide as they are sometimes called—is so intense that many potential meteorites burn up completely. Some fall in oceans or in difficult-to-hunt locations such as thick forests or mountain ranges. Some even land in areas that would make for perfect hunting grounds, if you could only get there—a fact demonstrated by the "Dugway" episode of *Meteorite Men* Season Two. In that instance we were certain that significant meteorites dropped in the middle of a top secret military testing range—a site so guarded it is off-limits even for regular military—peppered with unexploded ordnance and fiendishly confidential experimental weapons.

Every once in a great while, against the odds and to the unparalleled joy of meteorite hunters, a fireball will generously deposit real meteorites in a place that is almost perfect for hunting. Such was the case with the Alberta/Saskatchewan meteorite that later became known as Buzzard Coulee, after a lush, green, and steep-sided valley in a quiet corner of western Canada.

New fireballs always present a dilemma: should I stay or should I go? Did the meteorites burn up completely? Should we risk everything and jump on a plane in the hopes of being the first on the ground at the fall site, if there is one? Should we wait and see if anything is found by farmers or dog walkers before commencing an expensive and time consuming expedition?

[previous page] Lisa Marie Morrison, Queen of Buzzard Coulee, with one of her finds.
[above] The Buzzard Coulee strewnfield, on the first day of our hunt.

Winter comes early in Saskatchewan, and at the time of the November fireball I was, as usual, already immersed in several other projects. I decided to wait and see what might happen. My friends Sonny Clary and McCartney Taylor packed their bags and flew to Edmonton, Alberta. Mac need not have bothered packing, since the airline lost all of his luggage on the way out. As winter descended, and snow began to fall on the strewnfield, Mac gallantly hoofed it across freezing fields in the same lightweight shirt he wore on the flight in from Texas. Sonny and Mac made a few finds, freshly plucked from the gently rolling hills, established solid contacts with landowners, and then retreated back to the States as heavy winter snows enveloped the bleak landscape. They kindly reported the details to me, and I was invited to join them for a second—and, hopefully, considerably longer—hunt in the spring.

On the ground, entombed in ice and snow for the next five months, were possibly thousands of pristine black space rocks, lying just where they had fallen, gently and silently, onto a welcoming and comfortable bed of desiccated canola stalks. The meteorites slept through the long freeze while I—1,700 miles away in the more sensible winter climate of Tucson—counted down the days, weeks, and months until the spring thaw arrived.

I checked the weather periodically, but when Canadian snow falls on a strewnfield of small and medium-sized meteorites, they may just as well be encased in concrete. Nothing moved in the fall zone except for a few birds who left minute footprints in the snow, and the occasional hardy fox searching relentlessly for sustenance in the endless white. Every now and then, a courageous driver took a maintenance truck along ice-shrouded dirt roads, in order to check on the oil rigs that dot the landscape like giant skeletons. In turn, Sonny periodically checked in with the landowner who, he advised me repeatedly, was "The nicest guy you'll ever meet." Sonny reiterated several times that I was warmly invited to go up there with him when the ground thawed and stated, often, as he is wont to do with his never-ending positivism: "You know they're out there, Geoff, they just gotta be." Meanwhile, the frozen meteorites continued to doze, untouched and unknown, throughout the interminable winter.

One of my best friends in the world is Lisa Marie Morrison. A talented silversmith with a bohemian lifestyle, a devotee of cats, cocktails, and rock 'n' roll music, she drives the same model pickup truck that I do and is a fixture in Tucson's downtown club scene. She is also a space rock enthusiast, crafts the most beautiful meteorite jewelry, and heads my sales team each year at the gem and mineral show. When the spring thaw finally did commence, in April of 2009, it so happened that neither Sonny nor Mac were able to make the trip back to Saskatchewan, but Lisa—eager for an unexpected adventure in the Canadian wilds—offered to go with me. "I'm ready to leave tomorrow!" she said.

I was itching to get going. As the mercury crept tentatively up in Canadian thermometers, meteorites that had hopefully survived their long freeze unscathed would begin to emerge from the receding snow, their black exteriors popping out of the frigid ground, like seals bobbing their heads from the water off the coast of California.

Lisa accompanied me on one unsuccessful meteorite hunting trip to Mexico a couple of years earlier. Speaking fluent Spanish, she served as interpreter and helped me stagger through the blinding heat of Sonora in July. We found nothing of note, but discovered that we traveled well together and there was never an argument about what type of music should be blasting out of our vehicle's CD player.

[above] Lost in the landscape of Buzzard Coulee.

Every decade or so the plans for an expedition just seem to fall effortlessly into place without a prolonged planning drama or gargantuan expense. I spoke with the landowner whose property encompassed a significant portion of the fall zone, and he confirmed that about 70% of the winter snow cover had disappeared. Nobody else wanted to go with us, so we found a non-stop flight from Phoenix to Edmonton, drove up I-10, got on the plane, and headed for Canada.

Lisa started laughing to herself as she peered out of the window, watching Arizona disappear into the distance.

"What's so funny?"

Lisa's mother, Norma, who is a great friend of mine and also my copy editor, is a sweet and kind lady who is quite religious in a gentle and non-proselytizing way.

"Well, Mom said she was going to ask her entire church group to pray for us in the hope that we have a successful expedition."

"Oh, well, that's thoughtful."

"Does that bother you?" Lisa asked.

"Are you kidding? I'll take all the help I can get on this one. All we need is one decent late snowfall, and we'll have to come right back home with nothing."

Edmonton has a pretty little airport. Friendly, not too busy, with a kind of authentic "Welcome to Canada" warmth in its timbers. I have been to Canada many times and it is so close, geographically, and so similar, culturally, to the States that arriving "up north" does not exactly feel like visiting a foreign nation. Lisa and I were, therefore, somewhat surprised when we were pulled from the immigration line and taken into the little back room for a very thorough third-degree shakedown. Uniformed

154

officers wanted to know where we were going, how long we were staying, and so on, down to the minutest detail. I told them I was a science writer, Lisa was my photographer, and we were visiting a friend in Lloydminster to do some research on the previous year's meteorite fall.

"And how long have you known 'this friend'"? the immigration officer asked, in a rather sarcastic and threatening tone.

"I've actually never met him in person. We've chatted on the phone, and exchanged a number of emails and he invited us to visit him and see his property."

"And where else will you be visiting?"

"Nowhere. Just an overnight here in Edmonton and then on to Lloydminster to see my friend."

"You're staying in Lloydminster. Is that correct?"

"Yes, just Lloydminster."

"And what is it about Lloydminster that is so interesting you've come all the way up from the United States?"

"Birds."

"Birds?"

"Yes, I'm a birder. I'm interested in the local birds, and also seeing my friend, of course, and then the meteorite fall, so we have an action-packed trip planned."

I have traveled enough to know that you do not mess around with customs and immigration officers. They can, and will, detain you purely out of spite if they wish, and will most definitely dismantle your travel plans if you have any attitude. Despite that, and being now rather tired and irritable, I was doubtless a bit sassier than I should have been.

"Officer, we are both U.S. citizens and business owners. We have no criminal records and we are here on a short visit to research an event of scientific interest. Is there anything out of order with our passports?"

She glared at me, as if to say: "We ask the questions around here."

"Are you carrying any commercial merchandise, or valuables that will be left in Canada?"

"No, just a few personal items; two cameras, a laptop, and some scientific equipment. It's all used and I have receipts with me."

"Are you transporting any illegal drugs, currency, or pornography?"

"No, we're really trying to travel light on this one."

"Have you been to Canada before?"

"It's my colleague's first visit here, but I've been many times. I used to date a girl in Toronto, but she married a Canadian. Can you imagine?"

And so the grilling continued for a good half hour before we were finally released into the rapidly emptying airport, without the slightest hint of explanation or apology. Oddly enough, nobody thought to open our bags—which was almost certainly a good thing—as I suppose the three professional metal detectors, multiple GPS units, and various rock hammers and other unusual gear would only have made our already somehow-suspicious presence even more of a case for prolonged interrogation.

On the short bus ride to the hotel, I exclaimed so loudly that it startled the other passengers: "What the hell was all that about? It was ten times easier to get into Russia than Canada."

155

Canadians are so welcoming and easygoing that I found this small inconvenience to be more puzzling than it was annoying. I still cannot come up with any explanation for our short detainment, except that we were, possibly, mistaken for some other persons who were of interest to the Canadian government. I was so bemused by the entire event that I almost completely failed to notice how cold it was. Late April in southern Arizona feels like a very hot summer to most people; late April in Saskatchewan feels like the dead of winter to most other people. During the three-hour flight from Phoenix, we experienced a temperature drop of ninety degrees. We exited our truck in Arizona wearing t-shirts, but entered the airport bus wearing cold-weather parkas.

I became immediately smitten with Edmonton, a river city of irresistible charm, rich in bridges, interesting shops, and old British-style pubs. It reminded me of London. But there would be no sightseeing or lollygagging on this trip. My father, then in his eighties, visibly ailing but fighting valiantly against Parkinson's Disease, was making the arduous trip from Europe to see me in Tucson. I needed to be home in five days to pick him up at the airport, and that would give us less than three days in the strewnfield.

Lisa and I left Edmonton early the next morning and the drive to Lloydminster took several hours. We checked in to our hotel, had an espresso, then went to meet Charles who, together with his son, owned hundreds of acres of prime land right in the middle of the strewnfield. Charles was welcoming and extremely courteous. A professional photographer with a classy Old World air, he sat with us, produced detailed maps of his property, showed us roughly where Sonny and Mac had already hunted and, after a short and no-nonsense discussion, he granted us unlimited access to his

[above] My first Buzzard Coulee meteorite.

land in exchange for half of what we found. I normally do not agree to hand over such a large find percentage to landowners but, Charles was, as Sonny had predicted, "the nicest guy you'll ever meet," and I did not have it in my heart to dicker with him. In addition, if we were lucky, extremely lucky, and found an untouched zone within the strewnfield, meteorites would be, by all accounts, lying happily on the surface and ripe for picking. We required no equipment other than magnet canes, and there would be no digging.

After shaking hands with Charles, thanking him profusely and with real sincerity for his kindness, we headed for an outdoor outfitter. The temperature had plummeted further and Lisa and I realized that the cold weather gear we had with us would be of little use, even at the tail end of this savage Canadian winter.

We found a quaint store in Lloydminster and were greeted by a smiling red-cheeked lady who asked us what we needed.

"Everything," I replied.

It may seem obvious, but clothing that one might acquire in the Sonoran Desert does not quite cut it in Canada. In the overfilled and fascinating shop, we found the most remarkable puffy woollen socks—each pair no doubt requiring at least a third of the output from one well-padded adult sheep—and caps of similar consistency, and the best fleece jacket I have ever seen which still accompanies me on all cold weather jaunts.

Unable to think of any other tasks that might further delay a start to the real action, we took our rental car which, at that precise moment was still looking rather smart, off the main paved road and onto the first of a maze-like series of rough tracks still pockmarked, here and there, with piles of snow and ice. It was already late in the day and we had little hunting time before nightfall. There is a quandary of emotions at such a time. I had been looking forward to this moment for months. I was buzzing with energy and slightly nervous; or was that just anticipation? There could be mete-orites everywhere in Charles' vast field; a hundred stones waiting for us to pick them up, or there might be nothing but snow and cowpats. Failed missions and unfulfilled dreams had engineered a shell of realism around my eager heart and the mean side of my brain urged caution and sense. Don't get too excited. But those bleak and gravel-covered miles still could not slide by quickly enough. We would know soon. In this situation—a very recent and significant meteorite fall in an area almost ideal for hunting—there could be no middle road. The Buzzard hunt would be an astounding success, a pocket full of meteorites every hour, or a complete failure with nothing, or next to nothing, to be found.

Twenty minutes from the edge of the strewnfield, the monochrome sky hissed and threw a blanket of snow and hail across the landscape. Wind blew in at 45 degrees and ice pellets crackled against our car like popcorn and sandpaper. Visibility dropped to less than thirty feet and the snow began to settle. Charles' property lies in the center zone of the strewnfield, where we could expect to find meteorites between about 30 and 80 grams; grape-sized to golf-ball sized. It does not take much snow to cover a grape. We realized that, in less than an hour, everything we cared about could become thoroughly hidden and remain that way for weeks.

"Great! Snow! Thank you so very much." I shook my fist at the car ceiling, as if one of the weather gods actually had time to watch me at that very moment.

"What are we going to do?" Lisa asked. "This is awful."

"Well, we've come this far, we might as well drive through the strewnfield, get our bearings and see if there is any clear ground."

The snow eased up slightly, but only slightly. We took a hard-to-see right onto a steep track, as Charles had indicated, and rolled down a long slope to the very southern edge of his property. The road leveled out and we pulled over beside some railroad tracks. About a half inch of snow had already accumulated. I turned off the engine, and we sat there in the cold like two penguins in a bucket. And just as suddenly as it began, the snow ceased. I pulled on my fleece and my parka, and my balaclava and my emergency reserve woollen cap, two pairs of gloves, and climbed out onto what might as well have been the tundra. Ahead of us, and below, lay a spectacular vista: A steel-grey river wound through a deep and rounded valley, plump with leafy evergreens and long grass. A hawk whistled overhead, or was that a buzzard?

It was brutally cold, but no snow was falling and nothing had accumulated on the steep slope to our east.

"What do you think?" I asked Lisa.

"I'm game if you are."

"Well, I didn't come all this way to sit in a car, and this looks as good a place as any. Let's hike up those slopes. There's hardly any snow on the sides."

We assembled our magnet canes—simple wooden dowel rods from the outfitting store, with a powerful neodymium magnet affixed by a strand of camo duct tape—and stepped into the strewnfield.

In all honesty, not more than four minutes elapsed before Lisa called out, somewhat quietly, and most certainly in an I-can't-possibly-believe-it-tone: "Is this one?"

I remember being a bit annoyed and thinking to myself: "She doesn't know what she's doing. She can't possibly have found something already." But, after all, it was only her second meteorite hunt, and I would be patient while explaining that she had, in fact, found a piece of magnetite or some other annoying rock that sticks to a magnet but is not a meteorite.

She stood uncertainly on the side of the hill, one leg higher than the other, braced against the steep slope, wearing a comical red cap and overly long scarf, with a childlike and quizzical expression on her face, staring at her magnet cane. Affixed to the cane was a rock. A meteorite rock, actually. A pristine, complete, and gorgeous 79-gram stone, covered in fusion crust, clung manically to her magnet. It was about the size of a plum, and had socked itself into the side of the mud slope, upon landing.

"It was just there," she exclaimed, pointing. And I could see the plum-sized indentation from which the stone had been plucked moments before. "It just jumped onto my magnet."

She seemed slightly dazed.

"Is it . . . is it a Buzzard Coulee?"

I looked at it more closely. "Oh, most definitely. Our first catch of the day, and your first ever meteorite. Congratulations!"

I could not possibly have been more astonished if she had suddenly revealed that she was not a human being at all, but rather some sort of sophisticated robot. Less than five minutes into her first fireball chase she had found a perfect, desirable, and very valuable meteorite. I stared at it in wonder for some time.

"This is unbelieveable," I said. "You just got here! How did you find that?"

We laughed and joked around, took a few photos, weighed and bagged the piece, and then I bounded further up the hill, desperate to make my own discovery. I was not about to let Lisa show me up in this friendly but obsessive contest.

Rounding the top of the hill I noticed an odd-shaped rock sitting, with some degree of ignominy, I imagined, in a pile of rabbit droppings.

"That can't be one," I said out loud, to nobody in particular. "Sitting right out there in the open." But it was. A 139.1-gram stone, roughly the size of a tangerine, broken in half during flight, wrapped in fusion crust as black as charcoal, resting upright, plain as day in a pile of rabbit turds. I photographed it, picked it up delicately, kissed it on the one side that had definitely not been adjacent to any rabbit pellets, threw my magnet cane way up into the air, and let out a howl.

Lisa and I found three more meteorites, smaller but still wondrous, before darkness swallowed up the tan, grey, and beige fields. We drove back to the hotel, tired but jubilant, and discovered a bar and restaurant in the lobby that stayed open late, and which immediately became the scene of several hours of celebration.

Anxious to build upon our initial finds, we rose very early and enjoyed delicious French-style egg salad sandwiches on miniature baguettes—that transported my memory momentarily back to childhood summers spent in Paris—for breakfast, filled a thermos with strong coffee, and retraced our steps from the previous evening. As if by magic, or possibly the divine intervention of Norma's church group, all of the previous day's snow had miraculously vanished overnight. We returned to the site of the original finds but, after a careful search, located no other stones.

[above] A complete Buzzard Coulee stone lying, untouched, precisely where it fell.

The canola fields were crisscrossed, at regular intervals, by gravel service roads that led to isolated oil wells, each one perhaps a mile or two away from its neighbor. We followed a few of those tracks, stopped and hunted at various locations, but only found one tiny stone. The property was enormous and it would take years to search it thoroughly. Within a few days, however, tractors would arrive and begin tilling the soil for that year's crop. Any meteorites still on the ground would almost certainly be buried forever as a result of the strict necessities of agriculture.

Understanding strewnfields is a science. When multiple meteorites fall at the same time, in the same zone, their distribution can be studied and recorded. The more finds that are made, the better we can extrapolate where other meteorites might be. Lisa and I were, without doubt, solidly within a field of extraterrestrial stones but, despite the immediate success late on our first day, we were striking out on our second. A strewnfield map will, at best, only tell the hunter where other meteorites might be. For every find that I have made as a result of study and extrapolation, I have probably made five based on hunches, educated guesswork, or blind luck. We stood in a canola field where faded and crumpled stalks stretched to the horizon in every direction. The massive fireball hurtled right over our heads five months earlier, dropping sculpted black stones in a course and pattern defined by gravity, mass, inertia, and atmospheric resistance.

Wind arced across the landscape, rustling the dead stalks with a whooshing sound that reminded me of pebbles sighing on an empty beach. And wind, too, I thought. Wind, strong wind, could also affect the direction of small stones as they fell, silently, through miles of cold air.

I must have been locked deep in thought when Lisa walked over, tapping her magnet cane on the ground.

"What are you thinking?"

"Well, look at this." We walked back to the car and I pulled out my topo map. "We're right about here, directly under the path of the fireball, as best we can determine. We found five stones that way yesterday, towards the bigger end of the strewnfield. There should be stones everywhere around us, but we're finding nothing. What if smaller stones were blown slightly to the east, by wind?"

"You have good instincts, follow them. It worked yesterday."

We got back in the car and headed north for about a mile. Each gravel track that bisected our path looked much like the next, but for some reason I liked one of them more than the others. I turned right, east, and followed the track up a hill, through puddles and mud, and arrived in a hidden bowl-shaped valley almost completely surrounded by low hills. The track ended at a circular patch of gravel where an abandoned oil well had once labored at some time in the past. It looked like a deserted helipad. I stopped the car, got out, and surveyed the circle of moody hills. Lisa climbed out and stood beside me.

"What do you think, Commander?"

"I like it. Let's go."

We walked north, Lisa moving slowly and methodically while I strode briskly towards the nearest hill. A minute passed and Lisa shouted out: "Geoff, I've got one!"

I turned and started walking back, slightly irritated because she had interrupted my reverie, and as I walked briskly in her direction, I saw, directly in front of me, a 60-gram meteorite, black and curved, like a sea purse, resting on a bed of stalks.

"I've got one too!" I yelled back, as it clicked to my magnet, realizing I never would have seen it if Lisa had not called me over. A minute later we found another, and then another. We walked in a straight line from the car to the top of the nearest hill—perhaps an eighth of a mile—and recovered seven more, one of them magnificently carved by ablation into the shape of a shark's fin.

Around the banks of a miniature lake, tucked between gloomy hills, we found eleven meteorites in the space of twenty minutes. We searched the lake too, as best we could, joking that we might find the world's first underwater meteorite, but if anything did land in the water, it remained hidden from our magnets among the silt and weeds.

Our three-day haul totalled, astonishingly, more than one hundred meteorites. While I found more pieces overall, Lisa dazzled us both when a black Idaho potato-sized rock, sitting brazenly in the middle of a clearing in the fields, clung—defying gravity—to her magnet. At 314.8 grams it was the biggest find of the expedition and one of the largest and finest stones recovered on that seemingly endless property.

According to law, all meteorites found in Canada must remain within the country unless granted an export permit. On our final morning in Saskatchewan, we met with Charles once again to divvy up our finds. A gentlemanly and trusting person he invited us to keep any stones we particularly liked and leave him with "whatever seems fair."

Our last stop in Lloydminster was the post office. All of our rocks would go to my friend Pam who lived in Toronto—one of the two giggling girls I had met on that high school geology field trip, back in 1978. Leaving our precious astral treasure behind in a foreign country was as excruciating an exercise as I have endured but, in due course, and thanks to the generous assistance of a Canadian meteorite collector who filled out the paperwork for us, every one of our stones received clearance to complete one final journey—this time by airplane—to the United States.

Lisa drove up to my office when the package arrived. Several months had elapsed since the expedition. As we opened the parcel and reacquainted ourselves, one by one, with every single stone, it felt almost as if we were finding them all over again.

The Buzzard Coulee expedition was Lisa's first successful meteorite hunt. Her largest rock went to the Oscar E. Monnig Meteorite Collection in Fort Worth, Texas, where it will be preserved and admired for all time. Lisa proved herself a capable hunter and a fine traveling companion. Steve and I would return to Buzzard the following year to film a Season One episode of *Meteorite Men* but, by then, the cultivators had done their work and new finds were scarce.

For me, Buzzard was almost certainly a once-in-a-lifetime event. It was almost too easy, and once—as we scampered through chilly fields, like school kids, eyes wide and scooping up, every few minutes it seemed, the cast-off progeny of the Asteroid Belt—I said to Lisa: "Make the most of every moment. We will never, ever, experience anything like this again."

On the flight back to Phoenix I went over my field notes and marveled at the sheer number of finds we made during an expedition that was both short, and organized at the last minute. Despite being an atheist-leaning agnostic, I turned to Lisa and, smiling, suggested that she ask Norma if the church group might please be willing to pray for us on all future expeditions as well.

SEVENTEEN

SEVEN HUNDRED POUNDS

You're the senorita with the lipstick
Swirling dreams with each stroke
Can you lend a bum a dollar, can I bum another smoke?
The consulate is busy, yeah the embassy is a joke
I'm stuck in this country, and I'm running out of luck
And I wanna make a movie, let's make a movie

From "Let's Make a Movie"
By Lach

AFTER OUR ADVENTURES MAKING TELEVISION shows for Travel Channel, PBS, and National Geographic, I wanted more. Steve and I went back to one of the production companies we had recently worked with and pitched the idea for an ongoing series. We put together a list of one hundred interesting meteorite sites worldwide, suggested hunting techniques, equipment, and guest stars, and compiled everything into a secret document. There was some interest in our idea, but the company eventually came back to us and reported that such a show would be expensive and complicated to make, and might be a little on the weird side.

Over the next few months, strangely enough, we received several inquiries from other producers with similar ideas, though theirs were clearly half-baked and, again, nothing came of it.

During the winter of 2007 Steve and I were contacted by Ruth Rivin, executive producer at the prominent production company LMNO in Los Angeles. Ruth immediately came across as a serious and accomplished professional with a genuine interest in our work. She had seen an article about Steve in the *Los Angeles Times* and asked if we might have any interest in making a series about our work. Ruth seemed a little surprised when I express mailed our existing outline to her for delivery the next morning. *Meteorite Men* was Ruth Rivin's idea, and without her dedication and vision the show never would have existed.

After a few months of talks, producer Elizabeth Meeker flew to Tucson for a one-day desert shoot during the 2008 gem show. LMNO cut a brilliant five-minute demo reel from the footage. Looking back, some years later, the initial exploratory concept was so well executed, and so on target that it could probably be cut right into an existing episode and nobody would notice.

That July, LMNO owner Eric Schotz, Ruth Rivin, Steve and I received an invitation to fly to Washington, D.C., and meet with senior executives at some of the world's top cable networks. We thought it best to go as ourselves, so rather than dressing in suits, Steve and I turned up in the lobby of the Discovery building in full field gear, carrying a bag holding ten thousand dollars in meteorites. We walked into the lobby in Silver Spring, Maryland, and I was startled and impressed by the *Tyrannosaurus rex* skeleton that dominated the space.

"Steve, look! They have their own dinosaur," I said. "This is definitely the place for us."

Science Channel liked the demo reel and ordered a one-hour pilot episode. Veteran television producer Bob Melisso was brought in to work full time on the project. Randall Love, a cinematographer of exceptional talent and experience who has worked for Lucas films, Disney, Pixar, the BBC, and HBO, among others, served as Director of Photography and Ruth remained on board as one of the executive producers. Bob is a thoughtful and energetic man with a wry sense of humor and great smile, and would be equally at home as a professor of film history as he is developing and directing television. His experience included numerous other science shows, and Bob immersed himself completely in the project. In the space of five minutes I knew we would become great friends.

After months of pre-production, discussions, and planning, shooting commenced in late September. We were going back to Brenham. The plan had always been to film

[previous page] Our 273-pound find at Brenham. [above] Filming the final scene at our secret Alpha Site. [following page] The 35-pound Admire pallasite found on camera while filming at the Alpha Site.

the Brenham segment first, and then move on to the secret Alpha site, both locations being situated in Kansas, and we hoped both would produce pallasites. Although Brenham and Alpha meteorites are both from the same class, they are unrelated.

It is important to remember that meteorite hunting is always a gamble. You never know what you might find, if anything. Making a successful pilot entailed not only finding a meteorite, but finding a spectacular meteorite, on camera, and within a very narrow window of time. There would be only one chance to get it right.

One day before departure bad weather at Brenham forced us to reschedule at the last minute, and film at Alpha first. The entire crew stayed only a heartbeat ahead of appalling storms all through the week of shooting. I am accustomed to hunting through rain and mud, but high definition cameras do not much care for moisture, and our pulse induction metal detectors would not function properly on wet ground.

With three 4WD trucks, two ATVs, two giant metal detectors and enough other assorted hunting equipment to keep a small army occupied, we covered hundreds of acres of ground and filmed in plowed fields, forests, rolling hillsides, abandoned farms, on unmarked dirt roads and in howling Kansas winds. Elizabeth Meeker returned to work with the team, as did jib operator Scott Jolley, who had worked with us on the recent *Cosmic Collisions* shoot for Discovery Channel.

Shooting commenced on October 8, 2008, in a sunny field in northern Kansas. With only two days to complete the dig, we started early, and the very first scene ever filmed for *Meteorite Men* was Steve unlocking the gate that led to our hidden site. We found two spectacular masses on camera: 35 pounds and 109 pounds—both of which are well documented on screen—but there was a third. As we excavated the second and larger find, the day was coming to a close and we barely had sufficient light to complete the shoot. As the sun disappeared and the crew began packing up their gear, we had a serious problem to contend with. Call time the following morning was at 6 a.m. Our tight schedule dictated that we must load the trucks, drive several hours to the Brenham site, move into a new hotel, and participate in a briefing for the second half of the shoot. Before any of that could happen, Steve and I had to make a decision: What to do about the other target, still buried in the ground?

Meteorite hunters are not agreeable to the idea of leaving an unidentified object behind. You never know what it might be, and the suspense nags at you and bothers you until a shovel finally makes contact with something. In addition, there is always the chance that somebody else might happen to come along and stumble upon your find before you have the opportunity to return. Earlier in the day, our detector passed over something at the north end of the field that made it wail out in delight, much as I imagine a robotic opera singer would; but with our hardworking road crew limited to a twelve-hour day, there was no time to dig it. As the crew headed off to the shelter of the hotel and the promise of a hot meal, Steve and I, together with the landowner, our friend Jason Philips, and location photographer, Caroline Palmer, drove three trucks to the far end of the field, positioned them around the source of the unknown signal, turned the headlights on, and started digging.

Unlike most of the other targets located at Alpha, this one would not come easily from its resting place. It was, in fact, the deepest meteorite we ever encountered there, and it required hours of labor to uncover it. The site lay some distance away from major roads but, periodically, a vehicle still drove by. With no street lights anywhere

in view and the only illumination coming from the headlights of our parked vehicles, I often wondered what those drivers must have thought as they motored by and witnessed such a spectacle: our trucks arranged in a lazy semicircle in the dead of night, headlights on high beam and starkly pinpointing busy figures digging industriously around a large hole in an empty field. Farmers do not usually work at night and it certainly would have been impossible to miss us, spotlighted as we were out there in the dolorous Kansas night. That final dig at Alpha turned out to be worth every minute of nighttime effort. We unearthed a large 79-pound pallasite—one of our best finds from any of our expeditions.

Despite heavy rains during the previous few days, by the time we arrived at Brenham the ground had dried quite nicely, the sun was out, and we were on a mission of gravity. Two red ATVs were provided for our use, and blasting around the fields on them with the giant detector in tow, with the camera and jib following our every move, is one of my happiest memories out of all our television adventures.

In that one sprawling and furrowed field, ninety minutes west of Wichita and almost directly across a little dirt road from where Steve and I made our first joint Brenham finds back in 2005, we ferreted out three new targets, and they were all big. Sometimes in movies and television, events are shown in an order that is different from the way in which they originally occurred; such editorial decisions may be employed to add drama or to improve the storyline. In the Brenham segment of the pilot, everything seen on screen is just the way it happened.

Our first target was a whopper, if our detector was to be believed, and we were reasonably certain that a monster space rock lurked beneath our feet.

[above] Our unplanned night dig at Alpha produced a spectacular 79-pound gemstone-laden meteorite.

The return signal definitely emanated from deep underground, so after a failed effort to uncover it with shovels, Steve called in the backhoe. Later, once the 30-gallon oil drum stuffed inside a 55-gallon oil drum appeared ceremoniously above ground, Bob Melisso said to me: "Nobody could ever doubt that was all absolutely real! It would be impossible to fake that overwhelming look of disappointment on your face. That was great!"

I did not feel great at that moment, but we went on to find two astonishing meteorites in close proximity to the oversized rusty cans. The first was 273 pounds, and it remains a personal record for me; the second was 230 pounds. The Brenham shoot produced the largest single haul Steve and I made as a team and, combined with the Alpha finds, we uncovered more than 700 pounds of space rock in five days. It was not a bad way in which to kick off a television series.

Additional shooting took place at Arizona State University's Center for Meteorite Studies in Tempe, where we met admired meteoriticists Dr. Meenakshi Wadhwa and Dr. Laurence Garvie. Steve drove the finds all the way from Kansas to ASU and his wife Qynne filmed some of their cross-country journey with a hand held FlipVid camera, and a few of those scenes appeared in the episode.

Previously unaware that Dr. Garvie was a fellow British ex-pat with a twinkle in his eye, an extremely dry sense of humor, an occupation as a meteorite specialist and, like me, a great interest in desert cacti, I wondered for a moment if he might be my separated-at-birth twin. Laurence became a good friend and colleague, and appeared in many later episodes. The support and assistance given by Laurence and his colleagues added a valuable scientific aspect to the programs and Laurence, in particular, devoted an enormous amount of time and effort to the show.

Unable to clean the big pallasites prior to filming our science day at ASU, Laurence, Steve and I took them to a parking area behind the lab, and I set about stripping off the rust and dirt with an electric drill and wire brush. I put on welder's gloves and a black rubber full-face respirator. Highly amused by this, Laurence said I looked like Darth Vader, as I put the spinning brush against the surface of the first mass, sending a cascade of sparks showering across the surrounding concrete.

The *Meteorite Men* pilot episode first aired on May 10, 2009, on Science Channel. I threw a broadcast party at my home in Tucson and it was attended by many notable members of the meteorite community. The 230-pound Brenham and the 35-pound Alpha finds were both on display in the living room. I found it a pleasantly strange experience to first watch them emerge from Kansas dirt on screen in high definition, and then invite my human guests to run their hands over the gnarled and pitted surfaces of those other guests who had traveled so very far to be there for the premiere.

EIGHTEEN

EAST OF WEST

Sidewalk's slick with rain that is falling
"Mirar, mirar" someone is calling
42nd's lights almost blind me
Can't let a stranger fall in behind me
We're having fun
Civilized fun
Not like it used to be

From "Civilized Fun"
By Paul Martino and 4 Way Ping

ANYONE WHO TOOK PART in the Great Texas Fireball Hunt of February, 2009, will remember it for as long as they live. Meteorites, some of them worth thousands of dollars were lying on the ground in plain sight, and within a few days they would be collected or plowed under.

On the afternoon of February 15, while my Aerolite Meteorites team was hard at work breaking down our showroom following more than two weeks as exhibitors at the 2009 Tucson gem and mineral shows, a spectacular fireball was caught on film by a cameraman covering a sports event in Austin, Texas. As fireballs often do, it seemed, visually, to be "just over there"; but was, in fact, approximately 120 miles away from the man filming, and somewhere over McLennan County, near Waco.

Forty-five minutes after receiving news that our friends Dima Sadilenko and Doug Dawn had found several freshly-fallen meteorites along the projected flight path, Steve Arnold was in the car headed from Arkansas to central Texas. He drove all night and arrived in the vicinity of the suspected strewnfield shortly after dawn. Deprived of sleep, Steve spent all of that day hunting without success. On the second day he found a small, complete, fusion-crusted stone meteorite lying in the middle of a seldom-used side road and called me immediately.

I got up at 4 a.m. the next morning, packed my gear quickly, and headed to the airport with my long-time friend Suzanne Morrison, the meteorite hunter I first met at Gold Basin and now the Director of Operations for Aerolite Meteorites. We rented a Toyota truck at Dallas, Love Field, and blasted down Interstate 35E, eager to get to the fall zone as quickly as possible.

I often wonder what we used to do before cell phones. We never could have found our colleagues out there without one. I was on the line with Steve for much of the trip, and as we neared the small town of West, Texas, he told me to leave the highway at an obscure exit and "look for us by the side of the road." We found Steve's car parked, predictably, in a crazily haphazard manner on the side of a grass bank, and were delighted to learn that our great friend Sonny Clary was on the ground with Steve and both were in hot pursuit of the new fall.

"Welcome to the strewnfield," Steve boomed, shaking our hands—dressed as usual in a khaki shirt, baggy blue jeans, florescent-yellow sunglasses, and sneakers.

Our first duty involved interviewing a friendly farmer who witnessed the fireball and heard multiple sonic booms, while out trimming a tree. He pointed to the exact spot where he saw the brilliant bolide, and he was quite adamant that at least one of the meteorites rocketed straight over his head, leaving behind a slowly fading smoke trail.

We followed Steve to a site east of West—and I know that sounds wrong but it isn't—where a rival team had recovered a few meteorite specimens. More of our friends were arriving by the hour, and we hunted with them until sunset, with no luck. We did, however, have the unexpected pleasure of meeting Hopper, the Meteorite Dog, a sweet and diminutive female collie mix who somehow located a 71-gram stone meteorite. She proceeded to deposit the extremely valuable stone upon the porch of a family that she mistakenly thought of as her owners. The dog was a stray and local farmers were considering having her put down; one demented individual even took pot shots at her with a rifle. Our friend, Ruben Garcia, who appeared with us in the *Cash & Treasures* show, adopted Hopper and took her back to Arizona with him where they now form one of the world's strangest meteorite hunting teams.

[above] The author and Steve Arnold in the Ash Creek (West, Texas) strewnfield.

Steve and Ruben took off late that evening to scout, and I really should have gone with them because Steve discovered a new area of the strewnfield just around dusk. Once he shared this information, everyone in earshot was eager to go back with him. We agreed to meet in front of a supermarket north of Waco at 5:30 a.m. the next morning, in order to arrive at the new site by sunrise. When Suzanne and I rolled up at 5:29, we were rather surprised to find four new vehicles waiting for us, each with several passengers. It was one of the greatest meteorite hunting teams ever assembled. In addition to Steve and Sonny, Ruben, Suzanne and myself, sitting in the cars was veteran hunter Mike Miller, who also appeared in *Cash & Treasures* with us, along with Rob Wesel and Patrick Thompson from Oregon, and Jason Philips from Illinois. Noted collector Jim Schwade joined us soon after, and Mike Bandli arrived from Washington State.

As the sun crept up through damp and hazy clouds on that first morning, we hit the ground hard. Sonny found three meteorites within ten minutes, and by 11 a.m., most of our team were carrying around one or more freshly-fallen space rocks, carefully placed inside plastic baggies. My first find was an 18.8-gram quarter stone lying face up, exposing its unexpectedly white interior, and I very nearly missed it. I was standing in the grass talking to Mike Miller and complaining that I had found nothing so far, when I spotted it sitting about eighteen inches from his right foot.

"Hey! Is that one?" I exclaimed. And it was—Earth's newest arrival from the Asteroid Belt.

We spent that day, and the following six days, hiking across fields, ravines, through woodlands, and along white gravel roads. As we fanned out and began mapping the strewnfield, I started to realize what a very unusual fall it was. After studying the fireball video, and noticing what appeared to be four separate fragmentations, I suggested to Steve that we should probably be looking for four overlapping strewnfields. We repeatedly found large and small stones mixed together, instead of sorted by size as we would expect in a conventional strewnfield where the largest masses typically travel the farthest.

Five miles north of what we considered to be the small end of the strewnfield— where we should have found medium-sized rocks—we discovered stones tinier than the ones at the small end. In addition, nearly all the stones were spaced far apart, and in only a couple of instances did we see two meteorites in close proximity. Stone meteorite showers often produce small clusters of falls that land near each other, such as Gold Basin, but even in the most densely packed section of the strewnfield, stones were, on average, about 0.2 miles apart.

Sonny and Steve hiked off on their own and found a perfect open area that definitely sat within the strewnfield. A cotton field with flat, hard, yellow oil, stalks remaining from the previous year's crop peppered the ground and many times we found glorious, perfect meteorites nestling among brittle shards of decaying plants.

The cotton field turned out to be such a remarkably meteorite-rich treasure trove that the entire group spent the next two-and-a-half days gridding every inch of it, and that field alone produced over sixty stones. Our team collected over one hundred meteorites total, from various different sites. Not only were we making numerous finds, but the vast majority of the stones were perfect 100% fusion-crusted individuals, lying undisturbed on the surface, exactly where they had fallen only a few days before. Numerous finds were oriented, and a few showed flow lines and rollover lips. The crust was so fresh it almost glowed blue-black in the bright Texas sun.

Other hunters, would-be hunters, and the curious rolled into town daily, hungry to try and find their own piece of cosmic debris. The farmer who owned the cotton field was as gracious and welcoming as could be and, understandably, did not want strangers driving or camping on his property. There were plenty of novices careening around in the fields trying to figure out exactly where we were hunting, and hoping to jump on our bandwagon. We did not want to abuse our landowner's hospitality, and we were also not very keen to share our magical little cotton field with anyone outside the group. It was producing new meteorites daily and we had worked hard to find it. So, each morning we assembled our small convoy of vehicles and inched, single file, along a narrow path, past the farmhouse and tucked all the cars and trucks under the shadow of a steep riverbank, where they remained completely hidden from view. I felt like a little kid, back sneaking through the woods in the England of my childhood, but this time in search of actual cosmic wonders rather than badger burrows: "Shhhh! Don't let anyone know where we are."

Most nights, our entire group assembled for a raucous dinner—eight, nine or ten hungry and thirsty meteorite hunters who had hiked at least ten miles across rough terrain in record high temperatures for that time of year. Mike Bandli kept his GPS attached to him at all times and clocked eighteen miles during one day's hike.

I was walking right beside Mike, early in the chilly morning of our sixth day on the ground, when he suddenly dropped to his knees, and shouted out: "Oh, my god, I found one!" He is an experienced collector, but it was his first ever personal find. He almost went into orbit for a moment himself, but kept his wits about him and immediately handed me his digital video recorder.

"Geoff, would you do the honors?"

It was a treat to document the joy of my friend's very first find. That night, at dinner, I stood up, asked everyone to charge their glasses, and officially welcomed Mike into the Brotherhood of Meteorite Hunters with considerable fanfare, at which point Suzanne advised me to add "and Sisterhood" to the title.

Sonny found a gorgeous oriented individual next to a wire fence that looks uncannily like a black flying saucer, but it was Suzanne Morrison who won the prize. While scouting near the northern edge of the strewnfield with Sonny, she came across a large complete individual, resting gracefully on soft grass, weighing 192 grams, completely crusted and highly oriented. A few feet away, she found a second exceptional stone of 151 grams. The larger Ash Creek is one of the most fabulous stone meteorites I have ever seen, and was later sold to a private collector for thousands of dollars.

I hiked well over one hundred miles and put almost 900 miles on the rental truck, while driving around the strewnfield. Most of the landowners we met were welcoming, and generous in giving permission to hunt on their properties, though we did encounter a few who shouted, and sent us away. One of our team was ordered off a property by a maniac with a shotgun. We were careful and respectful of our hosts' land, packed out all our trash, and kept landowners posted regarding our finds.

What could have been a leisurely hunt quickly turned into a race against time. Late February is planting season in Texas and an ominous shadow loomed over us. Once planting began, massive tractors would roll in and tear up the pristine flat surfaces in a matter of days, burying any remaining stones in the soft soil. We were driven to rescue as many of these new arrivals as we could, before they were lost forever, and that meant hiking the fields from dawn until sunset, or until our feet gave out.

One night, near the end of the trip, I was too exhausted to hunt past sunset, and started heading back to the truck an hour earlier than usual. On some odd whim, I decided to backtrack, and cut diagonally across a section of ground we had already covered. And there it was, plain as day: a triangular, 100% crusted, perfectly oriented stone half buried in the dirt. It had smacked hard into the ground, creating a miniature impact pit, and my was best find of the trip.

I returned to the Aerolite Meteorites HQ in Tucson with thirteen new arrivals to planet Earth in my field pack. Eleven were complete individuals, with one half stone and one quarter stone. The total recovered weight of all meteorites from the event was very low, likely less than five kilograms, and that is a tiny amount compared to many meteorite falls. Collectors were desperate to acquire a piece of this important witnessed daytime fireball and that fact demonstrated a new phenomenon. By 2009 there were many more people hunting for, and collecting, meteorites than when I started out fifteen years earlier. Most of those who scoured the fields of West were meteorite afficionados of some sort, and kept everything they found for their personal collections. As such, very little material made it to market and specimens immediately began changing hands for the astonishingly high price of $100 per gram. In comparison, a more common witnessed fall such as Gao-Guenie from Burkina Faso typically sells for $2 per gram. The meteorite was later officially named Ash Creek, but for those of us who were there, it will always be West, Texas.

At the time of the fall, only the *Meteorite Men* pilot episode had aired, and we did not yet know if we would be picked up for an ongoing series. I remember sitting in the dirt, in the cotton field, talking to our production company on the cell phone.

[above] Expert hunter Mike Miller contemplates the Ash Creek strewnfield, while Ruben Garcia searches.

I gently tried to convince them to send out a camera crew and capture our adventure, the race against time, and the feuding between rival groups of hunters but, understandably, they could not commit to the cost of a film crew when the future of *Meteorite Men* was uncertain.

When Science Channel did order a full season of the television series, we returned to West and, even though time had passed and the fields were, by then, thoroughly hunted, I still managed to find one excellent stone on that second outing, and on camera. It was interesting to note how much the later find had weathered during the intervening seven months.

West was full of firsts for me. Accustomed to long solitary hours swinging my detector, it was the first time I hunted with a large group of friends and the camaraderie and lively dinners were a far cry from camping far out in the desert. It was my personal record for the speediest recovery of a meteorite, following a witnessed fall. My finds lay on the surface of our planet for less than a week before I carefully picked them up and placed them in specimen bags. And it was also the first time I witnessed despicable behavior by other meteorite hunters. One group went around spreading rumors and lies about their rivals, while others vainly pretended to be a university research team in order to gain access to a prime piece of land. The landowner was too smart for that and sent them packing. Meteorites are worth money, and money was bringing out the worst in some.

The meteorite world had changed. The once small band of eccentric enthusiasts who knew each other, and helped each other, had mutated beyond all recognition into a global gold rush for riches falling from the sky, and not everybody involved was pleasant.

[above] The author recovering a freshly-fallen Ash Creek meteorite.

NINETEEN

ANVIL

Phaser by his side
He's relaying information
To the starship *Enterprise*
Going to the barber
Photo in his hand
He's going have a haircut, haircut, haircut
Haircut like Captain Kirk

From "Haircut Like Captain Kirk"
By Dave Hall, Graham K. Smith and Geoffrey Notkin

AS A SCIENCE WRITER I AM EXPECTED to treat the discipline, or should I say idea, of astrology with disdain or, at the very least, sensible skepticism. There is no logical reason why Venus rising in a certain constellation (and we all know that constellations do not exist in an actual spacial sense but are, rather, distant stars that only appear to be in proximity to each other because of our particular vantage point here on Earth) could affect my chances to suddenly win the lottery, or unexpectedly hear from a long-lost friend. Despite all of that, I find the allure of astrology somewhat irresistible, especially when my friend Anne Husick emails me horoscopes from her favorite online source, and they appear to describe my current predicament or triumph with eerie accuracy. Before anyone writes in to tell me what a load of nonsense this is—or, perhaps, to salute me for keeping an open mind—let me please state that I do not actually think being born on February 1 entitles me to any particular character traits or skills.

I am an Aquarian, and one celebrated astrologer feels I am, therefore, likely to demonstrate the highest of ideals, have a strong moral sense, expect and demand absolute loyalty and perhaps even devotion from close friends. Apparently, and somewhat contradictorily, I am also believed to be spontaneous and unconventional, often prone to rocking the boat just for my own amusement or to upset the puritanically minded who, from the Aquarian perspective, might seem stuffy and unaware of how to really have fun. I am supposed to despise hypocrites and phonies. One astrology website

[left] On location for "The Tucson Ring Mystery," the first Season One episode of *Meteorite Men* to be filmed. Steve noted that the mountain behind us looks like the opening scene from *Raiders of the Lost Ark*.

spells out the things Aquarians most appreciate in life, those being adventure, fame, surprises, science and mechanical inventions, dreams, and—at the top of the list—themselves. I suppose I cannot help but reluctantly agree with most of these completely unscientific posits, except possibly the part about fame. Being recognized in the street was entertaining and uplifting the first twenty or thirty times, and I do enjoy talking to fans. I just wish some casual admirers would think of one question to ask me other than: "Where are you going on your next adventure?" I really don't know yet.

I, myself, had no clue what the "next adventure" might be, late in December of 2008 when an astrologically-minded friend insisted on reading my extended horoscope for the coming year. I imagined it would be much like the extended weather forecast: almost entirely inaccurate.

Our *Meteorite Men* pilot was slated to premiere in a few months' time, and I, obviously, had no idea what the coming year would bring. Who does? The horoscope was both lengthy and detailed, and it took my friend a good half hour to relate the entire tale to me. In the most confident, definitely-the-way-it's-going-to-turn-out tone it predicted that 2009 would not only be a great year, but perhaps the greatest of my life. Epic dreams were to come true, I would make amazing new friends, enjoy tremendous adventures, money would arrive, I was to become engaged in an important endeavor of great magnitude, and so on. Even my skeptical backbone—tempered and toughened as it had been by the abuses of English school and a couple of decades in the punk rock scenes of two continents—softened for a moment, and I thought to myself: "Wouldn't it be great if there actually was something to this astrology business and things do get that exciting?"

To my considerable surprise, they did.

[above] Preparing for the infamous jib shot in the Santa Rita Mountains, Arizona, 2009.

The *Meteorite Men* pilot episode had its premiere on May 10, 2009, on Science Channel. I felt puzzled and disappointed because Science did nothing to promote it, not even a trailer on their own network. I have since learned that this is just the way things are done, and I mean no criticism of the people at our network who treated us with great kindness and took a bold gamble by airing our most unusual series. In the world of television, pilot episodes are expected to stand or fall on their own merit. Many pilots are produced in a given year, and networks have limited time and resources for promotion. If a new television show is going to get picked up, the pilot must get good ratings, but it has to do so, seemingly, without anybody knowing about it and that concept strikes me as rather counter productive. But then, I am a meteorite specialist, not a television specialist. Or perhaps I should say I was not a television specialist back in the spring of 2009.

After founding Aerolite Meteorites LLC, I had the pleasure of issuing a standing order that my design firm, Stanegate Studios, would now devote all of its time and energy to Aerolite and, in short order, my meteorite company became my design company's sole client. Along with a few freelance designers and photographers, I oversaw every aspect of Aerolite's visual look: websites, business cards, logos, postcards, even the return address we used for shipping specimens to customers had to be just so. I had the benefit of years of experience in advertising, design, and marketing and—since nobody else seemed to be doing anything to promote our pilot—I committed myself to getting the word out, in every way possible.

My friend Caroline Palmer is an excellent photographer and I had already flown her out—at my own expense—to serve as location photographer while we filmed the pilot. I had plenty of superb images available, and I owned the copyright on all of them. I bought the domain MeteoriteMen.com, built a website, set up a Facebook page, and Caroline convinced me that getting involved with a budding new social media network phenomenon called Twitter was a good idea. A tech consultant introduced me to Ning, a modern, interactive platform designed to build online communities and, as a result, Club Space Rock—now the world's largest meteorite forum—was born in the Stanegate offices at around the same time.

During the first quarter of 2009 I put every single thing I knew into promoting the upcoming pilot. I designed *Meteorite Men* postcards and sent one out with every order we shipped from Aerolite. I posted news pieces in online astronomy forums, asked my friend and publisher Dr. Hobart King to include a *Meteorite Men* feature on his prominent science website, Geology.com (which was seen by tens of thousands of people), wrote blogs, and did interviews. One TV executive later told me, somewhat grumpily, that all my efforts probably "failed to reach a single Nielsen box," but he could not possibly have known if that was true. Who cares anyway? I gave myself the personal task of spreading the word about the pilot, near and far, and it worked. The ratings were good and Science Channel ordered a six-episode first season. That was the good news. The bad news: episodes were to be delivered in December and it was already late spring. We had six expeditions to organize, in two countries, and filming commenced early in September of 2009. Things moved very quickly after that and, for me at least, they would not slow down, ever, for the next three years.

During the several-month gap between the premiere of the pilot episode and the announcement that we would be doing a full season, our friend and original executive producer, Ruth Riven, was put on a different project, and that became a successful series, *The Little Couple*. As such, we would not work with her again, but we remained good friends, and I always felt a friendly presence in the distance, as if she kept a gentle and thoughtful eye on us from afar.

Returning to the fold and helming the first three episodes, was Bob Melisso who directed our pilot. I had already taken a great and immediate liking to Bob while we were working together in Kansas. A lean and waspish Italian-American with a slender hawk-like face, tight beard, bright eyes, and a wide and easy smile, he was a film scholar with a great deal of experience in science-related programing. Later, while focused upon the almost impossible task of hauling literally tons of heavy equipment up the side of a steep and rocky mountain, he exclaimed: "It's just like *Fitzcarraldo*," and from then on I called him "Werner," after Werner Herzog the great German auteur who directed the obsessed Klaus Kinski in that film.

Ruth handpicked her friend, Kathy Williamson, to serve as executive producer for the first season. Kathy would be our show runner, the person who oversees all aspects of the series at the production level, and would also direct Episodes Four, Five, and Six. I was most impressed that Kathy flew out to Tucson from Los Angeles, on the first day, to meet us in person and give us a pep talk. Kathy is petite, sophisticated, fiery, full of spirit and passion, and in the television business is sometimes referred to, in hushed tones, as "The White Tornado." She has won numerous awards in her career and exudes a compelling get-it-done energy. I felt that Kathy "got us" instantly.

[above] Excavating one of the satellite craters, Odessa, Texas.

It is impossible to talk about the television series in any detail without talking about Sonya Gay Bourn. A tall, attractive, and statuesque brunette with long hair, Sonya would be the only member of the road crew to work on all three seasons of the show. A writer, director, producer, and sometime professional stand-up comic, Sonya is a human dynamo. In rock 'n' roll she would have been our tour manager, but she did so much more than oversee the crew and logistics, and at various times during the coming three seasons of filming and 120,000 miles of travel, she would also serve as camera operator, medic, driver, surrogate mom, location scout, director, editor, researcher, wardrobe consultant, diplomat, and many other challenging capacities in order to get her hosts and crew back to friendly shores in one piece. Sonya, it seems, knows some important official, military liaison, or indie film producer in almost every town on the planet with a population of more than fifty people. Her influence and attention to detail live in almost every aspect of *Meteorite Men.*

I met Sonya, Kathy, and the rest of the crew, oddly enough, in my own house on September 8, 2009. As I live less than an hour's drive from the first scheduled episode's filming location, my home seemed a logical staging area, and it quickly filled with flight cases, high definition cameras, crates of water and first aid equipment, lights, food, coolers, survival gear, and personal suitcases. It all really was quite exciting for everyone, except my regal and impatient cat who was upset by the disruption to her scheduled nap time.

As Kathy discussed with us how she expected the season's work might unfold, there was—in the background—a great deal of commotion and whispering going on, and somebody ordered me not to look through the front windows of my own house. I became quite mystified. Later, with everything in place, Steve and I were ushered outside for the unveiling of a carefully planned surprise, and one engineered particularly for my benefit. Squatting magnificently on a trailer, after being driven all the way from its birthplace in Tennessee, sat the impressive Hydratrek, a go-anywhere tracked vehicle that Sonya nicknamed the *Rockhound.* I have been fascinated by tanks and amphibious vehicles since I was a child and the *Rockhound* was both. Half jokingly, some months earlier, I sent an email to one of our producers asking if he could "Please get me an amphibious vehicle for the show." The last thing I expected was to actually see such a thing, but Steve and I spent the later part of that day—the very first day of *Meteorite Men* the series—driving our turretless tank up and down the sandy washes near my home, like two big kids with the greatest toy of all time. The *Rockhound* was used, in varying degrees, in the first three episodes we filmed: "The Tucson Ring Mystery," "Odessa Crater," and "Ash Creek Fireball"; and again, much later, in the "Homestead" episode of Season Three.

For several weeks after completing location work for Season One, the *Rockhound* remained at my house awaiting shipment back to Tennessee. My neighbors, who already find me somewhat odd, were perplexed by the 3,300-pound bright yellow monster in my driveway, and visiting friends were thrilled when I offered to take them out for "a spin in the tank before sunset."

Filming in the Santa Rita Mountains outside of Tucson in late summer is a hazardous undertaking. The average daily temperature at that time of year hovers around 110 degrees Fahrenheit, and fans of our work often ask me why we film in the desert in the middle of the summer, as if it was my idea or something that I had any control over.

When a production company has an idea for a new television series, they might create a short film at their own expense, sometimes called a sizzle reel and usually about five minutes long that, hopefully, demonstrates the concept of the show in an engaging manner. Meetings are then set up and that reel is shown, by a senior producer, to the development staff at television networks in an attempt to generate interest. If the network is suitably impressed, they may instruct the production company to make a pilot episode; if the pilot does well in the ratings, the network may order a full season. The network puts up most or all of the money to make the programs, and the production company does the actual work in creating the show: hiring crews, arranging travel and accommodation, supervising editing, music, scripts, graphics, credits, and a million other tasks, all of which need to be carried out according to a strict timetable.

A few months after filming begins, a rough cut of each episode is delivered to network executives for approval. The network may come back to production and say they want more action, or less narration, different music, or a funny bit with a dog. There might be a period of discussion about those requests and episodes may be recut one or more times. Eventually, everyone, or nearly everyone, is happy and a broadcast date is scheduled. This process is costly, complicated and time consuming. While the hosts and crew are on the road filming, say, Episode Four, the post-production team is already hard at work editing Episodes One and Two.

There isn't any extra time for mistakes or for redoing things. The scheduling of television programs is planned far in advance, so when the network says episodes are to be delivered in December, it does not mean January. In order to get the Season One shows to our client on time, we had no choice but to work extremely quickly and that entailed filming near the height of a blazing southern Arizona summer.

It is important to note that the hosts of a show, or "talent" as we are called in the industry, typically have little or no say in what actually makes it to screen. Steve and I did, however, work closely with production during the development period for each season. We had the specialized—and sometimes secret—knowledge of strewnfields, hunting techniques, and more than thirty combined years of experience to draw upon.

We shot the first three episodes back to back—one in Arizona and two in Texas—between September 8 and September 24, 2009. It was both gruelling and fantastic. We had one day off and spent it doing laundry and trying to find spare parts for damaged equipment.

If there is sufficient light, and there was, film crews expect to work 12-hour days. Several times we went longer in order to capture a critical shot. People who work in television really want to do it, and I discovered immediately that despite long days spent at an accelerated pace, rushed lunches in the oven of the desert, the danger of snakes and heatstroke, and endless duties that are demanding both physically and mentally, nobody ever complains. I suppose that, if you are a complainer, you do not get hired a second time, and word does get around in the business.

"The Tucson Ring Mystery," was the first episode filmed, though not the first to air, and it was not even part of the original short list of Season One locations. The Tucson Ring is an iron meteorite weighing 1,400 pounds and lives, today, in the Smithsonian National Museum of Natural History in Washington, D.C. It is a spectacular celestial sculpture with an overly large natural hole, giving it a ring-like appearance. Along with two other masses (one of which has since been lost), the Ring is believed to have been found sometime prior to 1845 in the Santa Rita Mountains southeast of Tucson. For many years it was used as an anvil in a blacksmith's shop, and eventually made its way to the Smithsonian during the 1860s. The Tucson Ring is one of the most visually remarkable meteorites in the world; on the rare occasions when small samples, removed long ago for analysis, are made available on the collectors' market, they sell for hundreds of dollars per gram. One could argue that the Ring is the most valuable single meteorite in existence.

The most intriguing part of the story concerns the original find location, referred to in old journals and diaries as "The Valley of Iron." It is claimed that only three masses, out of many, were removed. If that is true, other pieces from the Tucson Ring fall are lying somewhere up there in the wilds. As a result, meteorite hunters, prospectors, and the curious have combed the ragged mountains and canyons for decades in the hope of finding the Ring's missing family. Such a discovery could be worth millions.

It was really my fault that we were working out there in the awful heat—well, my fault and also the fault of my friend Warren Lazar—and it all came together at the last minute. Warren is a famous rock 'n' roll musician, composer, and part time gold miner, and he looks the part, too, with his long David Bowie-like hair and dashing outfits. For many years Warren and my late, great friend Jim Kriegh of Gold Basin fame, were close pals and hunting partners. A few short weeks before we started filming Season One, Warren related to me a near-incredible tale about his role in the greatest mystery in all of meteorite lore.

A prospector named Leon spent years in those hills, using unconventional techniques while searching for rare metals. In the course of his work he discovered numerous

[above] Returning to harbor after a day of filming on Lake Mead, Arizona.

pieces of iron and marked the find locations on a map. When Leon passed away, he bequeathed the map to Jim Kriegh, and when Jim passed away, the map was handed down to Warren Lazar. Warren offered to share it with me.

We spent many afternoons up in the mountains, in harrowing terrain, and were very nearly struck by lightning during a thunderstorm. Using metal detectors, we found a number of promising iron fragments. So certain that one of them was the real thing, I called production and stated: "If this isn't a meteorite I'll stand on my head for a week." They gave the episode the green light and we started filming shortly thereafter, near Box Canyon in the Santa Ritas.

With our meager luxuries—a rickety sunshade and coolers packed tightly with damp sandwiches and Gatorade—Steve constantly made wisecracks about when his personal trailer might be arriving and asked, repeatedly, if he would have his own makeup and wardrobe girl for the next episode.

On the afternoon of our first location day, our crew was in the process of setting up a complex and somewhat risky shot in which Steve and I motor right to the edge of a precarious cliff without actually falling into the canyon below. We ran a couple of practice drive-ups and I managed to not once propel us over the cliff after which we would have rapidly plummeted to certain death. With everything in place Dave Marlin, our primary camera operator, got on his walkie-talkie and asked Bob Melisso to come over and check the shot. Bob had been sitting in the command truck for several minutes, vigorously applying sunscreen. He hopped out of his vehicle and walked past my truck towards the jib.

I started laughing. "Steve," I said, "look how much sunscreen Bob has on his face."

Dave was yelling at Bob and pointing up at the jib.

"Bob! Come and let me know if this shot is okay," he called out again.

Bob glided by, then wheeled around and stuck his head right in through my open driver's side window. His face was so encased in sunscreen he looked like a man made entirely of whipped cream.

Dave called out a third time and Bob squinted over at the jib, perched madly at the very edge of the cliff like a bat hanging from a suspension bridge, and then peered back at me with an insane expression on his face, heavily caked in white cream, and I was laughing so hard I could barely breathe. He opened his eyes wide, like a crazy person, and barked at me: "And they called me out of my trailer for *this*?" It became adopted as a popular catch phrase, and all through the production of *Meteorite Men*, whenever something went wrong, Steve or I would repeat Bob's comment.

Shortly after completing the jib shot, we saw the bear.

When our convoy of vehicles roared up to the filming site for the very first time, I asked Bob and Sonya if I might give a short safety briefing. While several members of the team were experienced with desert operations, others had come directly from offices in Los Angeles or Seattle and I did not want any casualties.

"Listen up everyone, please!" I began. "This is a hostile environment. Watch out for rattlesnakes. They live here, and so do scorpions, desert centipedes, fire ants, black widow spiders, and numerous other things that will bite or sting you and some of them are deadly. Walk slowly, and keep an eye out for snakes. Don't turn over rocks or logs unless you are wearing gloves. And watch out for cactus, especially the cholla and barrels. Some of those spines will go right through an army boot."

"Tell them about the coyotes," Steve piped up.

"We do have coyotes, but they're wary of people and we probably won't see any."

"What about wolves and mountain lions?" Steve asked, wryly.

"Oh, yes, the wolves and mountain lions." I smiled. "Do stay alert, but they don't really live in these parts."

"What about bears?"

"Oh, yes, most definitely. You should watch out for bears as well, very dangerous." By this point I was, I thought quite obviously, winding everyone up, just for fun, because the idea of seeing a bear in the Santa Ritas is preposterous.

"Oh, my god! Are there really bears out here?" a young production assistant asked, already clearly wishing he had remained safely in California.

"I wouldn't be overly concerned, but do keep an eye out for rattlesnakes and scorpions, seriously."

A few hours later, we completed the tricky truck and jib shot, with Bob's face still covered in layers of sunscreen. As the crew started to disassemble the jib, my friend Suzanne Morrison who was doubling as a P.A. and location photographer yelled out: "Holy cow, look at that!"

A large and fierce-looking black bear bounded across a hillside immediately to our north. I could not have been more surprised, and it remains the only wild bear I have ever seen in Arizona.

The poor P.A. looked absolutely terrified and was by then, no doubt, also worried about wolves, lions, and possibly monsters as well. He kept close to the trucks for the remainder of the shoot.

I thoroughly enjoyed almost every moment of filming Season One. After Tucson, we headed to the Odessa Crater in Texas, the same site that Steve and I visited on our second joint expedition back in 1998, and it almost felt like going home. The admirable Tom Rodman was still there and the crater remained much the same, except for a lovely, modern museum that now stood beside it. Various scientific groups and universities gave us, on loan, some of the most sophisticated hunting equipment available anywhere in the world, including ground penetrating radar and a state-of-the-art unexploded ordnance detector designed for the military. With $250,000 in borrowed equipment we found nothing at all; it was Steve's expert eye that saved the expedition. He noticed something dark stuck in a gravel road close to the crater. It turned out to be a moderately weathered Odessa meteorite. Around it were hundreds of others and, using nothing but steel rock hammers, we pulled eighty pounds of space rocks out of the road, which goes to show that sometimes, when hunting for meteorites, the simplest approach is still the best.

Next up would be another familiar site, although we had been there much more recently: Ash Creek, the site of "The Great West Texas Meteorite Hunt." Seven months had elapsed since our first search there, when our team came home with about one hundred stones. Our second outing was far less successful: many hunters had scoured the area during the intervening months, and we found only two meteorites on camera, although mine was much larger than any of the thirteen fresh stones that I found the first time around.

In October the team headed for Mohave County and we filmed one of the most visually striking episodes at Gold Basin, a location already so well known to us from

[top] Getting my crew ship-shape onboard the S.S. *Meteorite Men*, Lake Mead, Arizona, 2009.
[above] The talented and charming Bob Melisso directs a jib shot during the "Odessa Crater" episode.

previous hunts it almost felt as if we were working in my own back yard. After months of negotiations the U.S. National Park Service graciously gave us permission to hunt inside the relatively untouched National Recreation Area surrounding Lake Mead, well within the boundaries of the strewnfield. For years Jim Kriegh and I spoke of trying to get to the north shore of the lake, an almost entirely inaccessible area where we were certain meteorites lay in abundance. The north shore is so hazardous—liberally populated by the Green Mojave Rattlesnake with its deadly neurotoxin, and laced with precipitous cliffs and ravines—that the Park Service only cleared us to work there if we were, at all times, accompanied by a ranger who was an expert in desert survival.

My idea, all along, had been to take the amphibious Hydratrek across the lake and make a D-Day-style landing on the north shore. The waters in Lake Mead are calm and I expounded over and over again what a spectacular scene it would make. Unfortunately, the Park Service was having none of it, fearing our antics would encourage others to attempt the same thing in their own amphibious vehicles. I do not actually know anyone else who has one, but there you go. Next we tried to get the okay to land our team by helicopter on the north shore, but that was dismissed by almost everyone except Steve and me as being far too dangerous. I knew a pilot who claimed he could do it, "Any day of the week, in the dark, and with sunglasses on," but, again, that idea did not travel very far.

In the end, we used a half million-dollar houseboat to make the perilous landing. Steve and I lived aboard the ship for several days and had more fun than at any other time in all of the filming we did. I had my staff bring up a captain's hat which I wore at all times while underway. I made Steve say, "Aye, aye, Captain," at the end of every sentence and also sometimes required him to speak in a pirate accent. I had driven up from Tucson with my guitar in the back of the truck, so I sat on the boat's top deck, each evening late into the night, playing songs that echoed out across dark waters.

During our first attempt to gain a beachhead on the far side of Lake Mead, I piloted the boat into Little Burro Bay, a narrow and steep-sided channel full of submerged boulders. One of our viewers later described how much he enjoyed the scene: "You trying not to crash this half-million dollar boat into the cliffs or run it aground, with everyone telling you what to do, and Steve standing on the shore yelling at you. Now that's television!"

Christo Doyle, our executive producer at Science Channel flew in for the shoot. A young and energetic TV professional, he pitched in like an experienced desert hand, piloting the boat, hiking the mountains with us, carrying gear, and even found his own meteorite. Christo went on to great success as the executive producer of *American Chopper*, *Gold Rush*, and several other hit shows.

As we were working on restricted Federal land, an academic sponsor needed to sign on in order to validate the scientific aspect of our hunt, so we agreed to donate all finds to our colleagues at the Oscar E. Monnig Meteorite Collection in Texas. It was worth it for us just to experience hunting in virgin terrain, rich in meteorites. I wanted Christo to have the meteorite he found and I tried my best to acquire it for him, but our permit was quite strict and every find had to remain permanently in the museum's care. When I returned home, some months later, I sent Christo a different Gold Basin, of similar size and shape from my own collection, as a memento of his adventure in the desert with us.

My favorite *Meteorite Men* episode is the very first one that aired, "Buzzard Coulee & Whitecourt Crater." It was the only Season One show filmed outside of the United States, and it ended up being very different from what we expected. My friend Lisa and I were so successful at Buzzard Coulee in Canada earlier that year, everyone thought it a good Season One location. By the time we arrived at the site, it was the middle of October. The brutal Canadian winter arrived early that year and headed squarely in our direction.

On the second day of filming temperatures dropped to around 10 degrees Fahrenheit and the crew had to wrap heat packs around the cameras to stop them from freezing. Steve and I found a few Buzzard stones, but many people had searched the ground since Lisa and I were there and a freak snowfall the next day covered any that we missed. With snow lying everywhere and our equipment on the verge of failing we had to pull back to the hotel with only half an episode in the can.

Meanwhile, Bob Melisso was back at headquarters in Los Angeles, frantically making calls to meteorite specialists in Canada. About a day's drive northwest of us lay the recently discovered Whitecourt Crater. Approximately 1,100 years old and extraordinarily well preserved, the impact site had only been recognized two years earlier. A protected zone was quickly established to safeguard the unique feature and the Canadian Government warned of a $50,000 fine for anyone caught damaging the crater or removing meteorite fragments from the restricted area. We considered it entirely off limits until Bob called with the amazing news that eminent Canadian

[above] Steve Arnold and the author preparing to visit Whitecourt Crater for the first time.

scientist Dr. Chris Herd from the University of Alberta had invited us to visit the crater, with cameras, and do some hunting. We would be among the first people, ever, to see this untouched site.

Whitecourt is miles from the nearest road and Sonya hired a fleet of ATVs to carry Steve and me, and the crew, along tortuous snow-covered paths, deep in the woods of northern Alberta, to a place of startling grandeur and wonder. Whitecourt is a perfect bowl-shaped crater a little over one hundred feet in diameter. Stating its width makes it sound small and two dimensional, like something from a geometry text, but it could easily hold a large country house.

The crater was shrouded in snow, and the trees growing inside it were stripped of their leaves. It was an otherworldly scene and I was so in awe of this locus of our planet's interaction with the cosmos that, when we hiked down to the floor, all I could think of doing was lying down on the ground and looking up in the direction from which the meteorite had come, eleven centuries earlier.

We ended up with only a few hours of hunting time at Whitecourt, but we found some marvelous meteorites. Exploring the wintery and pristine crater remains one of the best memories from any expedition of my career.

October 30, 2009, was the final shoot day for Season One. We closed with "The Dry Lake Bed" and had the pleasure of again hunting with our friend Sonny Clary, who made the initial discovery there, and his dog Brix. Sonny claims that he has trained his dog to find meteorites, and whether or not that is true, Brix is most

[above] Nearly going into orbit after finding my first iron meteorite at Whitecourt Crater, Alberta.

certainly the only German Shepherd I have seen riding an ATV.

Sonny agreed to take us to a secret site where he had made an incredible find, some months earlier. While exploring a remote dry lake bed he discovered scores of meteorites—all of the same composition—lying on the alkali-rich surface, and in close proximity to each other. Steve and I were the very first people, after Sonny, to hunt there, and the circumstances were almost too good to be true. We believe that a single large meteorite landed on the lake bed, thousands of years ago, and as a result of weathering, broke down into a multitude of fragments. Meteorite hunting was, literally, never so easy. We ambled through a lunar-like landscape, picking up space rocks with our magnet canes, every few steps.

Against all odds we found meteorites in every one of the six Season One episodes. I have occasionally been asked, by people who found it hard to believe that we were so successful in such a short period of time, if we planted any meteorites. While a certain amount of artistic license was used, here and there in the editing and in order to create drama in the narrative, we really did find all of those rocks. Both our production company, and our network, were adamant that *Meteorite Men* should be real and that we should not fake any finds, not that we would have been willing or able to do so anyway. The search for meteorites is, for me, a quest for knowledge, meaning, and adventure. I wanted everything to be as authentic as possible, and it was.

[above] A handful of stone meteorites found while filming "The Dry Lakebed" episode in Nevada.

When *Meteorite Men* is no longer showing around the world, I will still be a space rock professional. Our reputations, and the reputations of the people we worked with, were much too important to even flirt with the idea of doing anything unethical.

For the next two seasons we would travel with a much larger crew and visit faraway continents. While the later episodes are, perhaps, grander in their scale and visuals, there is something special and endearing to me about those first shows. We were a small, dedicated and efficient team, close-knit, determined, and sometimes numbering only six, including Steve and myself. We traveled fast, adapted well, went with the flow and managed, somehow, to complete six expeditions in eleven weeks. Perhaps the horoscope had been right after all. 2009 was a hell of a year. I made extraordinary new friends, saw wonderous sites, and I consider filming Season One to be the greatest adventure of my life.

By the start of 2010, the final cuts were delivered to the network, and the first episode premiered on January 20. Just a few days before that, and shortly before Steve and I entered the period in our lives where we would be recognized almost daily on the street, I gave a meteorite lecture to a lively audience as part of the Science Café program, run by Arizona's prestigious Flandrau Science Center. The late O. Richard Norton whose book, *Rocks from Space*, had been so very influential upon my career in meteorites, and who became a personal friend in the late 1990s, was a former director of the Flandrau. I felt honored to be working with the center that had been so important to him.

Following the lecture, I happened to meet a woman of extraordinary beauty, charm, and poise. Libby was a professional ballet dancer and, fortunately for me, had a great interest in astronomy and rocks. I had with me a modest collection of meteorites on display as an accompaniment to my talk. Libby walked over to examine them. We spoke only briefly, but I was already smitten. Our first date was at the broadcast party for Episode One of Season One, in Tucson's astronomy-themed Sky Bar. We have been together ever since. For the first time in my life I experienced the strange but joyous feeling of caring about a person more than my work. Ahead of me lay fifteen more episodes, and many months of travel, adventure, and hardship, but, throughout all of it I had, finally, a real reason to come home.

If Libby and I stand on the flat roof of my house outside of Tucson in the evening, we can glimpse the Santa Rita Mountains, faint and dusty with distance. The iron fragments that Warren Lazar and I found on our initial scout for "The Tucson Ring Mystery," and most of the other pieces Steve and I uncovered on camera, were not meteorites after all. Luckily, nobody remembered the foolish offer I made about standing on my head. One small piece turned out to be the real thing—and a fascinating one too, completely new to science—but, alas, not part of the legendary Tucson Ring.

The mystery remains, and I still occasionally head up into those lonely hills in search of the lost Valley of Iron.

TWENTY

TIME IS AN ILLUSION

On my way to wild places
We spent some time eye to eye
But wasn't it always
Just a perfect copy that I knew?
And today in my walled and sunny garden
I can almost dismiss it all as another hazy view

From "Radiate, Baby"
By Geoffrey Notkin

WHEN THE NEWS ARRIVED that we would be making a second season of *Meteorite Men* and that five episodes were to be filmed overseas, there were two things I yearned to do above all others: See Australia's Henbury Craters and return to Chile's haunting Atacama Desert.

During earlier episodes while working at sites that Steve and I already knew, such as Ash Creek and Gold Basin, we enjoyed a marked advantage in our mission to recover meteorites. It takes time to get to know the land, to superimpose a two-dimensional strewnfield map created in a lab on top of a living landscape, test and calibrate equipment, and sometimes just figure out where you are actually standing, compared to where you might want to be standing. Where we go there are often no road signs.

On February 27, 2010, just as we were commencing serious planning for our upcoming travels, Chile was savaged by a powerful earthquake. With a magnitude of 8.8 it ranked as one of the most powerful seismic events ever recorded. Since the epicenter sat close to the capitol of Santiago, there were concerns that damage to the airport and infrastructure might impede travel in the country. Chile, however, is a big country and in a telephone conversation with production, Steve made an amusing point: "When there's an earthquake in Los Angeles, they don't close the airports in Ohio. Those are the kind of distances we're talking about."

We knew Chile, and knew meteorites could be found at Imilac. The idea of returning to that strange and miraculous orange desert with the accumulated knowledge of the intervening years, and superior hunting equipment, kept me awake at night. And, perhaps, I would at last get to see Monturaqui Crater. I lobbied hard for Chile and, in the end, we were given the green light.

How Chile had changed, and yet, remained the same. Antofagasta, hardly recognizable as the rundown outpost where we took shelter after our breakdown at La Pampa in 1997, now boasted modern hotels, rental car offices, chic restaurants, and a larger airport. We arrived in early August—which is winter in the Southern Hemisphere—and a bracing wind blew in from the frigid South Pacific. Seabirds called out as we drove along the rocky shore, and I felt as if I had slipped back into a happy and familiar dream.

Steve and I had aged since we said goodbye to Imilac; but when our trucks galloped up that long ochre slope once again and parked beside the old campsite, nothing had changed, nothing at all. The impossible sky remained the same enamel blue, and the hills to our west still slumped against the horizon like giant sleeping camels, far off in the clear and precise mountain air. I walked to the exact spot where I pitched my tent and tied it to our haggard Toyota in the ferocious wind, back when I was still thirty-six years old. I recalled precisely how my sun shade had been whipped away by that sudden gust—just over there, it was—and stared at my own footprints preserved, evidently forever, in the uncaring and impassive Atacama sand. While thirteen long and memory-filled years elapsed in our temporary and measurable lives, the hands of the great meteorite clock that remains hidden from the quotidian world of humans had moved forward, imperceptibly, about one minute.

The Imilac strewnfield is situated so far from civilization, camping with the entire crew became our only option. In addition to Steve and myself, our convoy consisted of senior producer Sonya Bourn, our director, two cameramen, two sound men, a camera tech, a mountaineering survival expert, a medic, a chef, and two drivers. In all of our travels it was one of only two times when we had a cook on staff, and I cannot state too strongly how reassuring it felt to have a real cooked dinner waiting for us after twelve hours of hiking, digging, and filming at 11,000 feet.

A huddle of abandoned and roofless miners' cabins made of rough stones was selected for base camp. We rushed to get tents set up before the blackest of nights descended upon us and by 9 p.m. the temperature had plummeted to 24 degrees below freezing. Standing beside a roaring fire on the stone floor of an ancient cottage, in the middle of the immense Atacama Desert, I looked at the huddled figures around me and had an epiphany: all of these people were here, and all of this time, effort, and money had been expended because of a dream I had as a child. I suddenly felt an intense camaraderie for this odd band of talented professionals, most of whom had traveled all the way from California because they believed in what Steve and I were doing.

We found plenty of meteorites, but most of them were small. Large meteorites, lying starkly on the surface, had been picked up long ago, but space gems still lay in the dusty earth and they looked exactly like the ones we had found in 1997. Again, I felt as if nothing had changed. I could have always been at Imilac, and the passage of time nothing but an illusion.

The second night we made camp at the abandoned Imilac train station, and in the morning I asked if I could slink off for a few minutes to take a photo of the old Imilac sign.

"There's an old sign?" our director, Marvin Blunte asked. "Let's film that."

The sign was rusty, 40 inches long and crudely fashioned into the shape of an arrow out of hammered pieces from a steel oil drum. The word "Imilac" is painted upon it in orange and appears as if scrawled by a child. Riddled with large bullet holes, the weatherbeaten sign was bolted onto a metal pole buried in a pile of sand, and had doubtless watched over the unchanging desert for scores of years.

To the north of Imilac lies Monturaqui, an ancient crater blasted out of the desert by an iron meteorite 100,000 years ago. For thirteen years I had gazed upon photographs of it after we failed miserably to locate the site in 1997. And I am not in the least bit surprised that we failed. The drive to the crater was so arduous it took us hours to cover a few dusty miles, and the convoy suffered repeated flat tires. During one pit stop the chef got a kettle going and handed around small white paper cups with a thin, pungent, and steaming hot tea.

"Coca leaves," he said.

The source of the drug cocaine, coca leaves in their natural state are perfectly legal in Chile and have been enjoyed for centuries by mountain dwellers because tea produced by boiling the plant's leaves is a gentle stimulant and cures altitude sickness. The tea tasted delightful and I felt invigorated.

[previous page] The Imilac strewnfield; it's a big country.
[this page] Mountains overlooking the Imilac strewnfield.
[following page] The Meteorite Men at Monturaqui Crater, Atacama Desert, Chile, 2010.

As a joke I ran over to the chef, pretending to shake and yelled at him: "Gimme some more of that tea, *I must have more!*" I wanted to take some back with me to the States but everybody shook their heads sternly and the chef said: "No. America customs don't like the coca leaves."

Monturaqui is a monument to the power of the cosmos, and to what one cast-off asteroidal remnant can imprint upon the features of our home planet. Our cameramen knew how long I had wished to see it and they wanted to capture my initial reaction on tape, so I waited for ages, a mile or so back, while they set up the shot. Finally, Steve and I drove up, got out of the truck, and I was literally speechless. I just could not think of anything to say, sank down on my knees and stared in wonder at the sun-toasted remains of an inferno that occurred a thousand centuries before. I find all meteorite craters magnificent. They are the scars left on our world by the detritus of other worlds, but Monturaqui is different. There is no gift shop, no guards, no guides, no fences or admission fees, or rules and regulations. It is just a crater, alone, brooding, ancient, and timeless.

We set up camp on the floor of the crater, and what an experience for a seeker of meteorites to sleep in the hollowed-out space that one of them formed long before there were cars, or roads, or countries.

As the day drew to a close, I opted to sit by my tent and watch the shadows travel crazily, and speedily, across the crater walls.

Just after sunset I noticed Steve partly hiking and partly sliding, fast, like a maniac, down the side of the crater towards camp.

"Where have you been?" I called out.

"Geoff! Geoff! Look what I found!" he shouted.

From the deep pockets of his baggy coat, Steve produced handful after handful of impactites—earth rocks melted by the crater-forming event, with tiny fragments of the original meteorite imprisoned within them forever.

"It was amazing! Just as the sun started going down, the light changed and I could see the rocks everywhere. They stood out so well. I collected all of these in about ten minutes."

I had missed out. Call time was 7 a.m. and Steve and I made a pact to get up before sunrise—no matter how cold it might be—to see if the gentle pre-dawn light might create a similar phenomenon.

That night I slept in a small tent, in an extreme cold weather sleeping bag, with thermals and fleeces, and a wool cap, and I was the happiest boy in the world. Although I passed a week inside the vast Popigai Crater in Siberia eleven years earlier, the manageable size of Monturaqui could be firmly grasped, seen, and understood. It was the only night of my life that I spent feeling fully cradled in the wondrous embrace of a feature created by the fury of the cosmos.

I woke at 5 a.m., put on my gloves, took the canteen I had kept with me in the sleeping bag all night so the drinking water would not freeze, quietly unzipped my tent and tip-toed over to Steve's.

"Oi, Steve," I whispered, so as not to wake the crew. "Are you up?"

A grumbling and mumbling emerged and he eventually fell out of his tent, in the darkness, onto the cold and hard desert floor, bundled up like a giant mummy.

In almost total darkness we clambered up the precipitous and—in some places near-vertical walls—and surfaced at the rim as the first tangerine hint of dawn shimmered in from the east. The effect of pale early morning light on the rocks surrounding the crater was nothing short of extraordinary. Once-molten impactite fragments appeared much darker than the ordinary stones around them, and we picked one up every few feet. One extremely dark speck, about the size of a peanut, caught my eye. I touched it with a magnet and it stuck enthusiastically. I pulled out my glasses, awkwardly because of my bulky gloves, and examined the coal-black stone chip more closely. It was, without a doubt, one surviving shard of the original meteorite, almost weathered away by the cruel action of 100,000 years of desert wind and abrasion. I scoured the landscape, and found more—lots more.

All remnants of the original Monturaqui meteorite ever found, combined, weigh about four kilograms, making it one of the rarest iron meteorites on the planet. On that chilly morning, in the narrow sliver of time between complete darkness and the beginning of our shoot day, we added about 400 grams to the total known weight— roughly ten percent, in weight, of all Monturaqui specimens ever found.

As the sun bounded over the horizon, unfettered daylight began arcing across the slopes beyond the crater and as it touched the surface, the strange low-light effect ceased. We ran away from the creeping sunlight, like vampires, searching for patches of shadow and hoping to pick up just a few more pieces. Once the ground became fully illuminated, any remaining meteorites and impactites instantly vanished back into a dry ocean of shattered terrestrial stone. The pre-dawn hunt was over.

We climbed back down the crater wall, intent on arriving in time for the start of our work day. As we descended, our teammates were waking up and we could hear the faint rattling of pots and pans below us. The crew gathered together and all of them seemed to be staring at us. As we got closer I could tell they definitely were.

"What the hell are you guys doing?" our audio man, Ponch, called out.

"Oh, we got up early and went hunting," I replied, as we hopped over the last few boulders and bounced into camp.

"No, really, what were you doing up there?"

"Seriously, we got up before dawn and went hunting. We found tons of stuff."

Ponch shook his head and some of the other crew members laughed.

"Man," he said. "I already thought you guys were hard core, but you really must be completely nuts to go up there in the dark, in this cold, to look for rocks."

If we were nuts, at least we were nuts with a lot of meteorites.

During the 1997 Chile Expedition Steve and I enjoyed the local grape brandy, pisco. It is a wonderful drink: strong, flavorful, a little sweet, with a taste like wild mountains. The only Spanish Steve learned on the trip was: "Pisco y Pepsi, por favooooor."

One the way back to the States we wanted to take some home with us, so Steve bought two one-liter bottles in the little duty free shop at the Antofagasta airport. He put them in his bag and we went through security. The customs office stopped Steve, opened the bag, pulled out the bottles and said: "Senōr, you cannot take theeez on the plane."

"But I just bought them in duty free over there."

"That is the duty free if you are landing only."

"What?" Steve replied, incredulous. "If you can't take stuff from that duty free on the plane why don't you say something about it?" He was pretty annoyed.

"I am sorry, Senōr, it cannot go on the plane."

I watched all of this with some irritation and then asked: "Hey, can we drink them now?"

The security officer claimed he did not understand.

"Look," I said. "My friend just bought this booze from your duty free and you're telling him we can't take it on the plane, so I'm asking you if we can drink it now."

"I guess eeez okay."

So, right there, in the middle of security, we put two chairs next to the x-ray scanner, opened the bottles and toasted the second Chile adventure. Unfortunately for us, they were fitted with those glug-glug slow pouring stoppers which severely impeded our drinking, so we sat in the chairs sucking grape brandy out of them like they were baby bottles. A young woman next to us, running one of the security scanners, was laughing so hard she had tears in her eyes.

After a while, a senior officer walked over and he did not look pleased.

"Gentlemen!" he snapped. "You cannot consume alcohol here in the security."

"That guy told us we could." I pointed at the first officer who, now, also did not look pleased.

Some discussion ensued during which he insisted that they were only following "regulations ordered by your country," pointing at us, and I did not see how U.S. customs could have any control over what happened at the Antofagasta airport, but I also was not a hundred per cent sure I wanted to cause an international incident over it.

Reluctantly, we handed over the partially consumed bottles and went on our way.

Steve was laughing again.

"I thought you'd be really mad about that," I said.

"I don't care about the cheap pisco. I'm just glad the guy didn't see this $50 bottle of wine I had in the same bag." He produced a very large bottle of fine Chilean merlot and laughed so hard his face turned red.

"So," he continued, once he had his wits about him again. "Do you want to go to the real duty free, over there, past security, and get some more pisco?"

"Oh, most definitely."

TWENTY ONE

DOWN UNDER

A couple of years ago
I didn't feel like myself
I said, "Well, I must be something else"
Adults were huge dolls
Tenements were battleships
From alien worlds
And the sun came down
And I learned to sing about life

From "Coffee Black"
By Lach

FIRMLY SEATED AMONG MY TOP TEN FAVORITE SONGS of all time is the pop/reggae hit "Down Under" by the Australian rock band Men at Work. I would quote the words if I could, but copyright is a tortuous beast and I did not feel like doing the paperwork and dickering with a music business publisher in the hope of getting permission to pay them a hefty fee so I could reprint a few lines. The bizarre and humorous lyrics to "Down Under" and its hypnotic melody have whispered "Australia" to me ever since the song first came out in the fall of 1981, when I was still playing full time with my band Proper Id.

In September of 2010 we traveled to Australia to film the final two episodes of *Meteorite Men* Season Two. I spent an hour or so in the One World Alliance lounge at Los Angeles International Airport, contemplating the grand adventure that was about to begin, then boarded an imposing two-deck Airbus for the 14-hour flight to Sydney. From there I continued to Alice Springs, a small desert city populated by artists and adventurers—not on the way to anywhere, and that reminded me of my own adopted home of Tucson—to meet up with Sonya and Marvin. While they went over the details of our vehicle rentals, I stole a half hour and wandered through Alice's arts district, rich in mystical Aboriginal paintings and wood carvings.

I promised myself that if I ever made it to Australia, I would return with two things: an excellent leather bush hat with crocodile teeth, and a didgeridoo. I had no trouble finding the hat in Alice. I chose carefully and when Steve predictably, a few days later, began berating me—"Oh, I see it's now okay for the vegetarian to have a hat with crocodile teeth on it"—I smugly presented my documentation. The teeth in my hat band were all naturally shed by crocodiles who lived happily and safely in a preserve. The discarded fangs were later collected, I imagine, by daring humans.

Steve had missed a connecting flight, so we were one person down, with several vehicles to ferry a couple of hundred miles to our base camp. Sonya asked if I minded making the drive on my own.

"Are you kidding?" I replied. After spending about twenty-four hours on planes, and in airports, a little solitude was most appealing.

In Australia they drive on the left-hand side of the road, just like England, and I could not have felt more completely at home in a strange land. As I rolled out of Alice Springs on that September evening, alone in a tough, waterproofed, go-anywhere 4WD truck with a snorkel attached to the side, and headed into the unknown wilderness and towards the Henbury Craters, I put my personal *Meteorite Men* 2010 Road CD in the player and listened to "Down Under," at full volume, and with all the windows down, seven times in a row. As the sun set, the sky burst into a melange of orange and violet, and the red soil of the Australian Outback lit up as if on fire. Australia and I shouted "G'day" to each other at last, and the grandeur, beauty, and boldness of that vast unspoiled frontier in the Southern Hemisphere filled my heart with unspeakable joy.

Home for the next week would be a rustic place, part road house and part log cabin motel, next to the highway, and entirely in the middle of nowhere. It was simple and comfortable, and about seventy miles from the craters I had longed to see for over a decade. On the run from Alice to our motel I had to drive, somewhat frustratingly, right by the turnoff to the craters, and I let out a cheer when the sign for Henbury flashed by in my headlights.

I rose before dawn, and sat on a little wooden chair, mesmerized, as the wild Australian sun began to light up puzzling and angular trees that could have been a science fiction movie set. The first thing I really noticed were the birds. Wild parrots were everywhere, some as large as chickens. Impertinent blackbirds with starched black

[previous page] The author standing in one of the smaller meteorite craters at Henbury.
[above] Sunset in the Australian Outback.

tails and long slender talons, so very similar to the magpies of my youth in England, clambered and clattered across the tin roofs of our cabins.

Only few days earlier I was working north of the Arctic Circle with Steve, digging for iron meteorites in the Swedish tundra during our "Muonionalusta" episode. I now found myself, literally, at the other end of the world. Henbury would be a completely new site to us. Although I had studied maps and photographs for years, it takes time to become familiar and comfortable with a new hunting location. Certain areas were off limits, while others had doubtless been picked clean by earlier hunters. I asked for five scout days prior to filming, but there was not sufficient time or money. I was given two days, and those were later reduced to one following a last-minute schedule change. And then Steve missed his flight. I, therefore, got to spend most of the scout day, blissfully alone, at one of the most magnificent natural exhibits of scientific wonder on Earth.

If there is one site, one location, one quintessential and unmissable place on our blue planet where the force and majesty of meteorites have utterly and absolutely made their mark—as if the cosmos branded Earth's face with a Titan-sized blacksmith's hammer, and said: "I was here"—it is Henbury. Although the 1997 Imilac expedition with Steve inspired me and pointed me down a long and sometimes treacherous road of adventure, pockmarked with successes and failures, it was, without a shadow of a doubt, my close encounter with that alluring Henbury iron at the Smithsonian, in 1998, that irrevocably committed me to a life of meteorite hunting. Not only did I need to have a Henbury meteorite, I needed to find my own.

Henbury meteorites are the color of the desert in which they fell: iron-red, sanguine, and scarlet, and are twisted into harrowing and mesmerizing shapes—a timeless reminder of a furious impact upon our planet more than forty centuries ago. The angle of fall was extremely steep, a fact shown by the remarkably close proximity of the fifteen known craters (not twelve, as is stated in the literature). The smallest is comparable in size to a New York City bathroom; in other words, not large. The four biggest craters are shouldered tightly up against one another; they share a common rim, along which awed visitors can walk. It is the only place in the world where a person can stand at the locus of four meteorite craters simultaneously.

Henbury was first recognized, officially, as a crater field in 1931. Ranchers had known about the site long before then and it still lives, mysteriously, in Aboriginal legend as an evil place to be avoided. I hoped to interview an Aboriginal elder, on camera, about the myths surrounding the area, but Jason, our Outback survival expert, told me that nobody would speak of the place to outsiders.

In the '60s and '70s it was still possible to find meteorite fragments on the surface. A few unscrupulous collectors dug into the crater walls, and drove trucks outfitted with magnets into the depressions. In order to protect this unique site from damage and erosion it was designated as the Henbury Meteorites Conservation Reserve and collecting specimens is no longer allowed. Except by us.

The Australian National Park Service generously granted us permission to hunt around the craters, but not inside them, which was fine, because at Henbury, explosions propelled fragments out and away from the sites of impact.

Sonya and Marvin were eager to get a feel for the area before we began filming. The three of us drove the one-hour stretch from our base camp to the Henbury turnoff, and then traveled about thirteen kilometers down a rough gravel track.

September is late winter/early spring in Australia and although Henbury is a site of monumental importance to meteoriticists, impact specialists, and astronomers, it is not exactly on the must-see list for the average tourist. Roughly half way between Alice Springs and the world famous site of Ayers Rock (now known by Australians as Uluru), Henbury attracts the curious and the obsessed; a few of the former, and a very few of the latter.

It began to rain. I saw two kangaroos in the distance and five or six large parrots, evidently puzzled by the unfamiliar moisture falling from the sky. The Outback is dry, very dry, and rain is unusual. Heavy rain is almost unheard of, and on the rare occasions when it does cascade onto the red desert, washes flood, and sand turns into a gurgling, treacle-like mass, eager to snare the tires of vehicles, and the shoes of hikers.

During our visit, the Henbury area received its heaviest rains in thirty-five years. Locals sometimes call that part of the Northern Territories "The Big Red" but, for the week we spent there, it became "The Big Green." Plants sprang up everywhere, and as water accumulated in the craters, exotic birds by the thousands came to drink.

On that first day I was so unconcerned about the weather, I barely noticed the rain. In fact, it turned out to be a blessing. Sonya and Marvin dropped me off at the entrance to the preserve—a cute little picnic area and information board—and said they would return in a few hours. Weather evidently deterred the few tourists who might have been journeying between Alice and Uluru that day and I was left to commune with the place that had lived in my thoughts for a third of my lifetime.

A one-kilometer-square area encompassing twelve of the craters, and all of the large ones, is marked by a tidy and precise wire fence. That is the heart of the preserve and we would not be allowed to hunt within its confines. The preserve extends for some distance in all directions beyond the fence and all of that was ours. After Sonya and Marvin's truck trundled off down the now-muddy track, I left my detectors and tools under a bush, outside the fence, opened the single narrow gate, walked down a neat gravel path, my 5.11 Tactical boots crunching on egg-colored pebbles, and walked into a wonderland of cosmic mayhem.

Not another soul ventured into the preserve that day. It was just me, and the craters, and birds who chirped happily from rain-slicked trees, observing my deferential and deliberate journey among the ancient remains of cosmic bombardment.

On the east side of the concentration of craters lay a marshy area, dotted with spindly trees, swaying in the wind. As I trudged through the clinging mud, my boots made a sucking sound with each step, as if the ground was trying to seduce me down into the underworld. I grasped one of the narrow tree trunks to steady myself, and noticed three little birds, bright green, talkative and flirty, perched directly above me. "Are those budgies?" I said out loud.

Budgie is the British word for parakeet. I kept budgies as pets, when I was kid, but I had never seen them in the wild. With their bright plumage, ivory-colored beaks, and round, black, quizzical eyes, they appeared curious, irreverent, and absurdly happy. They chattered at each other, and at me, and with more who began to arrive by the hundreds and thousands to bathe and drink at Henbury.

Later, while I was hunting outside the preserve, a vast flock of these mischievous miniature parrots soared and frolicked above me, like a swarm of brightly-colored flying fish. I was a lone figure in the landscape, with no trees or buildings around me.

The throng of birds wheeled, dived, and careened directly towards me, precisely at eye level. Entranced, but also fearing a high-speed collision, I pointed my metal detector up into the sky and they parted, barely over my head, and split perfectly as if they had many times rehearsed their dazzling and pitch-perfect choreography, into two lightning streams of vivid green and yellow, blazing past by me like feathered rockets.

I remembered standing in the Louvre, in Paris, and gazing upon the *Mona Lisa* for the first time. How well we all recognize that image and how strange it is to know it, and also not know it, when the original work is actually viewed in real life. I recall thinking that she was smaller than expected. The Henbury Craters were, in the same way, familiar strangers, and much larger than expected.

Years of studying maps and photographs had fixed every detail of the craters' dispersal and arrangement upon my memory. Even though I walked along seemingly unknown paths for the first time, I could just as easily have been in my own garden, or in my local pub, so perfectly aware was I that the four large craters lay in this direction, and the smaller clusters lay over there, towards the Bacon Range.

Partly as a result of research and planning, and partly trusting my own hunch regarding where undiscovered meteorites should still be, I knew exactly the spot at which I wanted to begin my hunt. I left the fenced-in area, retrieved my detector, tools, and GPS from their hiding place and began my hike. I was on a mission. I did not bother to turn on my detector, or sweep the ground as I walked. I would know when I arrived at the correct place.

I came to a gentle slope, its surface old and element-beaten, and covered with plates of terrestrial stones, shattered into elongated wedges by millenia of weathering. I turned on my Fisher F-75, ground balanced it, and moved purposefully across the floor of brittle rocks. Within minutes my detector found me a target, a small one, but with an audio return clear and sharp against the sighing wind and rain. I scraped through the rough ground, and a little orange shard, a hardened droplet from an asteroid's core, climbed onto my magnet and glistened. It was only a minute piece—4 or 5 grams—but it was my first Henbury.

Twenty minutes later the detector spoke again, but this time loudly, demanding that I find what lay buried beneath my feet. After a few seconds of digging, my rare-earth magnet pulled a chunk of crimson iron from its four-thousand-year hiding place, and it clung there as if it knew exactly where it was designed to be, like a old key slotting back into a familiar padlock. At 56 grams it was the size of a walnut, not massive or particularly valuable, but still brilliantly warped by the unmeasurable forces of impact into a swirling sculptural form, unlike any other in existence.

How does a heart react when a challenge, long dreamed-of, is accomplished? It might feel joy; it might feel vindicated; it might dismiss the victory as not really good enough, and promptly assign a new, and hopefully more satisfying task. I was so caught up in the moment, I cannot fully remember what my heart might have said, but I imagine it could have been: "Here you are, where you have always wanted to be, this instant, this minute sliver of time, on Earth, connected by effort and luck and determination, through time and space, with the heart of an asteroid, in the rain."

The purpose of scouting is not exactly to give me quiet time to find meteorites for my personal collection. The idea is to determine good hunting zones, in advance, so we can make the most of our time when the cameras and crew arrive. I found one good piece, and several small ones together, among the broken rocks, and—with some difficulty—tore myself away. There were more unknown meteorites in the ground, just there, I was sure, and I would leave them undisturbed for Steve and the cameras.

I spent the rest of the day sampling other areas, marking promising zones on my GPS, and watching the budgies cavort across grey skies. I found several more meteorites, and each time I came across a good area I collected one or two pieces, recorded the exact location, and moved on.

Late in the day, Sonya and Marvin returned, satisfied with an assortment of shoot locations that would add local color and context to the expedition. I saw the white 4WD truck lumbering towards me from far away, hoisted my pack back onto my shoulders and headed back to the meeting point. I was standing by the access gate to the central preserve when they arrived.

"How's it going Meteor Man?" Sonya asked as the truck pulled alongside.

"Couldn't be better." Slowly, and with exaggerated panache, I pulled a wet and dirty specimen bag from my pocket and held it up so she could see the twenty or so meteorites sealed inside: "I think we gotta great show!"

Two months earlier, Steve and I spent a few days filming an episode of the hit television series *American Chopper* in New York State. We visited the Orange County Choppers headquarters, where Paul Teutul Senior's team of engineers were hard at work designing and building a *Meteorite Men* custom motorcycle. Many of OCC's creations end up as show bikes that remain on display in museums or private collections. I remember the OCC engineers being excited at the thought of building a bike

[above] Trying out the *I Robot* motorcycle at Orange County Choppers HQ.

that would actually be used in the field. They constructed a 900-pound, three-wheeled monster, painted bright orange, with racks for our metal detectors and tools, and a central tower to house our sophisticated tracking GPS unit. The "Meteorite Men Bike" episode of *American Chopper* premiered on September 2, 2010. At the same time, the bike itself was locked in a specially-built crate en route for Australia.

The OCC bike appeared in "Alpha Site, Kansas," the first episode of Season Two, and Paul Senior delivered it to us, personally, in a farmer's field. We promptly covered the beautiful machine in mud and dirt when we used it to drag a 223-pound meteorite out of the ground. It also appeared in the "Wisconsin Fireball" episode and would, doubtless, have been the star of both our Australian episodes had it not been for the appalling weather.

Steve and the motorcycle arrived in the Outback at about the same time; Steve massively jet-lagged but eager to hunt, and the bike carefully stored in a towering and teetering moving truck that did not look as if it would do well on the rough tracks leading to Henbury.

We managed one full day of filming with the OCC bike before the real rains came. Much of the interior of Australia is made up of dirt tracks. Australian off-road vehicles are designed specially to cope with the extreme conditions typical of the Outback and are routinely fitted with snorkels—an exhaust pipe that goes up the side of the passenger door and expels fumes over the top of the vehicle. A truck with a waterproofed engine compartment and properly-fitted snorkel can churn through water deep enough to partially cover its windows. I know this from experience.

[above] At the Alpha Site in Kansas with the *Meteorite Men* bike and Steve's giant detector.

Twice each day, our entire road team ran a 13-kilometer gauntlet from the main road to the craters. The evening trip was always worse because, it seemed, water collected during the day and a flooded section of road that was under a foot of water in the morning might be under three feet by late afternoon. As a result, we were sometimes forced to end our shoot days earlier that we would have liked, for fear of getting stranded by rising flood waters.

During the course of making the Henbury episode, we conducted four separate rescues of stranded tourists who were unprepared for the dismal road conditions. The most challenging involved freeing a Volkswagen van, full of happily intoxicated hippies, from the gluey mud; the most amusing featured an Irish motorcyclist who was attempting to cross Australia, solo, on a small and underpowered dirt bike. With his motorcycle firmly entrenched in a sheet of creeping mud, he busied himself collecting dry brushwood in the hope of building a ramp or roadway to dry land. At first he refused our help, claiming he was fine, but we insisted, and eventually freed his bike from the morass. Instead of thanking us he asked if we had any beer we could give him.

Resilient and mighty though the OCC bike was, it could not get down heavily-flooded roads, and neither could the moving truck it had arrived in. The engine is slung low on the bike, and driving a hot motor into cold water is not a good idea, although that did not stop Steve from trying it several times.

Steve is adventurous by nature; some might say reckless. On the third day of filming, we managed to get the bike part way along the track to Henbury, in order to get some driving shots. To my considerable misfortune, Steve was driving, while I hunched, somewhat fearfully, in the passenger compartment. Marvin wanted a dramatic shot of us cruising along the flooded road. On the first pass, Steve took it slowly and we emerged relatively unscathed.

"That wasn't bad," I said, foolishly.

This prompted Steve to turn around and hurtle through a stream, a second time, at top speed. Our velocity, and the angle of the guard panel in front of me, were such that a sheet of freezing cold, muddy, and filthy Outback road water blasted me in the face like a fire hose, filling my eyes, nose and mouth. It must have made for some spectacular footage that was, unfortunately, not used in the broadcast episode. After that, I declined to ride any further on the bike at Henbury, if Steve was driving.

I consider Henbury to be one of our most successful expeditions. We found hundreds of fragments, my largest being more than half a kilo. On the final day of filming I was off, as usual, in the rockiest, most difficult-to-get-to spot I could find, swinging my detector awkwardly under brambly bushes. At a particularly precipitous spot my F-75 let out a shrill yelp and I looked down to see a button-sized Henbury meteorite on the ground, just in front of me.

"Why would a little piece like that give you such a strong signal?" I asked the detector.

I put my rock pick next to the little iron, expecting it to jump onto the attached magnet, but instead the pick was almost pulled out of my wet and slippery hand, down onto the iron, where it stuck. I tugged, quite hard, and out of the ground emerged an astonishing orange and red meteorite in the shape of an elephant's head. Like an iceberg, most of the rock had been hidden below the surface.

I have seen larger Henbury irons, but none finer. Of everything we ever found, on any expedition, anywhere, it was my favorite piece. In time, the Australian government kindly granted us export permits, and "The Elephant" remains in my private collection, a happy reminder of our muddy but magnificent days at Henbury.

From Alice Springs, we all flew to Adelaide, then on to the small town of Ceduna, where we rented a trio of off-road Toyota Hilux diesels—one of the finest vehicles I have ever driven. Each sported an orange flag on a pole about twelve feet high. When I asked the rental agent about the purpose of these flags, he informed me they were so the "big dumpers" (dump trucks) would be able to see us "out there in the bush."

"How big are the dumpers?" I asked, feeling a little uneasy.

"Big enough so they can't see ya without one o' those flags, mate," he replied.

Dotted along the route of Australia's transcontinental railroad is a series of tiny hamlets. The propellor-driven aircraft of earlier decades did not have sufficient range to traverse the country from east to west, so a series of refuelling stations and small airports were constructed and supplied by train. Forrest is one of them. Its quiet aerodrome could have stepped directly out of a World War II fighter plane movie. A monolithic corrugated iron hangar—home to an inquisitive white-faced barn owl, perched high up among aging beams—sagged slightly with age, but remained grand and imposing, dominating the airstrip and taking my imagination back to an age when aviators wore white silk scarves and leather flying helmets. Forrest was the last taste of civilization before our final Season Two destination—Mundrabilla.

The Nullarbor Plain is a limestone plateau, a primeval former seabed covering some 200,000 square kilometers. Nullarbor means "no trees" and it is one of the emptiest places I have ever seen. Grey limestone extends, in every direction, to the horizon and beyond. Kangaroos and wild camels wander the treeless expanse, as do giant lizards and some of the world's most dangerous snakes. It is also home to the Mundrabilla iron meteorite.

Mundrabilla is an enigma. It is unlike any other meteorite and is described as "anomalous," in that it does not fit conveniently into any existing class. Several multi-ton pieces were found in 1911 and, since then, thousands of smaller, zoomorphic irons have been recovered in the strewnfield, which is one of the largest in the world. The original Mundrabilla masses were rich in silicate minerals, filling the spaces between iron elements that are shaped like slugs and snails and raw peanuts. As the masses hurtled through the atmosphere, it appears that some of the silicates melted, and scattered worm-shaped iron meteorites over hundreds of square kilometers.

We followed a rough track from Forrest to an abandoned railway stop where a battered sign announced we had arrived at Mundrabilla.

Mundrabilla is so far removed from habitation that camping was our only option. The hard-working crew set up a mess tent, latrine, and even a portable shower which was a nice idea but did not work very well, especially in the wind. We were joined by Dr. Andy Tomkins, a young and enthusiastic meteorite specialist from Monash University in Clayton, Australia. It was a rare opportunity both for us to work in the field with an academic expert, and to actually camp inside the strewnfield. Mundrabilla irons were, literally, strewn here and there over an area of stupefying proportions. Each evening, as the camp fires got going and food was cooking, I knew I would see Andy wandering a half mile or so from camp, spending every possible minute on the hunt for space rocks.

[top] A Henbury iron meteorite, tucked between terrestrial rocks, exactly where it fell thousands of years ago.
[above] One of four impromptu tourist rescues that we carried out at Henbury.

[top] At the disused Mundrabilla railway siding, en route to the hunt site.
[above] A Mundrabilla iron meteorite, exhibiting a typical zoomorphic shape.

Camping is not something I do for fun. When meteorite hunting in remote locations there is sometimes no alternative, and if I am just hunting then camping is palatable. When working, however, and trying to look presentable on camera, spending five nights in a tent on a windswept plateau can become taxing. After days of trying to shower under a luke-warm plastic bag, shaving out of a tin cup, and attempting in vain to do something with my hair I was, perhaps, a little grouchy. Between us, Andy, Steve, and I had, after several days, found nearly a hundred meteorites, most of them about the size and shape of a cocktail pickle. By the final morning of the shoot I felt grungy, irritable, tired, and frustrated that a larger find had eluded us. I was also really missing Libby. We had not spoken in over three weeks.

As I wandered around the campsite, watching the sun squeak up over the endless tabletop of limestone, Sonya walked over to me with the satellite phone in her hand.

"Would you like to make a call?" she asked.

Sat phones are expensive and tricky to use. Out there in the Nullarbor, the phone had to be held at just the right angle, for just the right period of time, in order to connect. It was used sparingly to check in with production headquarters.

"What, on the sat phone?" I asked, surprised. "Isn't that only for emergencies?"

"You look like you could use a little cheering up."

I walked a few hundred meters from camp, dialed into the satellite, then keyed in the number to Libby's apartment—a world away.

It was morning for her too, but a whole day earlier. The surprise and delight in her voice sounded better than a good breakfast, a hot shower, and a big meteorite find put together.

"But, how . . . how are you calling me?"

"Dear Sonya very kindly lent me the sat phone. It's super expensive and I can only talk for a minute."

I described the wild landscape to Libby, told her about the camels and lizards, promised to email when I got back to town, and also promised to be back with her in a few days.

It is remarkable how much a few words with your sweetheart—separated by time and distance—can illuminate the day. I felt energized, and determined to give Mundrabilla one last shot.

The problem at Mundrabilla is the sheer size of the fall zone. Weeks would have been required to conduct even a partial search, so we came up with a risky plan. Steve, Andy, and I plotted—as best we could determine it—the flight path of the meteorite that had thundered over the Nullarbor thousands of years earlier. Rather than carry out a detailed search in a single area, we followed that line, drove one kilometer and searched on foot for exactly half an hour. Then we moved one more kilometer down towards the big end of the strewnfield, and started again. The further we went in the direction the largest pieces fell, the fewer meteorites we could expect to find, but our chances of finding a single big piece were marginally better.

Late in the day, our convoy stopped for lunch. As usual, I wolfed down my sandwich in five minutes and spent the remaining time hunting by eye with my magnet cane. After nearly an hour I heard the truck engines firing up in the near distance, and Sonya calling out to me to come on back.

I turned and headed towards the parked vehicles. Fifty feet in front of me a thin and twisted tree, lonely and out of place struggled to grow in the wasteland. It appeared so incongruous in the otherwise-flat landscape that I walked over, just for a look, on my way back to the makeshift lunch camp.

Plainly on the ground, beside the tree like a bronze statue in the sun, sat the largest Mundrabilla I had ever seen outside of a museum. The 870-gram piece was as spectacular as it was rare: almost nothing had ever been found in that size range. There were the few multi-ton giants, and thousands of tiny ones, but none in between. It was eventually granted an export permit by the Australian government and resides, proudly and permanently, in my personal collection.

Later, I told Libby that it was all thanks to her, and she had brought me the best of luck during the final hours of the final shoot day of Season Two.

I did get the didgeridoo. With no personal shopping time during our journeys across Australia, I was supremely lucky and found a nice one at the airport, shortly before departure for Los Angeles. The Qantas flight crew kindly allowed me to stow the four-foot, hollow and polished tree limb in the cabin. Marvin was one of the last passengers to board, and as he walked onto the plane, we both started laughing. He had one too.

Memory and music are powerful allies. There are, in my life at least, a precious few, most-loved, most-adored timeless songs that carry within them the ability to transcend the disappointments and difficulties of everyday life. Those recordings can—whatever unexpected tragedy or calamity might have befallen me—lift me up, put my spine and senses into some kind of order, and shunt me back on the tracks of existence and creation. "Down Under" is one of those songs.

All of this time, whenever I heard it, I would instantaneously be transported to the era when "Down Under" was released, and to the Id Mansion, as we called it—a fallen-down white suburban house in Rockland County, New York, surrounded by ordinary trees. My band, Proper Id, lived there together for a couple of heady years in the early 1980s. Those ingrained associative memories of songs we loved when we were first starting to embrace life as independent individuals never change; they are indelibly printed into our experience and understanding and enable us, sometimes and briefly, to relive our youth.

Except for this one time.

I was cooking dinner the other night and, on a whim, I played "Down Under" on my fancy iPod docking station—a technological wonder we could not have imagined back in the punk days. When I heard those pounding metallic drums and floating reggae guitar, my thirty-year point of reference reset and all I could see were quilted trees outside the sleeping half-town of Forrest, and Australia's sweeping, empty roads rushing past me in the impossible red sunset.

Ever since I watched an eccentric, fun-loving, traveling Australian man empty a bottle of laundry detergent into a geysir in Iceland in 1973 I wanted to be there, in that untamed final frontier of civilization. Nothing about Australia is small, or ordinary, or conventional. The people, the landscape, the wildlife—and, well, the meteorites too—are all better than they need to be. In all my travels it is the place I loved the most.

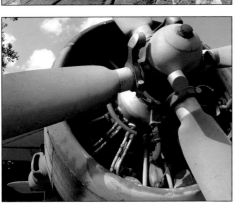

TWENTY TWO

THE LONG HUNT

None the wiser for the thoughts
That bring you down
Just the dream of bright lights
Buzzing 'round and 'round
Maybe one day they'll
Remember what they said
We saw green Marine light
Shutting out the red

From "Shutting Out The Red Light"
By Martin Brett

MY LONGEST AND PERHAPS MOST CHALLENGING expedition began very quietly at 3:30 a.m. on a Saturday morning. It would become the first half of the third season of *Meteorite Men*.

In order to be on the LOT Polish airlines 5:25 p.m. nonstop from Chicago to Warsaw, I had to catch a 6 a.m. flight out of Tucson. That meant a 3:30 alarm and a six-hour layover in the windy city.

Libby drove me to the airport, along with three large bags, including an 82-pound Pelican case loaded with metal detectors.

Once in Chicago, I was startled by an unexpected question.

"How goes the big meteorite hunt?" asked Mike, a reservations officer with a gentle Polish accent, who recognized me before I could hand him my passport. He was delighted to know we were filming in his homeland, and asked which towns I might be visiting. When I said I could not tell him because of confidentiality agreements, he said: "So, the project really is secret."

I noticed letter-sized flyers, seemingly designed in a hasty and urgent manner, fastened with tape to the front of each check-in booth. They bore a photograph of a horrific-looking industrial chainsaw, circled in red with a diagonal slash through it—the universal symbol for "No"—and an official notice stating that passengers must not take said items on the plane. The haphazard way in which the flyers hung from each counter made me imagine a panicked officer—just moments earlier—dashing franti-cally from one desk to the next with a roll of tape in one hand and wad of alert posters in the other, crying out: "Aleksander! Pawel! Listen to me, don't let any of chainsaw on plane!" as if this was somehow a recently devised security protocol.

I passed the slow hours of my layover in a shadowy VIP lounge, shared by LOT, EL-AL, Turkish Air and a few other carriers. It gave off the Old World vibration of a faded European gentleman's club. I chuckled to myself, remembering a scene in my most favorite of all science fiction tales—*The Hitchhiker's Guide to the Galaxy* by Douglas Adams—in which a mysterious and much sought-after character named Zarniwoop hides himself away in the First Class lounge of a derelict starship in a forgotten space port.

After boarding, one of the flight attendants promptly got on the intercom and delivered a heartfelt plea for forgiveness for our late start. She said she hoped we could still enjoy the flight, despite the terrible delay. She also said it was caused by "Passengers who had problems with documentation." We were only twelve minutes late.

After apologizing a second time, she strapped herself into one of those complicated backwards seats that aircrew use. They may look strange, but they are very sensible. In the event of a crash your back and the padded seat absorb the impact, rather than your stomach with the seatbelt cutting into it. I knew this from my Royal Air Force cadet days, when we flew in jets where all the seats faced backwards. The obvious safety benefits were explained to me by an officer onboard. When I asked why all aircraft were not built that way, he replied: "Civilians don't like to face backwards because they can only see where they've been instead of where they're going."

Evidently, the Royal Air Force will take whatever steps are necessary to protect its people, but if you are a paying airline customer, you're on your own.

Most of the flight crew spoke English, which helped, as the only Polish I knew at the time was the name of the airline, and the word "bialystok" which is actually a town, not a kind of bagel. At least in Poland.

On the morning of June 26 I arrived in Warsaw. At that moment, Steve and our Season Three show runner, James Rowley, were in Sweden scouting for the "Return to Muonionalusta" episode. I had enthusiastically volunteered to go to Poland with Sonya, ahead of the crew, to reconnoiter the mysterious and alluring Morasko meteorite craters—a little-known site that had intrigued me for years.

Nothing could have prepared me for how much I enjoyed Poland. The Poles are a noble and courageous people who were brutalized by both the Nazis and the Communists. Hitler and Stalin carved up their country like a cake at an engagement party, and Poland remained under the dictatorial heel of the Soviet Union for decades following the end of World War II. Despite this, the Poles are fun-loving and jovial, and speak with a musical and animated cadence.

After 21 hours on the move I arrived unsteadily at the Warsaw Sheraton, with my voluminous collection of luggage, and whispered a silent but sincere "thank you" to our travel coordinator who mercifully had the foresight to arrange an early check-in for me. And, I had an unopened bottle of authentic Green Buffalo Grass vodka in my bag, whatever that might be, which I apparently purchased from duty free on the airplane.

I should have gone immediately to sleep, but my hotel was less than a ten-minute walk from the Polish Academy of Sciences and I could not resist. A European colleague advised me by email that the museum boasted a small but important meteorite collection, and I must not leave Warsaw without inspecting it. My lack of sleep combined with a quick sampling of the vodka—which tasted like straw, rum, and tequila mixed together—had me feeling tired but elevated and I walked out into the brisk Warsaw sunshine, headed for the museum, and found myself in the most beautiful of city parks. I was amazed by the grandiose height of aged oak trees. They were most definitely more than 65 years old and I was surprised they were not obliterated during World War II.

When I arrived at the museum, it was closed.

I rose early the next morning, and while awaiting the arrival of our expedition vehicles, decided to try the museum again, even though everyone assured me that all museums in Poland are always closed on Mondays.

I walked through the leafy park for a second time and noticed some activity inside the museum buildings. The sign said Monday hours commenced at 9 a.m. It was 10 a.m. and the three staff members present were still getting themselves together. I was the only visitor, and some time passed before they allowed me into the main exhibit hall. A heavyset woman with a red and white hanky wrapped around her head frantically dusted everything in sight, as if the entire museum was being prepared specifically for my benefit.

The Polish Academy of Sciences is a charming and unpretentious place where specimens are housed in a combination of vintage hand-worked cabinets and small, modern display columns. The care that went into preparation was evident at every turn, particularly in a wall-spanning explanation of the family tree of fossils. I imagined a quiet and thoughtful Polish academic spending weeks or months assembling the finest examples of ammonites and fern fossils, and carefully mounting them on that wall. A labor of love.

After examining the geological display, the paleontology wall, and a luminous room entirely filled with colorful Baltic amber, I developed a sudden and unreasonable fear that the meteorite exhibit might be closed. I peeked through a heavy wooden door, only barely ajar, into a room that, at first glance, appeared completely dark and abandoned. As my eyes adjusted, I realized the low-lit space housed the meteorite collection. Everything about that tiny room was imaginative and atmospheric. Meteorite specimens were set in recessed, glass-covered vaults flush with the wall. Each exhibit nook was covered entirely in black velvet, with no ceiling or floor lamps. Tiny fiber optic cables, almost invisible in the darkness, transmitted concise pools of light onto the meteorites. They appeared to float in the vacuum of space and the effect was enthralling.

I gazed upon an entire cabinet devoted to the Polish fall of 1868 in Pultusk, captivated because when Pultusk stones are seen on the collectors' market, they are almost always pea-sized. In that peaceful and empty closet-sized room sat a magnificent 8.1-kilo monster and numerous other extraordinary examples of varying sizes.

I had breezed through the previous rooms fairly rapidly, but once I settled into the meteorite exhibit, I stayed for a while. I remained the only guest at the museum, and the woman who dusted the exhibits could not have been more suspicious of me.

I spent at least twenty minutes staring at Polish space rocks, in silence, and completely absorbed. The dusting lady walked in, several times, to look at me in a more-than-slightly-disapproving manner, making it quite obvious she assumed I was up to no good. She would watch me for a few minutes, walk out, walk back in, busy herself with polishing the handle of the exhibit room door, or pretend to find something particularly disturbing about one small section of the ceiling over my head.

I nearly handed her a *Meteorite Men* business card in a nonchalant manner, as if to say: "Please don't be concerned about anything, I *am* here on official business," but my natural tendency toward on-location secrecy wrapped itself around my shoulders like the claws of an old parrot. You never know when a minor official is going to post a notice on their Facebook page saying: "One of the guys from that 'Meteor Men' show on the television was in the museum today," and then, in a single moment, everyone with any knowledge of the field would deduce where we were and where we were going.

"Fixer" is a television term for a local expert who arranges transportation, film permits, ensures that hotel check-ins go smoothy, dialogs with area authorities, translates when necessary, and generally takes care of solving any and all problems that crop up while on location. It can be a demanding job, and is best suited to someone who has a lot of film experience, requires little sleep and has a patient and positive attitude. Our Polish fixer, Jan, was perfectly suited for the task. Thin and energetic, thirty-six, dressed in a tight black t-shirt and black tactical pants, with a shaved head, tight blonde goatee and petite glasses, he reminded me of my friend and fellow science writer Chris Cokinos, author of *The Fallen Sky*.

Jan spoke good English and was well versed in Polish history. After he, Sonya, and I packed out of the hotel he treated us to a high-speed driving tour of Warsaw. I knew 85% of the city had been demolished by Nazis during the 1940s, so I was puzzled by the abundance of elegant classical buildings. Jan explained that, following the war, much of the city was reconstructed in a determined attempt to recapture Warsaw's earlier grandeur.

[above] The Morasko crater preserve in Poland.

Jan is a worldly man who has worked on major feature films and traveled internationally, and I found his perspective on post-Cold War Poland illuminating. He pointed out hideous modernist apartment buildings: "They were the Communists' plan for how we should live; packed together in cramped concrete apartments with small windows."

The Russian-era buildings formed a grim and stark contrast to the rebuilt classical Polish architecture, and Jan told us, with ill-concealed glee, about a national scandal brewing: the Communist-built structures were starting to fall apart.

"The Communists built them to last thirty or forty years and now it's been thirty or forty years and nobody knows what to do about them. Eventually, one of these buildings will collapse and then our government will finally have to get involved."

The traffic in Poland is indescribable. It feels as if you are—always at any hour of the day or night—driving at rush hour through a heavily-congested town on the outskirts of London. Jan explained that there are no highways that cross the country (or lead to Warsaw for that matter), and that after many years of a focused, government-sponsored highway-building initiative they had managed to complete only 12 kilometers of working motorway.

"And we need 12,000 kilometers," he added for good measure. "So, the national pastime in Poland is complaining. This is our official sport, and if a group of people should be out in the evening drinking, and anyone mentions the weather, or the motorway system, then immediately will begin a long and angry conversation in which everyone will take part. In U.S.A., or Western Europe if something is not working, you look at problem and say: 'How can we fix this?' Here in Poland we would rather bitch about the problem for years and do nothing."

In spite of this, the Poles cannot help but maintain a sunny outlook on life, and perhaps the opportunity to indulge in an entertaining critique of national problems is one good reason for not fixing them.

Our drive of approximately 225 kilometers, which might have taken 2 1/2 hours back home, consumed eight hours.

"You see, this is main road in all of Poland," Jan said, as we inched along a single lane of tarmac that appeared to intentionally wind through the gridlocked center of every town. But it was a lovely early summer day in Poland, the windows were down, I was in a new country, and I also needed to familiarize myself with my latest Garmin Rino GPS. The manual was thick in pages and in my somewhat jet-lagged state, the technical details kept me happily occupied for hours.

Poznan, our base of operations for the Morasko expedition, is a fine city of cobbled streets, grand stone buildings, and multi-colored tramways. An undiscovered gem of Eastern Europe, it could have been the long-lost progeny of Amsterdam and Paris. At the hotel came the rather strange experience of meeting my friend Andrzej Pilski for the first time. He runs the Polish magazine *Meteoryt* and had been working as my Polish publisher and translator for well over a decade. In fact, the account of Chile's 1997 Atacama expedition was my very first piece to be printed in a foreign language, where it received the unusual title of "W Drodze do Imilac."

Andrjez is also a celebrated astronomer, observatory director, and a member of the Society for Barefoot Living, which means he never, ever, wears shoes, regardless of temperature or terrain.

"Is that my friend, Andrzej Pilski?" I asked.

"Is that my friend, Geoffrey Notkin?" he replied.

I shook hands with a man I had worked with, and corresponded with, regularly for twelve years but never actually seen face to face. Andrzej and I enjoyed a fine dinner of pierogis and white wine and I fell asleep sometime after midnight.

I awoke at 6 a.m., too excited by the prospect of seeing the Morasko craters for the first time to sleep any longer. During breakfast—an extraordinary serve-yourself buffet with exotic cheeses I would expect in Sweden, hot trays of eggs, tomatoes and mushrooms that belonged in one of London's fancier restaurants, along with bowls of nuts, seeds, fresh fruit, and dried fruit—I became puzzled by the prevalence of British accents in this seemingly out-of-the-way old city, until I discovered that an international bridge tournament had come to Poznan.

Thanks to the incomparable Polish traffic, it took us forty minutes to cover the paltry eight kilometers to Morasko. Professor Muszynski, a noted Polish academic and meteorite expert, waited for us beside a lovely old stone house belonging to the forester who owns the land upon which the Morasko preserve sits. The professor had intimate knowledge of the site, produced startlingly detailed strewnfield maps, and with a boyish enthusiasm invited us to join him on a private tour of the Morasko crater field.

The resemblance between the forests of Morasko and the woods behind my English childhood home was instantly both magical and disorienting. The birds were the same, as were the plants and trees, and the soft paths that wandered among tall cloud-obscuring pines and birches. I could not help but recall the World War II bomb craters lying deep in the forest back in Surrey, and how I imagined they might be meteorite craters when I was a kid. The actual meteorite craters at Morasko were nestled among calm, silent trees, so very nearly identical to the woods I played in as I child that I might as well have stepped into a time machine and traveled back to the sleepy town of Purley in the 1960s. To complete the illusion, several of the craters were nearly identical in size—just as bomb craters would be—and my childhood fantasy that those hidden scars of World War II were really meteorite craters seemed to transmute itself into conscious reality.

The largest crater dozed lazily, half filled with water, and lime-green algae covered its surface from one edge to the other, like an oversized pond from a British stately home. Sun filtered through high leaves, and birds chirped and hopped among the admirable and brooding trees.

Battles from World War I and II were fought across that land, as were earlier conflicts. The zone is crisscrossed by a complex network of World War I trenches that show a remarkable degree of preservation, and it was a German soldier digging one of those trenches who accidentally discovered the first Morasko meteorite in 1914. With military history fascinating me almost as much as meteorites, I might as well have been romping across an adult playground designed specially for me. The dugouts —gradually filled in by normal processes of deposition and erosion—remained about two or three feet deep. Three-sided abutments, once the sites of gun emplacements were clearly evident, as was barbed wire and other assorted debris of warfare. I have hunted in trash-filled zones before, many of them in fact, but I have never experienced anything like Morasko.

Professor Muszynski explained that, some years earlier, the university and a Polish meteorite hunter named Krzystof Socha hatched a private deal. Socha was granted exclusive access to the protected zone on the understanding that he would catalog all finds, and give half of them to the university.

While Socha hunted through 2005 and 2006, he dug, bagged, and recorded every single target, and the numbers were not encouraging: one meteorite recovered for two hundred pieces of man-made trash. In comparison, at Brenham in Kansas, we averaged one meteorite for every thirty meteorwrongs.

Socha carried out his work with such exacting precision that the areas he had already hunted might just as well have been signposted: "Don't bother looking here." Nothing remained in the zones Socha covered: no wire, no nails, no iron residue of any kind. One area, however, within the preserve remained untouched; Socha ran out of time, or perhaps patience, and Andrzej and I concentrated our efforts there. It was immediately apparent when we moved into the unhunted zone; you could not walk two feet without hitting a target. The most abundant finds were large lead bullets from the Napoleonic era, white in color, and many of them smashed and distorted as a result of hitting a tree or, perhaps, more gruesomely, a human bone. Although these lost implements of havoc gave off a shrill sound on the detector, they were difficult to recover; with no iron present they would not stick to a magnet and we had to carefully sift through damp soil to find them.

We passed the better part of two days wandering through the lime and teak-colored forest, hunting, and exploring the craters. It was one of the few times in all of Season Three when cameras were not present and I could fully enjoy the experience without interruption, or the constant need for OTFs ("on the fly" interviews, later edited into the final cut in order to explain and comment upon the action). Andrzej hunted by my side, using one of my detectors, and found one lovely meteorite weighing about 300 grams. He spent the entire time barefoot, walking through nettles, and over barbed wire, without injury or complaint.

In Poland, I came up with an amusing and vaguely devious game to play with our viewers. During our travels I posted a daily clue to Twitter, inviting our followers to try and determine where I was, using the hashtag #WhereAreTheMM. Anyone who guessed correctly would win a prize, but I did not want to make it too easy.

Clues included such useless tidbits as: "Eventually Geoff will say 'Get thee to a nunnery;'" because of the proximity of one to the Morasko strewnfield. From Poland I also posted: "A rare species of toad & a bird from home in one place." I expected to mislead contestants and have them start researching Arizona wildlife, while my reference was really to a song-addled robin I saw at Morasko, along with a spotted toad, both of which, again, reminded me of my youth in England.

Beneath my feet, meteorites slept in the peaty soil. We would return, a few weeks later with the full crew, to shoot the "Morasko" episode. With the aid of a Deepmax 5 detector, we uncovered a 75-pound iron meteorite from six feet below the surface. It was the deepest excavation we made by hand at any time in our careers, and also—by far—the deepest Morasko meteorite ever found, and the second largest.

All of that lay in the future. The gentle hours spent during the Morasko scout were among the happiest moments of the entire *Meteorite Men* adventure for me. I moved quietly, pensively, and often alone, through a dream-like landscape that was both present and past; an exploration of a remarkable meteorite site long admired from

[top] After almost three days of digging a single hole at Morasko, our prize was a 75-pound meteorite. It was the most deeply-buried specimen found at the site, and one of the largest meteorites ever recovered in Poland. [above] The *Meteorite Men* Season Three road crew at Pultusk, Poland.

afar, and a journey through memory back to the wistful and magnificent woodlands of my childhood.

After Morasko, Sonya and I transported—just the two of us—14 cases of equipment and personal belongings to Finland where we met up with the crew and filmed at the Ice Hotel in Kiruna, the inspiration for the frozen and glassy set of the James Bond film *Die Another Day*. Kiruna became the third Bond location we worked at during our travels, the others being the European Southern Observatory at Paranal and the town of Baquedano, both in Chile, and both featured in *Quantum of Solace*.

From Finland we continued to Sweden for the "Return to Muonionalusta" episode. Despite five arduous and extremely longs days of hunting (it was summer in the Arctic Circle and we experienced round-the-clock daylight), using the finest deep-seeking metal detectors in the world, we found nothing. I was later informed that our clever competition in Europe and Scandinavia downloaded illegal torrents of the Season Two "Swedish Meteor Balls" episode, figured out exactly where we were hunting—a not overly difficult task considering only one new logging road had been cut through the endless forest—and picked the area clean.

After Sweden we flew to Russia, and how Moscow had changed in the twelve years since my previous visit! The city now boasted modern American hotels, chic nightclubs, and even car rental agencies.

We were granted a rare day off, and really should have slept, but our camera tech, Andy Shuford, and I could not bear to sit in the hotel. We took the Moscow subway across town, visited Red Square, enjoyed a traditional Russian lunch, and stumbled across an exhibit of Russian space memorabilia at a shopping mall.

The next morning, once all of our production equipment was stowed in a cargo van, we jammed ourselves into a fleet of very small and very well-used Russian cars and headed to the beautiful Moscow Planetarium, a graceful deco-style building that had just reopened, following seventeen years of dereliction. I was mesmerized by their collection of cosmonaut patches and badges, and the vintage telescopes and optical equipment on display. Again, alas, that scene was cut from the broadcast episode.

Our team then embarked upon a terrifying five-hour road journey to the venerable town of Kasimov, established in the year 1152, where we would meet up with my Russian friends, and fellow meteorite hunters, Serge Afanasyev and Dima Sadilenko. Our local drivers spoke almost no English and propelled us in a reckless manner along narrow and tortuous country roads. After two separate near misses with oncoming traffic, Andy sensibly refused to travel in the front seat any longer.

Kasimov is authentic, uncontaminated rural Russia. Donkeys wandered the cracked streets and brightly-colored wooden houses seemed untouched since Medieval times. Our convoy pulled in to a local market in order to supply the team for the coming days in the field, and we could almost have been back at the turn of the previous century. Cabbages and potatoes sat in piles on creaking wooden tables, while dogs dozed between crates of onions and carrots.

One whole wall of the market was devoted entirely to vodka. There were scores of different brands and hundreds upon hundreds of bottles. I ran to the other side of the store and found Steve.

"You've gotta come look at this!" I said.

"Well, this looks like a good place to stock the bar," he laughed.

225

I picked up various bottles and noted that the average price was about $3 per liter. In a moment of brilliance Steve suggested that we ask one of the Russians to recommend a good label for us.

Confusingly enough, we had three Dimas and two Serges on the team. Dima Two, as we called him, spoke good English, and seemed like a guy who knew his drinks.

"Dima," I asked. "Would you mind telling us which is a good vodka?"

He wheeled his shopping cart over to the wall of bottles and started examining them one by one.

"This one is good, and this one. Oh! Byelley Bars ('White Bear'), this *very* good!"

He squinted at the price tag, nodded his head approvingly, and began dumping bottles by the armful into his cart, until it was completely filled.

"Hey, Dima! Leave a couple for us, would you please?" I said, feeling I must missing out on something of great importance.

Steve and I managed to get our hands on a couple of the remaining bottles, paid for them and some canned goods and water, and headed back to the vehicles.

Our somewhat dilapidated accommodation, when eventually found, was tucked away behind the Kasimov bus station, and not very popular with the crew. Its name, when spelled out in Russian, looked uncomfortably similar to "Hotel Douchebag," a fact quickly noted by our soundman Ponch, and so it became known for the rest of our stay.

Steve is a big guy and the five-hour drive had been hard on him, crumpled as he was into an uncomfortably small car. As we collected our gear from the vehicles, he asked if anyone wanted a drink, opened a bottle of vodka, and started dispensing the contents into paper cups.

We made a little toast and then noticed a police officer walking towards us, from the direction of the bus station. A small man, with a baggy ill-fitting uniform, and overly large cap lounging on the side of his head, he marched right up to us, beaming, stomped his booted feet, and plastered a hand across his forehead in a comical salute that made him look impossibly like the British comedian Benny Hill. And then he started yelling at us.

I speak a little Russian, but not enough to understand our transgression, so I found our interpreter. After some discussion, the officer saluted again, and marched back to the bus station. Our translator seemed quite annoyed.

"This very serious. Yor err lucky I make an apology with officer. Pliz not do again."

"I'm sorry," I replied. "What did we do to annoy that officer?"

"You drink in street. Iz problyem in Russia."

I was incredulous.

"Wait, we're being told off for drinking vodka in a parking lot, *in Russia*?"

I retired to my tiny room, with its tiny single bed, sponge-thin mattress, and yellow, flowery curtains that might possibly have delighted a seven-year-old girl, without further mishap.

The meteorites at Dronino are a rare type of iron, rich in nickel and known as ataxites. There are only a few sites on earth where one might be found. The forests around the strewnfield are the mushroom capital of Russia and prized fungi are collected there by gourmets for use in restaurants, and also by the poor, who have no other option. The first Dronino meteorite was discovered, by accident, in 2000 by a

226

[top left] Vintage astronomy equipment at the Moscow Planetarium. [top right] One of the giant biting flies takes a liking to Steve's neck, Dronino, Russia. [above] One of three rare ataxites we found at Dronino.

[top] Our special expedition vehicle, *The Mule*, near the Franconia strewnfield, Arizona, 2011.
[above] Sonny Clary, one of the world's great meteorite hunters, and his sidekick, Brix at Holbrook, Arizona.

man in search of mushrooms. It was recognized by Serge and Dima and classified at the Vernadsky Institute in Moscow. They made a deal with the local landowner, and kept the find site confidential for years. Steve and I were the first non-Russian hunters ever to work at the Dronino site.

Serge and Dima are not only some of the best meteorite hunters in the world, and are also accomplished academic meteoriticists. They were certain that Dronino was once a crater field, but centuries of farming had obliterated all trace of the impact sites. Our plan was to search around, and between, the likely positions of these vanished craters. The hunt began on a July morning, high summer in the Russian countryside, and it was hot. Our fleet of vehicles drove through waist-high grass and blooming wildflowers. Large insects buzzed back and forth, and I took them to be bumblebees, until one flew in through an open window. It was a giant fly, as big as a walnut, with hideous yellow compound eyes, and fangs. I had never seen a fly with fangs. We shrieked and shoed it outside, then rolled up all the windows, despite the heat and absence of an air conditioner.

The convoy wound down a narrow forest track, branches scraping along the vehicles' sides, and arrived in a clearing, occupied by colorful tents and a roaring fire—it became known as Camp Vodka. As we parked and exited, flies descended upon us like iron filings onto a magnet. Serge roared with laughter.

"The files are blind. They are attracted to heat. Get away from cars!"

The insects were fierce but slow moving. When they landed on an arm, or neck, the victim had a couple of seconds to brush them away before being bitten. A couple of times, Steve did not move quickly enough and the savage flies actually drew blood.

Only three days were allocated for location shooting at Dronino. After dealing with the daily drive in from Kasimov, vehicle and equipment problems, lengthy on-camera interviews, and Serge periodically deciding that he would rather jump in the river than hunt, our actual time spent looking for meteorites was whittled down to a puny seven hours. If, at the beginning, someone had said: "Hey Geoff, let's go hunt at Dronino, but you can only stay there for seven hours," I would have shaken my head and stayed home. Miraculously, despite the flies and the regular and requisite vodka toasts at lunchtime, and the paucity of hours spent in the field, we found three iron meteorites totalling 4.7 kilograms. Dronino was a success, but only barely, and by the narrowest of margins. A few days later, Dima Two found a mass weighing 20 kilograms, in the same zone, which demonstrated again, and very clearly, that time is the most vital commodity in the search for space rocks.

Later, when we took our Dronino finds back to the lab for cutting, they revealed an interior packed with intriguing amoeba-like inclusions, and are among my favorite pieces out of everything we found over the years.

Following the Russia adventure we returned to Poland and filmed the "Morasko" and "Pultusk" episodes back to back, and mostly in the rain. On the final day in Poland, exhausted after five weeks of shooting, and while being rushed to load up a vehicle, I fell down a flight of nine slippery stone steps, with a 70-pound duffel bag on my shoulder, broke a toe and suffered a concussion. I was lucky; it could have been much worse.

Back in the States, my doctor said I needed to rest up from the concussion and keep off my feet for several weeks. I told her that was funny because I was leaving for

Canada the next day. All through the episodes "Return to Whitecourt," "Mojave," "Sahuarita," and "Homestead," I was hiking on a broken toe. I developed benign paroxysmal positional vertigo as a result of the concussion (fortunately, it was only temporary) and during a scene at the University of Alberta I had to hold on to the wall to stop from falling over. I had lost all sense of balance and gravity.

In Iowa, the pain from my broken toe was so severe I had to take off my boot and sit on a grassy slope applying a topical anaesthetic, in the middle of a shoot day. Jeff Fisher, who directed the final four episodes of Season Three devised an ingenious solution to my temporary incapacitation. For fifteen minutes I sat on a low hilltop, while Steve gridded the field below me with his detector, and the whole scene was filmed as a time-lapse. When we were done, our cameraman Joe "Boots" Parker, a nature photographer and ex-Army ranger asked if I did a lot of yoga.

"No, I don't have the patience. Why do you ask?"

"I've just never seen anyone sit so completely motionless in my life!"

"Well," I replied. laughing. "You did tell me I should sit very still."

Unfortunately, again, that scene did not make it into the broadcast episode.

Our relentless travel schedule required us to use rental vehicles in the majority of our adventures. My beloved 1995 off-road Toyota Tacoma did, however, appear in two episodes of Season One, and I was keen to get it some additional airtime. I had already fallen in love with the Orange County Chopper *Meteorite Men* bike and wanted to keep it, but Science Channel paid for its design and construction, and the orange motorcycle now sits proudly in the lobby of Discovery Channel headquarters in Silver Spring, Maryland. I hoped to take the OCC bike to Sturges, the Tucson gem and mineral shows, and other events, but—even though I promised not to disappear into deepest Mexico while in possession—I was never allowed to borrow it.

We needed a memorable vehicle of our own that could be taken to public functions so, early in 2011, I began work on an exhaustive refit of my Tacoma. The entire body was stripped and sanded, and I had a custom paint shop in Tucson mix a color for me that was an exact match for Rommel's Afrika Korps desert yellow from World War II. All-Pro Off-Road in California built special bumpers and a bed rack. My friends at Dan's Toy Shop in Tucson put the whole thing together for me, then installed top-of-the-line shocks and suspension. Finally, I added Aerolite decals, a spray-on bed liner, netting, dune flags, a cab-mounted laptop holder, and an assortment of jerry cans, digging tools, first aid and survival supplies, and anything else I could think of. We ran a naming contest on Twitter and my friend, Michael Mulgrew, came up with the winning entry: *The Mule*. The newly-completed special expedition vehicle was featured in the "Mojave" and "Sahuarita" episodes of Season Three and continues to make regular public appearances around the country.

By November, our final shoot in Kansas wrapped, and I set out for home at last. I was reunited with Libby who waited for me, patiently, all those months. My petite calico cat, Bonnie, a 9/11 orphan I rescued in New York, pretended at first not to know me, but later relented, and reverted to her normal imperious self.

After three seasons and 23 episodes, *Meteorite Men* was over. We travelled roughly 120,000 miles—almost five times around the world—found space rocks on four continents, visited eleven countries, and half the states in the Union. I felt the timing and the decision were perfect. We went out on top and my most adored television show, the original *Star Trek*, also ended after three seasons, so that had already set the bench mark for me.

While Steve and I are the ones visible on the television screens, it is important to remember that literally hundreds of people worked diligently, behind the scenes, in order to make *Meteorite Men* a reality. I have a lot of admiration for our network and our production company. They had the backbone to stand behind a show that was, at times, difficult, complex, and even hazardous to make. And, between all of us, we succeeded in doing something that had never been done before in the history of the world. We made a TV series about rocks from space.

In three years Steve and I recovered hundreds of thousands of dollars worth of meteorites. Some of the best specimens went, as promised, to university collections in exchange for the privilege of hunting at restricted sites of national importance. Landowners were paid their cut of material found on private property, and I kept a few prized pieces for my personal collection. In the end, there was enough money left over to invest a little in Aerolite Meteorites, LLC, take Libby on a short vacation to London to see the Royal Ballet, and buy some salmon for Bonnie.

The truth is, it really never was about making money.

I hoped that our work might inspire and entertain, and introduce the world at large to the wonder of meteorites. I never expected that *Meteorite Men*, a reasonably cerebral program with significant science content, would become a major hit with viewers under the age of twelve.

A nice gentleman emailed the company offices recently, and ordered a meteorite. He explained it was a gift for his grandson. He showed his grandson our *Meteorite Men* pilot and reported: "All he can do now is talk about growing up to be a meteorite hunter."

The gentleman went on to say: "P.S.: Please tell Mr. Notkin that he has replaced Dennis Anderson, driver of the world-famous monster truck *Grave Digger*, as my grandson's favorite superhero."

I found this comment rather exciting, especially with my history in the comic book industry, and because I have always been quite the superhero fan; especially X-Men, Iron Man and Fantastic Four. Being a tech head, it was the gadgets and gizmos they use that really moved me, and I particularly liked the way in which Tony Stark initially devised Iron Man's chest plate for the purpose of keeping his heart going.

I wrote back to the grandfather, told him his email had made my day, and said we would be shipping him a signed *Meteorite Men* photo for his grandson in addition to the order. I like to send an extra little gift for kids who enjoy the show.

The next day I received another email from the gentleman.

"About the superhero thing: I made the mistake of explaining to my grandson that in as much as you, Mr. Notkin, can't jump higher than the tallest building or stop bullets with your bare hands, you cannot really be considered a superhero. My grandson then explained, very slowly so I wouldn't get lost, that while some superheroes were born with powers, like Superman, most are normal humans who use technical devices to make them superheroes. He said that made you just like Batman."

TWENTY THREE

132904

If there's one thing I've learned from all of my travels
It's that nothing ever turns out the way you planned
So I'm sitting here in the dust outside of Tucson
Still trying to do the best I can

From "Reset To Zero"
By Geoffrey Notkin

MY FRIEND ROBERT MATSON—an astrophysicist and meteorite expert with a genius-level IQ and movie-star looks—sent me an email with astonishing news. Asteroid 132904, discovered by him at the Mount Palomar Observatory, had been named Notkin and approved by the Minor Planet Society. It was the greatest honor ever bestowed upon me and I felt humbled. I telephoned my father, the devoted amateur astronomer who carried me out to his telescope when I was a child, and said I wished to share that honor with him.

I wanted to visit my asteroid, of course, but—in this lifetime at least—such things are not possible. I thought of Antonie de Saint-Exupéry's wonderful book, *The Little Prince*, with the title character standing on his tiny planet, no larger than a city bus, surrounded by minute craters, and watering his plants. Interestingly enough, in his book *Wind, Sand and Stars*, Saint-Exupéry, an expert aviator, described accidentally finding a meteorite after he made an emergency landing on a plateau in the Sahara Desert during the 1930s.

At some point in my travels I noticed the uncanny similarity between being on the road with a rock 'n' roll band and being on the road with a television crew filming an adventure series. Both are small groups of talented people, dedicated to their craft, existing outside the strata of conventional society, working long days and nights and

[previous page] The author and Steve Arnold with the Hydratrek *Rockhound* on the Iowa River, 2011.
[facing page] With my old friend, Paul Martino, outside Doc Hudson Guitar and Kustom, Tucson, 2012.

traveling to strange places in the hope of creating something that is good, lasting, and important. And maybe even entertaining people on the way, as a bonus.

The quiet little boy who fixated on finding things, and owning things, grew into the adventurous meteorite hunter driven to find a space rock so amazing and perfect it would solve all riddles, answer all questions, and clarify his role in an unexplainable universe. But nothing can answer all questions. In the pursuit of excellence, in the overwhelming need to do something worth doing, and in the desire to fulfill impossible dreams, we realize that the joy, meaning, and understanding we all yearn for are being surreptitiously handed to us by the very process of searching for them. In other words, the greatest discovery is found within the act of creating, of being, and of trying. You just have to notice.

As Winston Churchill said: "Action is character."

Not so long ago I received a most unexpected telephone call from Paul Martino, my dear old friend from the punk days who once sang with rival band 4 Way Ping. He shared the sad news that his adored wife had passed away, following a long battle with cancer. He was devastated and—just as I did in 2004—he planned on starting a new life in Arizona. Being an unconventional chap and never much caring for airplanes, he boarded a train in New York and headed west.

"I have a friend in Phoenix," he told me on his cell phone from the rattling railroad car. "I'm going to buy a house near him, what do you think?"

Phoenix is a major city that entirely lacks the funky charisma and friendly weirdness of Tucson. A boho rock and reggae intellectual like Paul would never, in a million years, be happy there.

"I absolutely forbid you," I told him emphatically, "to buy a house in Phoenix before you've spent at least a week with me here in Tucson."

I picked him up at the train station and he never left. Paul fell in love with Krista Khrome, a dynamic, larger-than-life rock singer and veteran of the Chicago punk scene, and they moved in together. Paul opened the Doc Hudson Guitar and Kustom shop on Fourth Avenue and quickly became an oracle among local musicians, due to his unmatched skills in building and repairing instruments. Paul, and particularly Krista, badgered me, relentlessly, but in the nicest possible way.

"Why are you not playing in a band?" Krista demanded of me time and again. "And don't you dare tell me you're too busy with television and rocks. You're old school punk rock man! What is this 'I don't have time for music nonsense'? Are you a wuss?"

In December of 2011 I grudgingly agreed to come out of rock 'n' roll retirement for a special show at Tucson's splendid Rialto Theater. As part of the annual Great Cover-Up, Paul, Krista, our drummer Ernie, and I did a performance piece, for a Tucson charity, as Cheap Trick, circa 1978. The Rialto is Tucson's largest and most impressive rock venue, and it was the biggest gig I had played since the early 1990s. It was also the first time Paul and I appeared together on stage in twenty-eight years. Yes, I was older, and, yes, a lot of time had passed, but who cares? I bought a new bass and played it hard. I leapt off the drum riser, kicked over my backup bass, threw guitar picks into the audience, and snapped right back into the rock 'n' roller I have, I suppose, always been.

I saw Paul last week and he is working on repairing and refinishing the acoustic guitar my mother bought in the 1950s. Yes, both my parents were musicians. Paul and I are thinking about putting a new band together. I like the name M.I.R. (Mercury In Retrograde), because every time things go wrong some astrology nut tries to comfort me by saying: "Don't worry, Mercury is in retrograde," as if a tiny planet, annihilated daily by its terrifying proximity to our boiling sun, could possibly have any influence on my scientific life. But, then again, what do I know? Stranger things have happened to me than being mysteriously directed by the weak gravitational force of a pulverized cosmic body.

The former members of my old band, Proper Id, are, today, more widely dispersed geographically than at any other time in our history. My roots are now happily in the Arizona that filled me with wonder as a child, and Jon Berger's are in New York where they have always been. Lach, his beautiful wife Anu, and their little boy Henry Strummer relocated to Edinburgh, Scotland, where he writes, records, and performs regularly. Norman continues to excel at everything he does, including writing, direct-ing feature films, translating, and causing trouble in Tokyo in his spare time. Despite all of that there are, incredibly enough, periodic whispers of an Id reunion, and record-ing sessions at a secluded studio in the west of England. Perhaps we will finally get to make the album we always wanted.

If there is an answer for me, it probably lies in the shadow of a camera obscura, amid that barely visible sliver of illumination we sometimes glimpse, just for a moment, at sunset or as we slide off into sleep—somewhere between a rock band and a space rock. When worlds collide.

Helping to train the next generation of space rockers at the 2012 Tucson gem and mineral show: Norma Morrison, the author, Suzanne Morrison, and Beth Carillo, with our brilliant young friend Nick.

AFTERWORD

ON MARCH 5, 2012, at approximately 3 p.m. Greenwich Mean Time my extraordinary father, Sam Notkin, passed away peacefully in his sleep at St. Vincent's Hospital in Dublin. He spent the last fifteen years of his life battling Parkinson's Disease.

If I inherited one thing from my father, it was determination. At times, his near total refusal to admit that he actually did suffer from a debilitating illness aggravated me. He often insisted on walking with his cane—excruciatingly slowly—from a restaurant, or to one of Libby's ballet performances, when any sensible person would have accepted a ride in a wheelchair.

Sam was taken by ambulance to hospital in late February, following a seizure. My brother, Andrew, and I flew over from the States separately. My interminable journey took me from Tucson to Chicago—where I nearly missed my connection due to a typical and unspeakably long line at security—and then on to Dublin where I arrived at 9 a.m. on a bright and sunny morning, sleep deprived and unsteady following eight hours surrounded by squawking infants and dazed parents. Andrew arrived a day ahead of me and—when we met at his quaint little hotel on Lansdowne Road—reported that Dad was agitated, hallucinating, and not entirely lucid. My brother was not even sure if Dad had recognized him, and I feared the worst; I may well have made it to Ireland too late to say goodbye.

When I walked into St. Christopher's Ward, my father—who was not a large man, but always a giant in spirit and character—looked frail and sad, but only for a moment. He saw me, and his eyes lit up as I walked over to the hospital bed. I asked if he had been causing trouble with the attractive nursing staff and he proceeded, with considerable difficulty, to tell me some characteristically bad jokes, despite the confines of his oxygen mask.

I wrote part of Chapter 19 of *Rock Star* in St. Christopher's Ward, while Dad slept quietly beside me. On that Sunday afternoon, his resilient old frame that had survived SS Panzer divisions during the Battle of the Bulge, a sizable piece of Nazi artillery shrapnel, and numerous other assaults and indignities, gently conceded the final battle. How many sons are lucky enough to be holding their father's hand when he slips silently into the void? I was never able to say farewell to my mother, and my

[facing page] My father's passport photo from the 1960s.
[following page] One of the meteorite craters at Morasko, deep in the Polish woods.

good fortune in being able to spend Dad's last few hours with him is something for which I shall always be grateful.

Since Andrew and I made the long journey to Ireland at no notice, I took with me whatever regular Tucson-friendly clothes happened to be nearby in the moment, that being my favorite faded jeans, sneakers, a couple of Aerolite Meteorites tees, and a pair of slightly tatty safari shirts. As a result, the day after Dad's death, I wandered the cobbled streets of old Dublin in a desperate effort to put together appropriate attire for the funeral. Later, when my father's wife, Kay, saw my new boots, light grey suit, shirt, and lavender tie, expertly picked out for me by a courteous men's department manager, she said I looked very fine and asked where I had found them. It was Cleary's, of course, one of Ireland's grandest department stores, and I am quite sure Dad would have approved.

The afternoon hung slightly chilly, speckled by sporadic rain, like an old tarpaulin stretched across a landlocked fishing boat. After completing my shopping tasks, I stopped at a venerable Dublin pub, Grogan's Castle Lounge—its dark and welcoming walls packed beyond capacity with countless original paintings—for a couple of pints of Smithwick's ale. I sat alone, outside, under an awning. As Dubliners walked briskly by on their way home from work, seagulls honked mischievously overhead, I realized that, inexplicably, and for the first time in many months, I was genuinely happy.

Even my nearly indestructible father had, just shy of his 87th birthday, finally succumbed to the ravages of Parkinson's. There would be no more suffering for him. His labyrinthine personal memories of New York in the 1930s, Paris and Brussels in the 1950s, London in the 1960s, Israel, Africa, Spain, Portugal, Iceland, Italy, World War II, and so many other lands and events were gone forever, as the empathic replicant, Roy Batty, says at the end of *Blade Runner*: "Like tears in rain." The rest of us would just have to carry on as best we could.

As I finished my last pint, I imagined James Joyce sitting in the same pub—or perhaps another one, just over there—scribbling through grey Dublin afternoons in a notebook, much as I was. Who knows what he might have been thinking? Who knows what anyone might be thinking as they walked by me, chatting with sweethearts on cell phones, or engrossed in the day-to-day minutiae of their own personal journeys and struggles?

My father first introduced me to the wonders of the night sky when I was just a child, and his two telescopes now live with me in the Sonoran Desert, where they enjoy black night skies of a striking clarity we could never have imagined from our rainy suburban London garden of the 1960s.

I delivered the eulogy at his funeral service, and closed my short talk with the tale of Asteroid 132904, and how the only way I could fully comprehend and absorb the extraordinary honor bestowed upon me was to share the dedication with my father.

Somewhere up there, in the maelstrom of asteroidal debris between Mars and Jupiter, is a somber little world with Dad's name on it. Even a man of my father's uncommon modesty would have to admit that is pretty cool.

ABOUT THE AUTHOR

GEOFFREY NOTKIN is the author of the award-winning book, *Meteorite Hunting: How to Find Treasure from Space*, as well as more than 150 published articles on meteoritics, paleontology, adventure travel, technology, and the arts. He is a popular columnist, and writes *The Logical Lizard* for TucsonCitizen.com.

He hosts the hit television series, *Meteorite Men*, on Science Channel, and has made numerous other programs for the BBC, PBS, A&E, TLC, Discovery, National Geographic, History Channel, and the Travel Channel.

Geoffrey is a widely published photographer and art director. His work has appeared in *Astronomy, Astronomy Now, Sky & Telescope, Wired, Reader's Digest, Robb Report, The Village Voice, Rock & Gem, Geotimes, Meteorite, Meteoryt* (Poland), *Seed, The Field Guide to Meteors and Meteorites, Arizona Daily Star, Tucson Weekly, Mechanical Engineering, American Theater Arts, Popsmear, Alternative Press, New York Press* and many other national and international publications. He is also an accomplished musician, and performed professionally for many years.

As owner of Aerolite Meteorites, LLC, one of the world's foremost commercial meteorite companies, Geoffrey has worked with, and provided specimens to, many of the world's major institutions including, The American Museum of Natural History, New York; The Natural History Museum, London; The Center for Meteorite Studies at ASU, Tempe; and the Oscar E. Monnig Meteorite Collection in Fort Worth. He is a fellow of The Explorer's Club, and a member of the Electronic Frontier Foundation, the International Dark-Sky Association, the Association of Applied Paleontological Sciences, and the International Meteorite Collectors' Association.

Geoffrey was born on 14th street in Manhattan, and grew up in London, England. He studied geology, astronomy, photography, writing, and design in London, Boston and New York, and now resides in the Sonoran Desert of southern Arizona, with one eccentric cat, a flock of semi-tame quail, and no children.